ISSUES IN
SCIENCE
EDUCATION

PROFESSIONAL DEVELOPMENT
Planning and Design

Jack Rhoton and Patricia Bowers, editors

National Science Teachers Association
National Science Education Leadership Association

NATIONAL SCIENCE TEACHERS ASSOCIATION

Shirley Watt Ireton, Director
Beth Daniels, Managing Editor
Judy Cusick, Associate Editor
Jessica Green, Assistant Editor
Linda Olliver, Cover Design

Art and Design
Linda Olliver, Director
NSTA Web
Tim Weber, Webmaster
Periodicals Publishing
Shelley Carey, Director
Printing and Production
Catherine Lorrain-Hale, Director
Publications Operations
Erin Miller, Manager
*sci*LINKS
Tyson Brown, Manager

National Science Teachers Association
Gerald F. Wheeler, Executive Director
David Beacom, Publisher

NSTA Press, NSTA Journals,
and the NSTA Web site deliver
high-quality resources for
science educators.

Issues in Science Education: Professional Development Planning and Design
Library of Congress Catalog Card Number 00-110014
NSTA Stock Number: PB127X2
ISBN 0-87355-185-0
Printed in the United States of America by IPC.
Printed on recycled paper

National Science Education Leadership Association

Susan Loucks-Horsley
1947–2000

For more than a quarter century Susan Loucks-Horsley provided leadership for the science education community. Honoring her achievements and contributions requires one only to pause and reflect on her professional research, books, reports, and presentations. Her accomplishments far exceed in quality and quantity what most of us could only wish to attain. There is another quality of Susan that we must recognize and honor. In Susan's life and work, she always conveyed a freshness of appreciation for the other person. This interest in other people complemented her written contributions and achievements. Susan left the science education community with this deeper and more profound contribution. Personally, she conveyed a belief that, given the opportunity, each science teacher had the potential to improve, and that each teacher wanted her or his students to learn science. Susan let all she touched know that she understood their concerns and recognized their daily struggles to change. She supported their dignity, integrity, and worth as individuals. Susan Loucks-Horsley clearly recognized that the central issue of reform is not educational material; the essential factor is how leaders think and respond to the personal concerns of teachers, how they learn, and what has meaning for them. The foreword she wrote for this book reveals her belief that ultimately it is the individual science teacher who will make a difference in students' lives. Her life made a difference in the lives of others; now we have lost one of our best and brightest. We are left with her inspiration and dedication. Fulfilling her vision passes to all of us. As we look to the future without Susan Loucks-Horsley, we can be thankful for her professional achievements and contributions, and we must be grateful for her personal inspiration and grace.

Rodger Bybee

On the evening of August 8, 2000, Susan Loucks-Horsley died of injuries sustained in a fall.

Contents

Part I.
Standards-based Reform and Professional Development

Rodger W. Bybee and Susan Loucks-Horsley
A survey of four of the *National Science Education Standards* most relevant to professional development—learning science; learning to teach science; self-assessment and continuous improvement; and comprehensive, sustained professional development—this chapter shows that *Standards* and professional development are mutually dependent. Professional development puts the *Standards* into classroom practice, and the *Standards* provide criteria for judging the outcomes of professional development.

Susan Loucks-Horsley and Katherine E. Stiles
This chapter explores a design framework used to guide professional developers through a planning cycle driven by and designed to meet the specific needs of the teachers and students. The cycle works by considering essential inputs unique to its users: content, knowledge and beliefs, critical issues, and strategies for professional learning.

Norman G. Lederman, Fouad Abd-El-Khalick, and Randy L. Bell
Despite differences in the pedagogical or curricular emphasis, student understanding of the nature of science is one objective agreed upon in all major reform efforts. This chapter provides a series of concrete, classroom-tested approaches and activities for promoting K–12

student understanding of the nature of science: the understanding that scientific knowledge is tentative, empirically based, and subjective; that it necessarily involves human interference, imagination, and creativity; and that it is socially and culturally embedded.

A Continuum of Standards for Science Teachers and Teaching

Steven W. Gilbert

The focus of this chapter is on an emerging continuum of science teaching standards for accreditation, licensure, and certification that are part of the New Professional Teacher Project (NPTP). The NPTP model expects teachers at all levels to engage in professional development that fosters long-term, demonstrable growth through a unified, articulated system of individual performance standards. Unlike other standards, those of the NPTP are competency-based rather than prescriptive; that is, they identify desired knowledge, performance, or dispositional outcomes but do not prescribe ways to achieve those ends. The chapter suggests that, if the science education community writes these standards and state licensing agencies recognize them, these standards will not only develop better teachers, but also help create a sense of teaching as a true profession.

Angelo Collins

Collins takes on the task of deciphering the acronyms associated with science education reform through profiles of the American Association for the Advancement of Science (AAAS), the National Science Education Standards (NSES), the National Board for Professional Teaching Standards (NBPTS), and the Interstate New Teacher Assessment and Support Consortium (INTASC). Studying, supporting, and participating in these organizations helps advance the profession of science teaching by providing opportunities and guidance for professional development. This chapter briefly samples other reform initiatives that, although further removed from the science classroom, also influence science education policy and practice.

Part II.
Planning for Professional Development

Thomas Gadsden, Jr., and Kimberly S. Roempler

Profiles two online resources that offer convenient access to professional development resources: the Eisenhower National Clearinghouse for Mathematics and Science Education (ENC) and the Educational Resources Information Centers (ERIC). ENC's Web site provides searchable online access to over 14,000 instructional and professional resources, grouped by grade level, subject area, cost ranges, and other criteria. ERIC's Web site is the primary source for abstracts of educational research and scholarly writings in fields of study such as information and technology, assessment and evaluation, and urban education.

Chronicles the development of the NSTA Pathways project. The Pathways publications make up a comprehensive professional development package designed to put into practice the vision of educational reform expressed in the *National Science Education Standards*.

Provides an overview of the professional knowledge base teachers need to implement the *Standards* and to impact teaching practice across their careers. Professional development must include opportunities that support continuous skill and knowledge acquisition guided by the concerns, interests, and motivations of individual teachers. The chapter identifies characteristics common to successful teachers, including sustained support, promotion of incremental change, and individualized design by and for teachers.

Explores the National Science Foundation's (NSF) effort to systemically reform science and mathematics education through systemic initiatives (SI): Statewide Systemic Initiatives (SSI), Urban Systemic Initiatives (USI), and Rural Systemic Initiatives (RSI). SIs differ from other NSF programs and projects in that they deliver support through annual cooperative agreements with NSF, rather than through grants. Most states select professional development as the primary strategy for reform, though each state uses various components of professional development in different combinations. This chapter profiles Ohio as a model due to its heavy investments in professional development and in assessing its SSI, three USIs, and one RSI.

Describes a successful teacher enhancement program, CC-ISTEP, developed by the authors to supplement the master of arts in teaching degree program at a liberal arts college. The program offers summer institutes and academic-year follow-up seminars that engage teachers in constructivist learning to foster effective pedagogical approaches by helping them to make sense of teaching by being active learners themselves. This chapter profiles the Summer 1997 Institute as a model for the program in practice, and offers general principles to guide others in the development of similar programs.

Part III. Assessment and Evaluation in Support of Science Education Reform

Foreword

Susan Loucks-Horsley

In the early 1980s, alarms were set off across the United States about the deplorable status of education, in general, and science education, in particular. In response, a flurry of activity led to many suggestions about what should be done. In the 1990s, various reform efforts at the local, state, and national levels blossomed, and change began gradually to occur. The *National Science Education Standards* and the *AAAS Benchmarks* emerged after long debates over what it is that students at various grade levels should know and be able to do in science. The notion that "less is more" gradually became a shared value.

Happily, few teachers today would advocate slavishly following a textbook as their science curriculum. Many teachers understand and value inquiry as an outcome for their students and a way of fostering important learning opportunities, and we are moving slowly in the direction of having a scientifically literate population. But, we must not become complacent. Although we have come a long way since the poor status of science education was presented to the American public in the 1980s, there is still a long way to go. Recognition of what our classrooms should look like and what our students should be able to do does not automatically translate into changes in the classroom or with our students. This is due, in part, to a lack of information. However, knowing what needs to be done does not mean knowing how to do it. This is where the critical role of professional development comes in, and it is essential that science leaders—at all levels—take on the challenges of being both the "leaders of learners" and the learners themselves. Unless teachers are being able to practice new ways of learning, teaching, and leading, this reform will fall far short of its potential.

Science teachers are the crucial link between the curriculum and students. Professional development is a concerted effort to help them understand and change their practices and beliefs as they improve the learning experiences they provide for students within their school and district. Professional development can also serve a broader purpose: to help teachers develop leadership and change agent skills. It prepares teachers to take a more informed and focused leadership role in fostering the implementation or improvement of the instructional program. Support for teachers is essential if teaching is to occur as espoused in the *Standards*, and if teachers are to expand their visions to influence others in their schools and districts. The nature of professional development programs in which teachers participate will, to a large extent, determine the changes in students' learning experiences.

As this book suggests, effective professional development programs and initiatives for science teachers have many characteristics in common. They help teachers see their students and classrooms differently as they learn to foster deep understanding of important science concepts, the skills and understanding of scientific inquiry, and an appreciation of the natural world. Effective programs engage teachers in ways that they, in turn, will help their students learn; support collaboration among teachers as they learn and craft learning experiences for their students; and help teachers examine their own practice and become "critical friends" to other teachers. Such programs support teachers over time so that they not only can change their practices, but also can sustain and renew those practices continuously.

Science leaders can broaden their own professional development role by thinking of themselves as designers of learning experiences—much as teachers consider their instructional goals, their students' needs, and the resources and constraints of their school and district, science leaders can craft long-term, multifaceted programs for teachers that reflect current research and the "wisdom" of other professional developers. For example, breaking out of the "professional-development-equals-inservice-workshops-and-summer-institutes" box brings science leaders into contact with a wide array of strategies from which to choose. These include case discussions, action research, coaching and mentoring, and examining student work. They can use student curriculum as a tool for teacher learning, helping teachers go far beyond the "mechanical use" of new curriculum materials as they deepen their understanding of science content, of student thinking, and of teaching strategies. As science leaders broaden their vision for professional development strategies, their designs begin to incorporate and even influence some of the other important elements of systemic reform, such as curriculum, assessment, and the development of a professional community. Examples in this book "push the envelope" of old conceptions of professional learning in ways that can fuel deep and sustainable changes in classrooms, schools, and districts.

This book is written for science leaders at all levels: teachers, science supervisors, science consultants, science coordinators, science specialists, administrators, higher education science educators, and policymakers. The comprehensive presentation promotes understanding of the circumstances in which professional development most influences student learning. It reviews programs in place that work, and it provides a wealth of practical ideas about actions to take in the professional development arena in order to implement and sustain reform in science education.

This is indeed an exciting time to be in science education. As we work together to strengthen our understandings and roles as leaders in the science education community, we at the National Science Education Leadership Association (NSELA) and the National Science Teachers Association (NSTA) welcome you to use the resources in this volume to build programs that enhance and enrich science teaching and learning in our nation's schools.

About the Editors

Jack Rhoton is professor of Science Education at East Tennessee State University, Johnson City, Tennessee. Dr. Rhoton currently teaches science education at the undergraduate and graduate levels, and has also taught science at the elementary, middle, senior high school, and college levels. He has received numerous awards for service and science teaching, and has been an active researcher in K–12 science, especially the restructuring of science inservice education as it relates to improved teaching practices. Dr. Rhoton is the editor of the *Science Educator*, a publication of the National Science Education Leadership Association (NSELA), and director of the Tennessee Junior Academy of Science (TJAS). He also serves as editor of the TJAS *Handbook and Proceedings*. Dr. Rhoton's special research interest is in the area of professional development and its impact on science teaching and learning. He is widely published and has written and directed numerous science and technology grants. He has received many honors including the National Science Teachers Association (NSTA) Distinguished Service to Science Education Award.

Patricia Bowers is the associate director of the Center for Mathematics and Science Education at the University of North Carolina at Chapel Hill, where she teaches undergraduates and provides professional development training for math and science teachers. She also works closely with the UNC-CH Pre-College Program, which recruits underrepresented groups into math and science fields. She has been the project director for numerous grants, including 12 Eisenhower grants, and has received awards for service and science education. Dr. Bowers was a Science, Mathematics, and Reading Coordinator at the system level and worked as a classroom teacher and guidance counselor at the school level. Dr. Bowers is currently president of the North Carolina Science Teachers Association, and secretary of the North Carolina Science Leadership Association. She serves on several committees for the National Science Teachers Association (NSTA), and is a former district director and current board member of the NSELA.

Preface

Jack Rhoton and Patricia Bowers

Nearly every major document advocating science education reform in recent years has focused on science content and concepts to be taught, how science teachers should teach, and guidelines for professional development. The vision of science teaching and learning espoused by school reformers presents a key challenge for teachers' professional development. The vision of practice and standards-based reform advocated by the nation's reform agenda requires that most teachers make a paradigm shift in their beliefs, knowledge, and teaching practices. The success of this agenda will hinge, in large measure, on professional development opportunities that will engage teachers in learning the skills and perspectives called for in the new vision of practice. Because teachers are the crucial link between the curriculum and students, professional development is a major element in developing teacher leadership and change agent skills. It prepares teachers to take a more informed and concerted leadership role in fostering the implementation or improvement of the instructional program, driven by the desire to improve student learning.

Effective professional development also provides occasions for teachers to genuinely address change and renewal and reach beyond the "make and take" and "idea swap" sessions to more global, theoretical conversations that focus on teachers' understanding of content, pedagogy, and learner. For long-lasting and effective change within the science classroom, professional development activities must plow a deeper furrow of inquiry into practice than is normally available to teachers.

Professional development must allow teachers to rethink their notions about the nature of science, develop new views about how students learn, construct new classroom learning environments, and create new expectations about student outcomes. Teachers will need not only to explore new ideas in professional development programs, but also to develop and inculcate habits that will enable them to continue professional development over time.

Even though a common vision is beginning to emerge about what effective professional development should look like, a large number of teachers have not had an opportunity to participate in such professional development in their working environments. However, there is a growing momentum for schools to examine teachers' professional development in light of standards-based reform. This publication positively addresses issues and practical approaches needed to lay the foundation upon which professional development approaches can work to build effective science programs in our nation's schools. In addition, it examines the linkage between professional development and effective science education programs.

The *Issues in Science Education* series shares ideas, insights, and experiences of individuals ranging form teachers to science supervisors to university personnel to agencies representing science education. They discuss how professional development can contribute to the success of school science and how to develop a culture that allows and encourages science leaders continually to improve their science programs.

Using nontechnical language, this text is intended to be accessible to a broad audience. It is written for science teachers, science department chairs, principals, systemwide science leaders, superintendents, university personnel, policymakers and other individuals who have a stake in science education. It will also serve as a supplementary text for university methods courses in elementary and secondary science education.

The 13 chapters in this volume, *Professional Development Planning and Design*, are organized into three sections. The intent of the book is not to provide an exhaustive coverage of each major theme but, rather, to present chapters that effectively address the issues of professional development. Each chapter in the text illustrates the utility of professional development for practitioners and addresses general issues and perspectives related to science education reform.

The first part of the book, "Standards-based Reform and Professional Development," consists of five chapters that set the stage of the book by examining the critical issues of professional development, the nature of science teaching and learning, the linkage between effective science programs and effective professional development programs, and strategies for professional learning. Part II, "Planning for Professional Development," includes five chapters that illustrate the planning and designing of professional development programs within the context of resources and preparing effective teachers. Part III, "Assessment and Evaluation in Support of Science Education Reform," consists of three chapters that focus on using achievement data to modify teaching practices, the development and use of assessment tools to capture evidence about what students know and can do that is not already documented in systemic reform, and professional development implications from TIMSS (Third International Mathematics and Science Study).

Meaningful and sustained change in science teaching and learning is fraught with many challenges and pitfalls. These challenges and obstacles demand effective professional development. The task of developing and sustaining healthy professional development practices is simply too complex for any one person to tackle alone. Therefore, this work is directed at all players in the science education community who have a stake in improving science teaching and learning. Moreover, administrators must create an atmosphere that supports and encourages participation in effective professional development programs. One of the greatest challenges of leadership is to develop a culture that creates "laboratories" of ongoing improvements. The final determinant of success in this effort will be measured through the quality of science programs delivered to our students.

Numerous examples throughout the book illustrate the utility of professional development for practitioners and others interested in the improvement of science teaching and learning. Many of the topics in this book are placed within the context of real world experience and combinations of original research. Some of the concepts covered include: standards-based professional development; the nature of science, assessment and evaluation, leadership, and professional development; strategies for professional development; learning and teaching critical thinking skills; using ENC and ERIC as a resource for professional development; diversity issues in teaching science; and science education in formal and informal settings.

As we honor the memory and life of Susan Loucks-Horsley, we cannot escape the fact that her name is synonymous with professional development. Her many years of service and dedication to the science education community resulted in a body of writing of marked excellence, inspiring each of us to work harder, think deeper and take action on the subject to which she devoted her life—improving science education in our nation's schools. It was for this reason that Pat Bowers and I asked her to write the foreword to this book and to contribute two chapters to this document. We recognized that her works and writings have been influential forces in shaping the thoughts and actions on the direction of professional development in science education. And it will be so for years to come. There was also a human quality that permeated her work. Through my professional collaboration efforts with Susan, I recognized that she not only radiated an unparalleled warmth, glow, and passion for her work, but also was equally dedicated to uplifting each person with whom she came in contact. She was interested in people as individuals and recognized and appreciated the importance and role of each science teacher in his or her struggle and dedication to create effective learning environments for all students. She also worked hard to support teachers in their individual environments. Her memory is destined to linger in our thoughts as we work to fulfill her vision. The science education community will forever be the better for her influence, example, and inspiration.

Jack Rhoton

Acknowledgments

This book would not have been possible without the help, advice, and support of a number of people. More fundamentally, the members of the NSTA/NSELA Editorial Board—Gerry Madrazo, Lamoine Motz, Carolyn Randolph, Susan Sprague, Emma Walton—reviewed the manuscripts and made valuable suggestions for improvement. We could not have achieved our goal without their assistance, and we are grateful. Our appreciation is extended to Shirley Watt Ireton, Beth Daniels, and Anne Early of NSTA Press, for their invaluable help in the final design of which you are now reading. No volume is any better than the manuscripts that are contributed to it; we appreciate the time and efforts of those whose work lies within the cover of this book.

We also want to thank and acknowledge the support, help, and suggestions of the NSELA Board of Directors. Special thanks to Becky Litherland, past president, for her suggestions and guidance in the early stages of the project. The support of president Jerry Doyle and executive director Peggy Holliday in the later stages of the project is gratefully acknowledged.

Finally, we would like to credit people who simply made room in their lives for us to do this work. We are indebted to the calm, good-natured support of the East Tennessee State University Division of Science Education office staff: Leslye Culbert and Connie Frances. Each of these individuals did excellent work in word processing and typing the many drafts of each manuscript. And lastly, a special thanks to James Kevin, ETSU adjunct professor, and Chris Bordeaux, ETSU graduate student, for applying their expert editing skills to each manuscript.

Introduction

Jerry Doyle
NSELA President, 1999–2000

The numerous and vexing issues facing the science education leader today have created the need for leadership skills and knowledge that go far beyond those demanded in any previous era. The exceptional leader must be knowledgeable about science as a human endeavor; must be conversant with new developments in learning theory and how they impact classroom instruction; must have practical skills in chemical hygiene and lab safety needed to maintain a safe environment for students and teachers; must have the analytical skills needed to build a comprehensive assessment program and be able to move student achievement scores to higher levels; must be on the cutting edge of recent developments in technology that can be useful in science instruction; must have exceptional people skills and be able to work with a variety of interest groups who care about the science program; must know the structure of the school organization and be able to keep funds flowing toward the science department; must know where to find grant money and write "winning" grant proposals; must be able to create a vision and long-range plan for the science program; and must be able to coordinate a comprehensive staff development program to make that vision a reality.

The exceptional science education leader can master this overwhelming list of "musts" only if key resources are tapped. Pat Bowers and Jack Rhoton have compiled one of these key resources needed in the office of every science education leader. This volume includes an impressive array of pertinent articles from key leaders in the issue domains mentioned previously. It is my belief that this book will make you a more effective science education leader.

National Science Education Standards as a Catalyst for Change: The Essential Role of Professional Development

Rodger W. Bybee and Susan Loucks-Horsley
Center for Science, Mathematics, and Engineering Education,
National Research Council

Rodger W. Bybee is the executive director of the Center for Science, Mathematics, and Engineering Education at the National Research Council. Author of numerous journal articles, chapters, books, science curricula, and textbooks, he also directed the writing of the content standards for the *National Science Education Standards*. Honors included the National Science Teachers Association Distinguished Service Award.

Susan Loucks-Horsley was director of professional development for the Center for Science, Mathematics, and Engineering Education and the National Institute for Science Education at WestEd. She has written numerous articles, chapters, and books in the areas of professional development and education change. Her honors include the National Staff Development Council's Award for Outstanding Contributions in Professional Development.

Although the momentum for standards in national education began to build in the early 1980s, it is only a decade since the first set appeared in 1989. Since then, standards have become a part of the educational landscape. In this chapter, we survey the origins of national standards; reflect on their power, in particular those in science education; and examine the role professional development must play if standards are to realize their potential to truly transform education. The link between standards and professional development is essential: Knowing where one needs to go is only the first step. Building the capacity for continuous learning for all students—a capacity needed to take us well into the 21st century—must follow. In this chapter, we use the four professional development standards in the *National Science Education Standards* to discuss and illustrate the nature of opportunities for professional learning that will help this country succeed in this ambitious goal.

The Historical Perspective

In 1983, the National Commission on Excellence in Education warned that our nation was at risk and recommended strengthening content in the curriculum and raising expectations of student achievement. In 1989, the president and governors met in Charlottesville, Virginia, and developed a set of national goals for education. Soon after the release of the national goals, some leaders recognized both the strengths and weaknesses of the broad and abstract goals. In his role as chair of the National Education Goals Panel, Governor Roy Romer of Colorado encouraged the development of policies to facilitate higher levels of student achievement. Those policies have become known as education standards. In order to act on the national goals, the educational community had to describe standards for precisely what students should know and be able to do as a result of their educational experiences (Ravitch, 1995; Tucker & Codding, 1998; Rothman, 1995). The need for voluntary national standards emerged. In the same year, the National Council of Teachers of Mathematics (NCTM) released standards for curriculum and placed the term *standards* into the lexicon of contemporary education. Since 1989, various groups and organizations have developed standards for civics, geography, history, the arts, and other disciplines including our own—science. The National Research Council's (NRC) publication of the *National Science Education Standards* (1996) followed the American Association for the Advancement of Science's publication of *Benchmarks for Science Literacy* (1993). Together these documents guide the science education community on its road to higher student achievement in science for all the nation's students.

The power of standards lies in their capacity to catalyze change in fundamental components of the educational system.

The Power of National Education Standards

The power of standards lies in their capacity to catalyze change in fundamental components of the educational system. They do so first by specifying **outcomes**: what all students should know and be able to do. Clarifying educational outcomes is a new emphasis for national reform, which often has consisted of modifying **inputs** in hopes of improving outcomes. Education has changed, in terms of time (length of school days, years), content (additional science courses), materials (new textbooks or activity-based programs), techniques (cooperative groups, project-based learning), and technology (computers in classrooms and the use of the Web). Although these inputs were meant to enhance student learning, it is also true that to be optimally effective all educational inputs must target a common purpose. If not—and this has been true in the past—the result is uncoordinated and unfocused individual changes—none of which can or will add up to fundamental change.

Establishing standards for student learning triggers questions about fundamental components, such as curriculum, instruction, and assessment, for these components most directly influence what and how students learn. Further, changes in one of these components require changes in the others. Think back to the Sputnik era of reform, which focused on just one component—curriculum—and gave little attention to the other fundamental components of assessment and instructional strategies, with disappointing results. Further, this era demonstrated that the most stable and sustainable changes have support from other components, such as school district policies, budgets, teacher education, professional development, and the community.

The *National Science Education Standards* included science content that is fundamental. However, they went beyond statements of student outcomes and addressed the fundamental components of teaching—curriculum content, instruction, and assessment—as well as the supporting elements of professional development, the nature of science programs, and system support. In setting such a broad array of standards, the *Standards* facilitated greater coherence among educational components, which, as the TIMSS so recently and so painfully indicated, is critical to enhanced student learning. TIMSS's depiction of the U.S. educational system as incoherent—with goals which only tangentially relate to instructional materials, which are not true to assessments, which are not aligned with professional development, and on and on—correlated with U.S. students' decreased achievement. In comparison with students in other nations, U.S. students rank at or near the bottom as they leave high school (National Center for Educational Statistics, 1996, 1998; Schmidt, McKnight, & Raizen, 1996). Standards have the power to counter educational incoherence by specifying student learning outcomes, which, in turn, catalyze changes in other fundamental aspects of school science programs. The *Standards* provided criteria for judging the extent to which national, state, and local policies, curriculum materials and multiyear programs, teacher education and professional development programs, and organizational structures are apt to help students learn science content.

Establishing standards for student learning triggers questions about fundamental components, such as curriculum, instruction, and assessment, for these components most directly influence what and how students learn.

The Role of Professional Development in Standards-Based Reform

Thompson and Zeuli (1999:1) succinctly stated the essential role of professional development:

> *It is now widely accepted that, in order to realize recently proposed reforms in what is taught and how it is taught [as described in national standards documents]…, teachers will have to unlearn much of what they believe, know, and know how to do while also forming new beliefs, developing new knowledge, and mastering new skills. The proposed reforms constitute, if you will, a new curriculum for teacher learning. If they do not specify precisely what teachers should know and be able to do, they do outline it rather clearly and exemplify aspects of it with a nearly literary vividness.*

Standards cannot directly change behavior or beliefs, but they can point the way by defining desirable goals, stimulating movement toward the goals, and reducing conflicts among the policies faced by educators at each level. They can begin to create images of what different components of the education system would look like if they were aligned with the desired outcomes for students. Although some have argued that policies (including standards) might serve to teach those who must carry them out, rather than solely as an effort to induce or constrain them to behave differently (Cohen & Barnes, 1993), teaching of both students and adults requires far more than attending to policy statements. There must be substantial effort to translate policies into school programs and classroom practices (Bybee, 1997). Without professional development, this cannot be accomplished.

> *Standards cannot directly change behavior or beliefs, but they can point the way by defining desirable goals, stimulating movement toward the goals, and reducing conflicts among the policies faced by educators at each level.*

Standards for Professional Development

The *National Science Education Standards* recognized professional development as a key component of the science education system, one often neglected when concentrating on the core elements closest to the critical teacher/student interface of content, teaching, and assessment. Professional development standards describe the opportunities teachers and other educators[1] should have in order to learn what they need to know and be able to do in order to assist students to achieve the content standards. The professional development standards consider two dimensions: the **content** of professional development—that is, *what* teachers need to learn—and the **pedagogy** of professional development—that is, *how* they should learn it. Learning opportunities that support teachers in teaching to the *Standards* consider each of the professional development standards, both in the **content** and the **pedagogy**. Next we review the standards briefly and provide examples of each of them in action.[2]

Standard A: Learning Science (Table 1)

Because the *Standards* call for students to acquire deep understanding of important, fundamental, science concepts, teachers need to know science as deeply—even more deeply—than their students. The teaching standards call for teachers to assess their students' understanding of natural phenomena, and to help their students change or enhance those understandings through new and multiple, often concrete, experiences. Without their own understanding of the science involved, teachers cannot do this; staying "one chapter ahead of the kids" may have been a survival skill in the days when textbook memorization was equated with learning, but this strategy will no longer suffice. This situation is reminiscent of the scenes in the *Private Universe* video series (Harvard-Smithsonian Center for Astrophysics, 1987), in which MIT

Table 1: Professional Development Standard A

Professional development for teachers of science requires learning essential science content through the perspectives and methods of inquiry. Science learning experiences for teachers must:

◆ Involve teachers in actively investigating phenomena that can be studied scientifically, interpreting results, and making sense of findings consistent with currently accepted scientific understanding.

◆ Address issues, events, problems or topics significant in science and of interest to participants.

◆ Introduce teachers to scientific literature, media and technological resources that expand their science knowledge and their ability to access further knowledge.

◆ Build on the teachers' current science understanding, ability, and attitudes.

◆ Incorporate ongoing reflection of the process and outcomes of understanding science through inquiry.

◆ Encourage and support teachers in efforts to collaborate.

(NRC, 1996:59)

and Harvard graduates cannot explain why there are seasons and how a seed can become a tree. If teachers do not understand the science involved in these everyday occurrences (or know how to teach them, which we turn to next), their students will learn no more than the graduates interviewed in these videos.

The research base on how students best learn and, subsequently, how they should be taught science concepts is becoming richer as several lines of study converge. One line of study—the research on cognition and conceptual change—emphasizes the learner's active construction of new knowledge based on existing knowledge, rather than through straight and rather simple acquisition. The conceptual change research underscores the tenacity of existing knowledge, which is difficult to replace by new ideas, and the importance of challenges to existing ideas and multiple opportunities to interact with phenomena (materials, events, representations) so that students will replace or enhance their old ideas with new ones based on scientific principles (Guzzatti, Snyder, Glass, & Gamas, 1993; Hodson & Hodson, 1998; King, 1994; Novak, 1998; Staver, 1994). The literature also contains extensive studies of students' scientific misconceptions—particular concepts for which students at certain ages have their own (often predictable) explanations, which are often not scientifically correct (Driver, Griesne, & Libeighian, 1985; Driver, Leach, Millar, & Scott, 1996; Driver, Squires, Duckworth, & Wood-Robinson, 1994). Finally, there are many studies of approaches to teaching and use of curriculum materials based on models for learning that draw on these lines of research (Anderson, 1998; Shymansky, Kyle, & Alport, 1983).

Research on cognition and conceptual change emphasizes the learner's active construction of new knowledge based on existing knowledge, rather than through straight and rather simple acquisition.

In order to build their pedagogical content knowledge, teachers need to know science, but they also need to understand how learning occurs and what kinds of experiences facilitate learning of science.

These lines of research support science learning that is based on inquiry into natural phenomena—investigation that in many ways mirrors scientists producing new knowledge. Some attributes of such investigation and, therefore, such learning environments are listed in Standard A (Table 1).

One example of a professional learning opportunity that addresses this standard is provided by several of the U.S. Department of Energy's national laboratories. High school teachers spend eight weeks as scientists, joining lab scientists on their teams and participating in their ongoing research, often on the frontiers of science, such as particle physics. As they work, they develop new inquiry abilities, come to understand the process of scientific investigation, appreciate the dead ends and uncertainties of science, use new technologies, and examine the scientific literature. Teachers deepen their understanding of science, build their inquiry abilities and understandings, and do so through their participation in scientific investigation.

In another example of Standard A in practice, elementary school teachers attending a two-week summer institute at the Workshop Center at City College of New York, work with scientists and center staff to develop and conduct science investigations using a scientific inquiry approach. Typically limited in their science background and lacking confidence in their abilities to teach science, participants learn by forming hypotheses, designing experiments, asking questions, recording and analyzing results, and presenting their findings. They strengthen their understanding of science content and how they (and later, their students) can learn it through ongoing sessions focused on classroom applications held throughout the academic year.

Standard B: Learning to Teach Science (Table 2)

Knowing science is only one part of being able to teach it. As deep as their knowledge of science often is, most scientists cannot teach science expertly. This is because they do not have "pedagogical content knowledge," the special knowledge and set of abilities possessed by expert teachers. Shulman (1987) described teachers with pedagogical content knowledge as knowing how students develop their understanding of a particular concept (e.g., density, photosynthesis); what they are able to understand and what they are apt to stumble over at certain stages of development; and through what examples, representations, experiences, etc., they will learn best. In order to build their pedagogical content knowledge, teachers need to know science, but they also need to understand how learning occurs, what kinds of experiences facilitate learning of science (i.e., pedagogy), and what learning environments foster the exploration and openness to new ideas that must accompany learning. A foundation for pedagogical content knowledge can be built through study of the literature

---

Table 2: Professional Development Standard B

Professional development for teachers of science requires integrating knowledge of science, learning, pedagogy, and students; it also requires applying that knowledge to science teaching. Learning experiences for teachers of science must:

◆ Connect and integrate all pertinent aspects of science and science education.

◆ Occur in a variety of places where effective science teaching can be illustrated and modeled, permitting teachers to struggle with real situations and expand their knowledge and skills in appropriate contexts.

◆ Address teachers' needs as learners and build on their current knowledge of science content, teaching, and learning.

◆ Use inquiry, reflection, interpretation of research, modeling, and guided practice to build understanding and skill in science teaching.

(NRC, 1996:62)

on learning and teaching, but teachers can only develop expertise through practicing and reflecting on their teaching practice (Shulman, 1987).

This is where professional development is critical, and the knowledge base is becoming stronger the more professional developers use and test a broad range of strategies (Loucks-Horsley, Hewson, Love, & Stiles, 1998). Strategies that appear most promising encourage teachers to examine their own practices, often by using curriculum materials that they use with their students. For example, in many large districts, elementary school science reform initiatives select and carefully implement a set of curriculum materials based on the *Standards*. Teachers attend a series of workshops spaced throughout the school year, where they experience the science units as learners, reflect on the successes and problems encountered in the units they have already taught, receive in-class assistance through demonstrations and coaching, and have easy access to materials through a support system that delivers and replenishes them without extra work by the teachers. After mastering the mechanics of teaching the units, which usually occurs in the first year of use, teachers collect student work, which they examine in professional development sessions to analyze student thinking, determine what students understand, and how they as teachers can assist in students' conceptual development. Curriculum-based professional development can be particularly effective when teachers do not have the understanding of content they need to create their own curriculum (Ball, 1996; Russell, 1996).

Another professional development strategy that addresses Standard B is the discussion of teaching cases, either written or video-based. Teachers in Cambridge, Massachusetts, worked with professional developers/researchers at the Technical Education Resource Centers (TERC) to view a video series entitled, "Sense Making in Science (TERC, 1997)." In one video, a class was experimenting to learn which objects sink and which ones float. The varied, often contradictory, and nonscientific explanations students gave of what differentiates sinkers from floaters left their teacher wondering what to do to help her students understand the ideas underlying the concept of density. Discussion of the case included what the students knew, what they didn't know, and what the teacher might do to extend their understandings. (See the Loucks-Horsley and Stiles article in this section for additional discussion of professional development strategies focused on learning science and learning to teach science.)

Effective professional development helps teachers learn and gives them tools for further, often less-formalized learning.

Standard C: Self-Assessment and Continuous Improvement (Table 3)

Effective professional development helps teachers learn and gives them tools for further, often less-formalized learning. One strategy that does both is action research, in which teachers determine what questions they are most interested in asking about their students' learning and their own teaching and pursue those questions by learning ways of collecting and analyzing data and sharing their results. In the Colorado College Integrated Science Teacher Enhancement Project, for example, K–12 teachers conducted action research as they built their content and teaching repertoires. A first-grade teacher's question regarding what would happen if she taught science first in the day rather than last resulted in significant changes in her teaching, as well as a published article on her research (Strycker, 1995). The K–12 teachers in this program pursued their own action research questions with support from scientists and project staff, then had the tools of action research to continue to pursue questions of importance to their teaching, long after completion of the program.

Coaching is another professional development strategy that provides teachers with tools for continuous improvement. There are numerous forms of coaching that can

---

Table 3: Professional Development Standard C

Professional development for teachers of science requires building understanding and ability for lifelong learning. Professional development activities must:

- ◆ Provide regular, frequent opportunities for individual and collegial examination and reflection on classroom and institutional practice.
- ◆ Provide opportunities for teachers to receive feedback about their teaching and to understand, analyze, and apply that feedback to improve their practice.
- ◆ Provide opportunities for teachers to learn to use various tools and techniques for self-reflection and collegial reflection, such as peer coaching, portfolios, and journals.
- ◆ Support the sharing of teacher expertise by preparing and using mentors, teacher advisors, coaches, lead teachers, and resource teachers to provide professional development opportunities.
- ◆ Provide opportunities to know and have access to existing research and experiential knowledge.
- ◆ Provide opportunities to learn and use the skills of research to generate new knowledge about science and the teaching and learning of science.

(NRC, 1996:68)

help teachers to help one another learn, and each form has particular skills and procedures that optimize its effectiveness. For example, middle-grade science teachers are particularly concerned about encouraging girls, as well as boys, and members of groups underrepresented in science (typically minorities and those from lower and working class families), as well as those well represented (typically white and those of middle class and professional families). Two coaching programs—Teachers Effectiveness for Student Achievement (TESA) and Gender and Equity for Student Achievement (GESA)—help teachers focus classroom observations on the amounts and kinds of attention that they give different students. This is eye-opening for many teachers, who believe they provide their students with equal opportunities to learn science. In reality, teachers limit the amount of time some students have to participate (e.g., they call on some more than others) and the level of demand they put on students' thinking (e.g., teachers ask some students to recall facts and others to create explanations for natural phenomena). Teachers participating in these professional development programs come to understand that they do not give all students equal opportunities to learn.

Standard D: Comprehensive, Sustained Professional Development (Table 4)
More and more professional developers are recognizing that teachers need opportunities to study the content and pedagogy they need to know over long periods of time, with coherence of content and context and in a way that allows for regular application and reflection (Loucks-Horsley, Hewson, Love, & Stiles, 1998). Yet there are still many "menu-driven" offerings: catalogues from which teachers can select two- to six-hour disconnected workshops and courses that have no connection to their teaching and their students. As consumers of professional development, teachers need to learn to demand more comprehensive, long-term opportunities to learn. Professional development providers (which can include teacher leaders, district administrators, higher education faculty, trainers and consultants external to school districts) in districts, universities, and other locations need to abandon their overwhelming emphasis on short-term workshops and institutes[3] and design better opportunities to help teachers truly transform their practice.

Long-term professional development programs and initiatives are appearing at every level of the system. For example, there are districts offering teachers 100 hours of professional development that incorporates implementation of new instructional materials; universities offering masters programs that focus on integrated science and curriculum development; and professional networks offering physics teachers the opportunity to share teaching strategies and dilemmas and learn new programs designed to engage more high school students in learning physical science. These and other approaches to teacher professional development incorporate Standards A–C in ways that are comprehensive and sustained, thus addressing Standard D as well.

Table 4: Professional Development Standard D

Professional development programs for teachers of science must be coherent and integrated. Quality preservice and inservice programs are characterized by:

◆ Clear, shared goals based on a vision of science learning, teaching, and teacher development congruent with the *National Science Education Standards.*

◆ Integration and coordination of the program components so that understanding and ability can be built over time, reinforced continuously, and practiced in a variety of situations.

◆ Options that recognize the developmental nature of teacher professional growth and individual and group interests, as well as the needs of teachers who have varying degrees of experience, professional expertise, and proficiency.

◆ Collaboration among the people involved in programs, including teachers, teacher educators, teacher unions, scientists, administrators, policymakers, members of professional and scientific organizations, parents, and business people, with clear respect for the perspectives and expertise of each.

◆ Recognition of the history, culture, and organization of the school environment.

◆ Continuous program assessment that captures the perspectives of all those involved, uses a variety of strategies, focuses on the process and effects of the program, and feeds directly into program improvement and evaluation.

(NRC, 1996:70)

Conclusion

Standards and professional development are critical companions. Professional development is needed for standards to move outside the very documents that contain them and eventually into the practice of every teacher and the learning of every student. Fortunately, standards for professional development provide criteria for judging whether the learning opportunities available to teachers and other educators are the ones that will lead them to support ambitious learning goals for all students.

Notes

[1] Although system change requires that all professionals acquire new knowledge and skills, in this section we focus on teachers as learners, especially because readers are more likely to work with teachers in professional development settings.

[2] Note that these examples are meant to illustrate the professional development standards, not to provide activities to adopt unless they fit a carefully crafted, long-term design for professional development. The Loucks-Horsley and Stiles chapter in this book discusses program design, describing how activities such as these and many others form a repertoire for professional developers that can be drawn upon, depending on teacher needs and the constraints and resources of the context.

[3] Note that we have not suggested that all short-term workshops and institutes are necessarily ineffective, but they should be part of a longer-term design by either individual teachers as they construct their long-term learning goals and activities or professional developers whose role it is to help teachers transform their teaching practice.

References

American Association for the Advancement of Science. 1993. *Benchmarks for science literacy.* Washington, DC: American Association for the Advancement of Science.

Anderson, R. 1998. The research on teaching as inquiry. Paper prepared for the Center for Science, Mathematics, and Engineering Education, National Research Council, Washington, DC.

Ball, D. 1988. Unlearning to teach mathematics. *For the Learning of Mathematics* 8(1):40–48.

———. 1996. Teacher learning and the mathematics reforms: What we think we know and what we need to learn. *Phi Delta Kappan* 77(7):500–508.

Bybee, R. 1997. *Achieving scientific literacy*. Portsmouth, NH: Heinemann.

Cohen, D., and C. A. Barnes. 1993. Pedagogy and policy, and conclusion: A new pedagogy for policy? In D. K. Cohen, M. W. McLaughlin, & J. E. Talbert (Eds.), *Teaching for understanding: Challenges for policy and practice*. San Francisco: Jossey-Bass.

Driver, R., E. Griesne, and A. Libeighian. 1985. *Children's ideas in science*. Philadelphia: Open University Press.

Driver, R., J. Leach, R. Millar, and P. Scott. 1996. *Young people's images of science*. Philadelphia: Open University Press.

Driver, R., A. Squires, P. Duckworth, and V. Wood-Robinson. 1994. *Making sense of secondary science: Research into children's ideas*. New York: Routledge.

Guzzatti, B., T. Snyder, G. Glass, and W. Gamas. 1993. Promoting conceptual change in science: A comparative meta-analysis of instructional interventions from reading education and science education. *Reading Research Quarterly* 28(2):117–159.

Harvard-Smithsonian Center for Astrophysics. 1987. *A private universe*. Video available from Annenberg CPB, S. Burlington, VT.

Hodson, D., and J. Hodson. 1998. From constructivism to social constructivism: A Vygotskian perspective on teaching and learning science. *School Science Review* 79(28):33–41.

King, A. 1994. Guiding knowledge construction in the classroom: Effects of teaching children how to question and how to explain. *American Educational Research Journal* 31(2):338–368.

Loucks-Horsley, S., P. W. Hewson, N. Love, and K. E. Stiles. 1998. *Designing professional development for teachers of science and mathematics*. Thousand Oaks, CA: Corwin Press.

National Center for Educational Statistics. 1996. *Pursuing excellence: A study of U.S. eighth-grade mathematics and science teaching, learning, curriculum, and achievement in international context*. Washington, DC: U.S. Government Printing Office.

———. 1998. *Pursuing excellence: A study of U.S. twelfth-grade mathematics and science teaching, learning, curriculum, and achievement in international context*. Washington, DC: U.S. Government Printing Office.

National Research Council. 1996. *The national science education standards*. Washington, DC: National Academy Press.

Novak, J. D. 1998. Teaching science and the science of learning. *Studies in Science Education* 15:77–100.

Ravitch, D. 1995. *National standards in American education: A citizen's guide*. Washington, DC: Brookings Institution.

Rothman, R. 1995. *Measuring up: Standards, assessment, and school reform*. San Francisco: Jossey-Bass.

Russell, S. J. 1996. The role of curriculum in teacher development. In S. N. Friel and G. W. Bright (Eds.), *Reflecting on our work: NSF teacher enhancement in K–6 mathematics*. Lanham, MD: University Press of America, Inc.

Schmidt, W., C. McKnight, and S. Raizen. 1996. *Splintered vision: An investigation of U. S. science and mathematics education*. E. Lansing, MI: Michigan State University, U.S. National Research Center for the Third International Mathematics and Science Study.

Shulman, L. S. 1987. Knowledge and teaching: Foundations of the new reform. *Harvard Educational Review* 57:1–22.

Shymansky, J. A., W. C. Kyle, Jr., and J. M. Alport. 1983. The effects of new science curricula on student performance. *Journal of Research on Science Teaching* 20(5):387–404.

Staver, J. R. 1994. Constructivism: Sound theory for explicating the practice of science and science teaching. *Journal of Research in Science Teaching* 35(5):501–520.

Strycker, J. 1995. Science first. *Science and Children* 32(7), 26–29.

Technical Educational Resource Centers. 1997. *Sense-making in science*. Portsmouth, NH: Heinemann.

Thompson, C. L., and J. S. Zeuli. 1999. The frame and the tapestry: Standards-based reform and professional development. In G. Sykes (Ed.), *Teaching as the learning profession: handbook of policy and practice*. San Francisco: Jossey-Bass.

Tucker, M., and J. Codding. 1998. *Standards for our schools: How to set them, measure them, and reach them*. San Francisco: Jossey-Bass.

Professional Development Designed to Change Science Teaching and Learning

Susan Loucks-Horsley and Katherine E. Stiles
National Institute for Science Education at WestEd and the National Research Council

Susan Loucks-Horsley was director of the Professional Development Project at the National Institute for Science Education, WestEd, and director of Professional Development and Outreach at the National Research Council's Center for Science, Mathematics, and Engineering Education. Her work focuses on policies and practices for effective professional development, standards-based reform in science and mathematics, and educational change. She has written numerous books, chapters, and articles in these areas.

Katherine E. Stiles is on the staff of WestEd, where she is involved in projects focused on professional development and evaluation in science education. She works with the National Institute for Science Education to examine models of effective professional development for mathematics and science teachers and with the National Research Council's Center for Science, Mathematics, and Engineering Education to disseminate the *National Science Education Standards*. Stiles also serves as program coordinator of the National Academy for Science Education Leadership, designed to enhance the knowledge, skills, and strategies of current leaders of science education reform.

In today's world of new discoveries and constantly evolving scientific knowledge, students must learn more than can be absorbed from simply reading about science—they need to *do* science, becoming critical thinkers and evaluators of what they observe and learn. This requires that teachers teach in ways that are often new and unfamiliar to them, and that they have the science content knowledge necessary to help them guide their students' thinking and understanding.

Currently, most teachers across the country continue to attend one-time workshops that rarely help them integrate new teaching strategies into their classrooms (National Commission on Teaching & America's Future, 1996). Changing science teaching and learning means changing the ways in which professional development meets teachers' needs.

What would this "new" professional development look like? Loucks-Horsley, Stiles, and Hewson (1996) examined national standards and related materials to determine whether the leading science and professional development organizations share a common understanding of and promotion for what a new vision of professional development should resemble. Their review indicated that these organizations do, in fact, share a common vision and suggested that the best professional development experiences for science teachers include the following principles:

1. *A commitment to the concept that* all *children can and should learn science in ways that reflect an emphasis on inquiry-based learning, problem-solving, student investigation and discovery, and application of knowledge.*

If teachers are to address the learning of all students, their professional development must engage them in learning major science concepts, understanding how children learn science, practicing and implementing new teaching strategies, and making informed decisions concerning science curriculum and instruction.

2. *The implementation and modeling of instructional methods to promote adult learning of science that mirror the methods to be used with students.*

Professional development must build on teacher' current knowledge and practices in science, introducing them to new information and strategies in ways that allow them to deepen their science content knowledge and build their pedagogical content knowledge (Shulman, 1987)—knowing *how* to teach science concepts and principles to students of all ages and developmental levels. Teachers need the opportunity to work collaboratively and reflect on what they are learning, and the time to practice the skills they are learning—the same opportunities they must give their students.

3. *Professional development experiences that build a community and culture of learning and enhance the capacity of teachers to become science education leaders.*

Community and leadership cannot occur if teachers remain isolated from each other. Departments and schools must institute policies and procedures that support teacher collaboration, risk taking, collegiality with other teachers as well as with experts outside of the school environment, and teachers taking on leadership roles within and outside of the school. Developing this community requires recognition that professional learning is a lifelong process that is best nurtured within the norms and culture of the school.

4. *Consciously designed structures that link professional development in science to other parts of the educational system.*

Aligning professional development with science standards, curriculum frameworks, and assessments can help ensure that what teachers are learning and implementing in their classrooms is consistent with the goals and policies of the school and district. Establishing consistency across all levels of the system reflects a commitment to long-term, sustained professional development that promotes student and teacher learning.

5. *Professional development programs that constantly review and assess their effectiveness and ability to meet their goals and align with their vision.*

Quality programs establish regular and consistent procedures for evaluating both short-term effectiveness (i.e., teacher satisfaction and engagement) and long-term impact (i.e., changes in science teaching, student learning, the school community) in order to continuously improve design and implementation.

A Framework for Designing Professional Development

Professional development that reflects these principles does not simply emerge; it results from a deliberate process of designing learning opportunities for teachers that enhance their science teaching and their students' learning of science teacher leaders, school or district administrators, curriculum coordinators, staff developers, university-based teacher educators, and outside trainers or consultants—have an important challenge. People who design professional development—including like teaching in a classroom, each professional learning situation for adults requires a set of strategies that address the goals, audience, and opportunities and constraints of the context—one size usually does *not* fit all.

There are several elements that need to be carefully considered when designing professional development. Figure 1 illustrates a design that organizes these elements in ways that suggest both how to *design* a new program and how to *analyze* the design of an existing program framework (Loucks-Horsley, Hewson, Love, & Stiles, 1998).

Four inputs are critical to consider when designing professional development: context, knowledge and beliefs, critical issues, and strategies for professional learning.

The four boxes through the center of the framework represent a planning and design process that guides the work of professional developers. This process emphasizes that designing professional development is strategic, thoughtful work and not simply a matter of always offering what is easiest, most expedient, or most attractive at the moment. At the beginning of the process, designers identify and agree upon goals and desired outcomes—all other elements of the design are guided by these. Laying out a plan that carefully considers all other elements and establishes a time line for the plan leads to implementation. Continually reflecting and evaluating at each step of the process enables designers to adjust continuously, as well as to return to earlier plans in order to make improvements.

This planning cycle guides the overall design of a professional development program or initiative; it is also used to monitor specific events to increase effectiveness. Thus, the four-step cycle can occur over several months or within the context of an hour-long experience. And it is not always a sequential process; often, designers find themselves in the midst of implementing a plan and want to "go backward" and rethink whether the plan meshes with their goals and desired outcomes.

The design framework includes four inputs that are critical to consider when designing professional development: context, knowledge and beliefs, critical issues, and strategies for professional learning. These inputs inform the development of a plan uniquely designed to meet the particular needs of the teachers and students it is intended for.

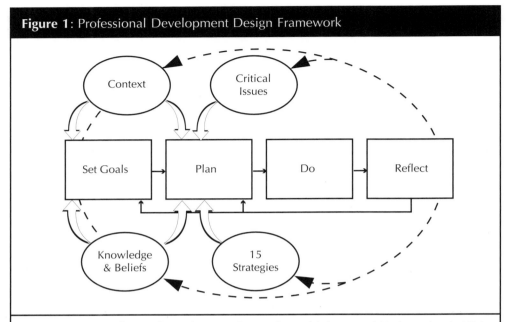

Figure 1: Professional Development Design Framework

From *Designing Professional Development for Teachers of Science and Mathematics*, (p.17) by Susan Loucks-Horsley, Peter W. Hewson, Nancy Love, and Katherine W. Stiles, with Hubert M. Dyasi, Susan Friel, Judith Mumme, Carey I. Sneider, and Karen L. Worth, 1998, Thousand Oaks, CA: Corwin Press. Copyright 1998 by Corwin Press. Reprinted with permission.

Context

Designers need to carefully analyze and understand the context in which their teachers teach and their students learn. The authors (Loucks-Horsley et al., 1998) identified several factors that constitute the context: the needs and nature of the students; the backgrounds, needs, and teaching responsibilities of the teachers; the resources available and the degree of community support; the organization, expectations, and current demands of the schools and districts; and the history of professional development that teachers have engaged in previously. When they understand all of these elements, designers are better able to develop a professional development program that fits the specific needs of the teachers and students.

Knowledge and Beliefs

Designers need not design professional development programs or initiatives from scratch nor need they work in a vacuum. They have a broad knowledge base from research and best practice from which to start. Specifically, Loucks-Horsley and her associates (1998) point to several areas in which there is substantial information that can and should influence the ultimate design: learners and how they learn, teachers and how they teach, the nature of science as a discipline, professional development and the principles that guide a design to ensure it is effective, and the change process that takes place in both individuals and organizations. Knowledge in all of these areas—knowledge that is grounded in research, as well as in the "craft wisdom" of experienced professional developers—influences the choices the designers make as they develop a plan.

Critical Issues

Critical issues are just that—critical. Although designers do not necessarily need to address all of these issues at the onset of a program, they do need to consider the important roles these issues may play as the program is underway. In some cases, neglecting one of these issues may block the success of the professional development. The issues are: ensuring equity, building a professional culture, developing leadership, building capacity for professional learning, scaling up resources, garnering public support, supporting standards and frameworks, evaluating professional development, and finding time for professional development. Knowing that these issues can influence the effectiveness of a professional development program alerts designers to pay attention to each of them at some point during the life of the program.

> *It is knowledge of the repertoire of strategies from which to choose that increases the effectiveness of the professional development program or initiative.*

Strategies for Professional Learning

No longer are designers limited to one-time workshops. There are numerous strategies that can be combined in different ways at different times to enhance teacher learning (Loucks-Horsley et al., 1998). Selecting among the strategies and knowing how to combine them at different points throughout a program depends on the knowledge of best practice, the particular context, and the analysis to critical issues discussed earlier. There is no one right way to select and combine the strategies; each situation requires its own unique model. It is knowledge of the repertoire of strategies from which to choose that increases the effectiveness of the professional development program or initiative. The Eisenhower National Clearinghouse for Mathematics and Science Education (1998) synthesized the work of Loucks-Horsley et al. (1998) and categorized the 15 strategies identified by these authors according to the nature of the strategies and the purposes of each (see Table 1).

Designs for Professional Development

The first half of this article has been about designing professional development—that is, using a process that ensures a more strategic, comprehensive, long-term, and informed professional development program. This focus implies that the resulting *design* is unique and must be developed from scratch, and that one combination of professional learning strategies is as good as another combination. Yet just as the professional development community knows a great deal about the individual strategies for professional learning, we are beginning to learn about professional development *designs*—particular combinations of strategies that seem to work for particular goals and contexts.

In this section, we describe some of these designs, framing the descriptions with the questions: What are some of the most pressing challenges that professional developers seem to be facing, and what designs are helping them meet those challenges?

The challenge to reach many is exacerbated by the need for each teacher to have more sustained time to learn, practice, and refine his or her knowledge and skills.

First, the challenges. One challenge is to strengthen the science content knowledge of teachers. This challenge is very complex. It involves helping teachers who have had no or extremely limited opportunities to learn science, such as the typical elementary school teacher and middle or high school teachers prepared to teach content areas other than science. It also involves updating the content knowledge of teachers whose content was learned in courses that viewed science as a body of information to be learned rather than a way of understanding and knowing the natural world. If the core of science is scientific inquiry and teachers have neither experienced nor developed the abilities of inquiry, they lack fundamental understandings needed to teach science to today's—and certainly tomorrow's— students. Strengthening the science knowledge of a large percentage of teachers is a major challenge for professional developers.

One of the critical issues noted above is another particularly demanding challenge: scaling up. Professional developers are challenged by the large numbers of teachers who have learning needs (which includes all teachers, although their learning needs vary). The challenge to reach many is exacerbated by the need for each teacher to have more sustained time to learn, practice, and refine his or her knowledge and skills. The challenge to professional developers is to do more for more teachers; thus, different designs are called for.

A third challenge for professional developers is promoting systemic reform. The image of the professional developer as one who finely crafts workshops for a relatively small number of teachers who come from a number of different schools or districts is becoming a thing of the past. Increasingly, professional development includes both individual teacher development and organization development (and here the organization might be the department, school, or district). It comes from recognizing that those few teachers mentioned above often return to schools where they have no support from administrators, materials to work with, colleagues to collaborate with, or goals to share and, as a result, never use what they learned in their workshops, no matter how good they are. Further, could they overcome these problems, these same teachers are often faced with a curriculum and assessments at odds with what they learned; school, district, or state mandates or priorities that work against using what they learned; and other professional development offerings that

Table 1: Strategies for Professional Learning					
Strategies	A	B	C	D	E
Immersion					
1. Immersion in Inquiry into Science and Mathematics: Engaging in the kinds of learning that teachers are expected to practice with their students—that is, inquiry-based science investigations or meaningful mathematics problem solving.	x	X			X
2. Immersion in the World of Scientists and Mathematicians: Participating in an intensive experience in the day-to-day work of a scientist or mathematician, often in a laboratory, industry, or museum, with full engagement in research activities.	x	X			
Curriculum					
3. Curriculum Implementation: Learning, using, and refining use of a particular set of instructional materials in the classroom.		x	x	X	
4. Curriculum Replacement Units: Implementing a unit of instruction that addresses one topic or concept and incorporates effective teaching and learning strategies to accomplish learning goals.			x	x	X
5. Curriculum Development/Adaptation: Creating new instructional materials and strategies or tailoring existing ones to meet the learning needs of students.		x	X		
Examining Practice					
6. Action Research: Examining teachers' own teaching and their students' learning by engaging in a research project in their classroom.		x			X
7. Case Discussions: Examining written narratives or videotapes of classroom teaching and learning and discussing what is happening and the problems, issues, and outcomes that ensue.		x	x		X
8. Examining Student Work and Student Thinking and Scoring Assessments: Carefully examining students' work and products to understand their thinking and learning strategies and identify their learning needs and appropriate teaching strategies and materials.		x	x	x	X
Collaborative Work					
9. Study Groups: Engaging in regular, structured, and collaborative interactions regarding topics identified by the group, with opportunities to examine new information, reflect on their practice, or assess and analyze outcome data.		x		x	X

(continued on following page)

A Strategies that focus on **developing awareness** are usually used during the beginning phases of a change. The strategies are designed to elicit thoughtful questioning on the part of the teachers concerning new information.

B Strategies that focus on **building knowledge** provide opportunities for teachers to deepen their understanding of mathematics content and teaching practices.

C Strategies that help **teachers translate new knowledge into practice** engage teachers in drawing on their knowledge base to plan instruction and improve their teaching.

D Strategies that focus on **practicing teaching** help teachers learn through the process of using a new approach with their students. As teachers practice new moves in their classrooms, they deepen their understanding.

E Strategies that provide opportunities to **reflect** deeply on teaching and learning engage teachers in assessing the impact of the changes on their students and thinking about ways to improve. These strategies also encourage teachers to reflect on others' practice, adapting ideas for their own use.

NOTE: A capital "X" indicates the primary purpose for each strategy and a lowercase "x" indicates one or more secondary purposes.

Table 1: (continued from previous page)					
Strategies	A	B	C	D	E
10. Coaching and Mentoring: Working one-on-one with an equally or more experienced teacher to improve teaching and learning through a variety of activities, including classroom observation and feedback, problem solving, troubleshooting, and coplanning.	x	x	**X**	x	
11. Partnerships with Scientists and Mathematicians in Business, Industry, and Universities: Working collaboratively with practicing scientists and mathematicians with the focus on improving teacher content knowledge, instructional materials, and access to facilities and on acquiring new information.	x	**X**			
12. Professional Networks: Linking in person or through electronic means with other teachers or groups to explore and discuss topics of interest, set and pursue common goals, share information and strategies, and identify and address common problems.	x	**X**	x		x
Vehicles and Mechanisms					
13. Workshops, Institutes, Courses, and Seminars: Using structured opportunities outside of the classroom to focus intensely on topics of interest, including science or mathematics content, and learn from others with more expertise.	x	**X**	x		
14. Technology for Professional Learning: Using various kinds of technology to learn content and pedagogy, including computers, telecommunications, videoconferencing, and CD-ROM and videodisc technology.	x	**X**	x		x
15. Developing Professional Developers: Building the skills and knowledge needed to create learning experiences for other educators, including design of appropriate professional development strategies; presenting, demonstrating, and supporting teacher learning and change; and understanding in-depth the content and pedagogy required for effective teaching and learning of students and other educators.		x	x	**X**	x

have little or nothing to do with what they have learned. If professional developers are indeed going to succeed in helping teachers become more knowledgeable and skilled in teaching, their professional development designs need to address this challenge of changing the system, not just the individual teacher.

If those are the challenges—building teachers' science content knowledge, scaling up, and promoting systemic reform—then what designs for professional development seem to hold promise for addressing these challenges? Just as there are no surefire models of effective professional development, there are no surefire designs to meet all these challenges. Yet there are some interesting combinations of strategies that appear to hold promise.

Strengthening Teacher Content Knowledge Through Study of Curriculum
As noted in Table 1, curriculum figures prominently in several professional development strategies. These curriculum-related strategies also combine in interesting ways with other strategies to address each of the challenges discussed above.

Curriculum is the way content is organized and delivered by teachers to their students. It includes the content, teaching strategies (including assessment strategies), and learning environments selected and used by the teacher (National Resource Center, 1996). It is typically determined by the textbooks that schools and teachers choose to use; but, increasingly, states and districts are concerned that students should have learning experiences across their K–12 school career that carefully build the knowledge and skills delineated in their standards documents. Therefore, in many cases, the science curriculum is determined by districts responsible for K–12 education and, when done well, creates the framework in which teachers can teach and students can achieve the valued outcomes.

Returning to the professional development challenge: In a context where teachers are limited in their own depth of understanding of the science content in ambitious standards documents, professional developers can begin by using a curriculum-related strategy. These include curriculum implementation, curriculum replacement units, or curriculum adaptation. We have not listed the strategy of "curriculum development," because this requires teachers who have high levels of content knowledge. Teachers can use curriculum materials that are carefully developed to provide students with experiences to help them achieve those standards. There are many materials that have been developed over the past five or more years with National Science Foundation funds and are available as alternatives to commercial textbooks. Research and experience are beginning to show that when teachers learn to use these new programs with their students, the teachers themselves learn important science content (Russell, 1996) and their students show learning gains (Cohen & Hill, 1998). The early professional development is typically in workshop or institute formats, with careful exploration of what content students learn from the materials and how teachers can use them. Subsequent professional development that sustains and deepens teacher learning over time uses the strategies of coaching or mentoring—in which teachers are observed using the materials and suggestions made for improving their practice—and examining student work, in which teachers share student products such as reports of their inquiries and responses to assessments and discuss the student thinking that is indicated by those responses. Case discussions, using either written cases or videos of teaching, are another strategy for deepening teacher understanding of what students are learning, which includes the science content the teachers sometimes do not know well. Early professional development emphasizes the mechanics and management of the materials; later, it focuses on student thinking and learning. This aligns with the development of teachers' questions and concerns as they implement new and challenging materials with their students (Loucks-Horsley & Stiegelbauer, 1991).

Scaling-Up

The above scenario in many ways addresses the second issue as well: scaling-up, or reaching a large number of teachers. A common set of curriculum materials—ones that carefully build student conceptual understanding over the grades—provides a focus for teachers within a grade level (because they are mastering the same materials and science concepts) and then across grades (where the issue of student concept development over time and articulation over time can be an important focus for exploration and discussion). This works best when professional development is school-based—that is, all teachers in the school have common learning experiences related to their curriculum materials, with opportunities to work out how these materials will be used with their students in their particular school situation.

[handwritten annotations at top: "different forms of summer institutes, workshops (local + ab regional mtgs) and combination of them to reach BSCS certification ? BSCS PD ? job-embedded"]

When professional development is school-based, there is more opportunity for it to be "job-embedded" (Sparks, 1994)—that is, learning is structured to occur at the same time as teachers are teaching, thus eliminating the need for large amounts of released time. Job-embedded strategies include action research, where teachers identify questions they have about their students and teaching, design an inquiry, gather data, and analyze the data to respond to their questions; coaching and mentoring are job-embedded, as is the gathering of particular kinds of student work. Although such strategies require protected time for teachers to meet together and process what they are learning, that time is on-site and can be in one- to two- hour segments, making it more cost effective than the alternative, "pull-out" professional development programs. A further advantage is that teachers' work together is firmly grounded in their common school and classroom contexts and relates to the students for whom they share responsibility.

> *Professional development designs that address the issue of scaling up also make use of the strategy of developing professional developers.*

Professional development designs that address the issue of scaling up also make use of the strategy of developing professional developers. This strategy begins with teachers or others who have been through sustained professional development in the curriculum materials and used them carefully over time, then provides them with knowledge, skills, and strategies for working with adult learners and supporting teachers as they change their practice. These professional developers are equipped to use a variety of strategies such as those described earlier; for example, they can conduct workshops and institutes, facilitate case discussions and examinations of student work, coach and mentor, and lead action research seminars. They learn to design professional development—that is, they can identify a set of goals, analyze the context, and select the most promising professional development strategy(ies). Building this capacity for supporting the professional learning of other teachers takes time; in this way, this strategy differs from some of the "training of trainers" strategies of the past, in which teachers attended workshops or institutes and were expected to return to conduct the same for their colleagues. Allotting the time and attention required to build new professional developers, especially among teachers, is another way to address the issue of scaling-up.

Promoting Systemic Reform

Finally, this combination of strategies contributes to systemic change. As professional developers use the design framework, they become increasingly sensitive to the other components of the system that must be attended to for teacher learning to both succeed and be sustained. In the combination of strategies noted above, for example, the inclusion of a carefully selected, standards-based set of curriculum materials as a focus for teacher learning has brought together two essential components of the system: curriculum and professional development. Instructional strategies and assessment are naturally included in professional development focused on this kind of curriculum.

In addition, when professional developers use the design framework, they develop the habit of continuous reflection and revision, a critical process in systems thinking. In the scenario above, this skill is spread widely among educators through the strategy of developing professional developers. It is not reserved only for the original planning team. Similarly, attention to the many inputs into design, the knowledge base, the critical issues, and a repertoire of strategies broadens the view of what needs to go into decision making and deepens knowledge of learning, teaching, and the change process. And it reinforces the need for sustained initiatives that touch a critical mass of educators strongly committed to a common vision. We have discovered that use of the framework for designing professional development helps educators learn how to design systemic initiatives, not just professional development.

Use of the framework for designing professional development helps educators learn how to design systemic initiatives, not just professional development.

Conclusion

Our work in professional development has only begun. Important questions remain about the efficacy of particular strategies or combinations of strategies and their ability to focus critical attention on learning and teaching of important science content, abilities, and habits of mind. The design framework and identified strategies are tools that appear to be useful for professional developers as they explore their work and labor to increase their impact. Indeed, they serve as lenses for inquiry into their complex and ever-challenging mission of increased learning for all.

References

Cohen, D. K., and H. C. Hill. 1998. State policy and classroom performance: Mathematics reform in California. *CPRE Policy Briefs,* RB-23-January. Philadelphia: University of Pennsylvania, Graduate School of Education.

Eisenhower National Clearinghouse for Mathematics and Science Education. 1998. *Ideas that work: Mathematics professional development.* Columbus, OH: ENC.

Loucks-Horsley, S., P.W. Hewson, N. Love, and K. E. Stiles. 1998. *Designing professional development for teachers of science and mathematics.* Thousand Oaks, CA: Corwin Press.

Loucks-Horsley, S., and S. Stiegelbauer. 1991. Using knowledge of change to guide staff development. In *Staff development for education in the '90s: New demands, new realities, new perspectives,* ed. A. Lieberman and L. Miller. New York: Teachers College Press.

Loucks-Horsley, S., K. Stiles, and P. Hewson. 1996. *Principles of effective professional development for mathematics and science education: A synthesis of standards.* Madison, WI: University of Wisconsin at Madison, National Institute for Science Education.

National Commission on Teaching & America's Future. 1996. *What Matters Most? Teaching for America's Future.* New York: NCTAF.

National Research Council. 1996. *National science education standards.* Washington, DC: National Academy Press.

Russell, S. J. 1996. The role of curriculum in teacher development. In *Reflecting on our work: NSF teacher enhancement in K–6 mathematics*, ed. S. N. Friel and G. W. Bright. Lanham, MD: University Press of America.

Shulman, L. S. 1987. Knowledge and teaching: Foundations of the new reform. *Harvard Educational Review* 57:1–22.

Sparks, D. 1994. A paradigm shift in staff development. *Education Week*, 16 March:42.

If We Want to Talk the Talk, We Must Also Walk the Walk: The Nature of Science, Professional Development, and Educational Reform

Norman G. Lederman, Fouad Abd-El-Khalick, and Randy L. Bell
Department of Science and Mathematics Education, Oregon State University

Norman Lederman is a professor of science education and director of the Academy of Excellence in Science and Mathematics Education at Oregon State University. He is a former teacher and author of over 100 journal articles and book chapters and has directed or participated in numerous funded teacher enhancement and professional development initiatives. He is editor of *School Science and Mathematics*, former president of the Association for the Education of Teachers in Science (AETS), and former NSTA Division Director for Teacher Education.

Fouad Abd-El-Khalick is an assistant professor of science education at the University of Illinois. He is a former teacher and author of several research articles related to teachers' and students' conceptions of the nature of science.

Randy Bell is assistant professor of science education at the University of Virginia. He is a former science teacher and author of several research articles an commentaries related to teaching and learning the nature of science.

Helping students develop adequate conceptions of the nature of science (NOS) is a perennial objective in science education (American Association for the Advancement of Science [AAAS], 1990, 1993; Klopfer, 1969; National Research Council [NRC], 1996; National Science Teachers Association [NSTA], 1982). Indeed, this objective has been agreed upon by most scientists and science educators for the past 90 years (Central Association of Science and Mathematics Teachers, 1907; Kimball, 1967–68; Lederman, 1992). Presently, despite their varying pedagogical or curricular emphases, there is strong agreement among the major reform efforts in science education (AAAS, 1990, 1993; NRC, 1996) about the importance of enhancing students' conceptions of the NOS. In fact, "the longevity of this educational objective has been surpassed only by the longevity of students' inability to articulate the meaning of the phrase 'nature of science,' and to delineate the associated characteristics of science (Lederman & Niess, 1997, p. 1)." Despite numerous attempts, including the major curricular reform efforts of the 1960s, to improve students' views of the scientific endeavor, students have consistently been shown to possess inadequate understandings of several aspects of the NOS (e.g., Aikenhead,

1973; Bady, 1979; Broadhurst, 1970; Lederman & O'Malley, 1990; Mackay, 1971; Mead & Metraux, 1957; Rubba & Andersen, 1978; Tamir & Zohar, 1991; Wilson, 1954).

Consequently, it is only natural to ask whether there are reasons to believe that the recent reforms in science education are more likely to impact students' understandings of the NOS than their predecessors. It is our view that the current reform documents' emphasis on the NOS are likely to have as little impact as earlier efforts. Two critical and interrelated omissions that have typified previous efforts are, unfortunately, evident in the more recent reform documents. There is not, and there has not been, a concerted professional development effort to clearly communicate, first, what is meant by the "NOS" and, second, how a functional understanding of this valued aspect of science can be communicated to K–12 stu-

In reality, the NOS represents much more than a small piece of the subject matter specified in the Standards.

dents. Perhaps the lack of professional development concerns related to the NOS is a consequence of the misunderstanding that the NOS is just a small aspect of subject matter understanding. After all, within the *National Science Education Standards*, the NOS is primarily addressed at the end of the long litany of specific science subject matter and processes that students are expected to "know and do." In reality, the NOS represents much more than a small piece of the subject matter specified in the *Standards*. NOS permeates all areas of the discipline-specific standards and is a critical component of the standards on "science as inquiry." Furthermore, an understanding of the NOS underlies the essence of the *Teaching and Assessment Standards*. And it is easily argued that a teacher who lacks adequate conceptions of the NOS and a functional understanding of how to teach this valued aspect of science cannot orchestrate the types of instructional activities and atmosphere or even assess students' progress as specified in the *Standards*. Indeed, a functional understanding of the NOS by teachers is clearly prerequisite to any hopes of achieving the vision of science teaching and learning specified in the *National Science Education Standards*. In the following sections, we will clarify the meaning of the NOS and provide a series of concrete, classroom-tested approaches for promoting student understandings.

What is the NOS?

The phrase "nature of science" typically refers to the epistemology of science, science as a way of knowing, or the values and beliefs inherent to the development of scientific knowledge (Lederman, 1992). Beyond these general characterizations, no consensus presently exists among philosophers of science, historians of science, scientists, and science educators on a specific definition for the NOS. This lack of consensus, however, should neither be disconcerting nor surprising, given the multifaceted nature and complexity of the scientific endeavor. Conceptions of the NOS have changed throughout the development of science and systematic thinking about science and are reflected in the ways the scientific and science education communities have defined the phrase "nature of science" during the past 100 years (e.g., AAAS, 1990, 1993; Central Association for Science and Mathematics Teachers, 1907; Klopfer & Watson, 1957; NSTA, 1982).

It is our view, however, that many of the disagreements about the definition or meaning of the NOS that continue to exist among philosophers, historians, and science educators are irrelevant to K–12 instruction. The issue of the existence of an objective reality as compared to phenomenal realities is a case in point. We argue that there is an acceptable level of generality regarding the NOS that is accessible to K–12 students and relevant to their daily lives. Moreover, at this level, little disagreement exists among philosophers, historians, and science educators. Among the characteristics of the scientific enterprise corresponding to this level of generality are that scientific knowledge is tentative (subject to change); empirically-based (based on and/or derived from observations of the natural world); subjective (theory-laden); necessarily involves human inference, imagination, and creativity (involves the invention of explanations); and is socially and culturally embedded. Two additional important aspects are the distinction between observations and inferences and the functions of and relationships between scientific theories and laws. We now *briefly* consider these characteristics of science and scientific knowledge.

Many of the disagreements about the definition or meaning of the NOS that continue to exist among philosophers, historians, and science educators are irrelevant to K–12 instruction.

First, students should be aware of the crucial distinction between observation and inference. Observations are descriptive statements about natural phenomena that are "directly" accessible to the senses (or extensions of the senses) and about which several observers can reach consensus with relative ease. For example, objects released above ground level tend to fall and hit the ground. By contrast, inferences are statements about phenomena that are not "directly" accessible to the senses. For example, objects tend to fall to the ground because of "gravity." The notion of gravity is inferential in the sense that it can *only* be accessed and/or measured through its manifestations or effects. Examples of such effects include the perturbations in predicted planetary orbits due to interplanetary "attractions" and the bending of light coming from the stars as its rays pass through the sun's "gravitational" field.

Second, closely related to the distinction between observations and inferences is the distinction between scientific laws and theories. Individuals often hold a simplistic, hierarchical view of the relationship between theories and laws, whereby theories become laws depending on the availability of supporting evidence. It follows from this notion that scientific laws have a higher status than scientific theories. Both notions, however, are inappropriate because, among other things, theories and laws are different kinds of knowledge and one cannot become the other. Laws are *statements or descriptions of the relationships* among observable phenomena. Boyle's law, which relates the pressure of a gas to its volume at a constant temperature, is a case in point. Theories, by contrast, *are inferred explanations* for observable phenomena. The kinetic molecular theory, which explains Boyle's law, is one example. Moreover, theories are as legitimate a product of science as laws. Scientists do not usually formulate theories in the hope that one day they would acquire the status of "law." Scientific theories, in their own right, serve important roles, such as guiding investigations and generating new research problems, in addition to explaining relatively huge sets of seemingly unrelated observations in more than one field of investigation. For example, the kinetic molecular theory serves to explain phenomena that relate to changes in the physical states of matter, others that relate to the rates of chemical reactions, and still other phenomena that relate to heat and its transfer, to mention just a few.

Science involves the invention of explanations, and this requires a great deal of creativity by scientists.

Third, even though scientific knowledge is, at least partially, based on and/or derived from observations of the natural world (i.e., empirical), it nevertheless involves human imagination and creativity. Science, contrary to common belief, is not a lifeless, rational, and orderly activity. Science involves the *invention* of explanations, and this requires a great deal of creativity by scientists. The "leap" from atomic spectral lines to Bohr's model of the atom, with its elaborate orbits and energy levels, is a case in point. This aspect of science, coupled with its inferential nature, entails that scientific concepts, such as atoms, black holes, and species, are functional theoretical models rather than faithful copies of reality.

Fourth, scientific knowledge is subjective or theory-laden. Scientists' theoretical commitments, beliefs, previous knowledge, training, experiences, and expectations actually influence their work. All these background factors form *a mind-set* that *affects* the problems scientists investigate and how they conduct their investigations, what they observe (and do not observe), and how they make sense of or interpret their observations. It is this (sometimes collective) individuality or mind-set that accounts for the role of subjectivity in the production of scientific knowledge. It is noteworthy that, contrary to common belief, science never starts with neutral observations (Chalmers, 1982). Observations (and investigations) are always motivated and guided by and acquire meaning in reference to questions or problems. These questions or problems, in turn, are derived from within certain theoretical perspectives.

Fifth, science as a human enterprise is practiced in the context of a larger culture and its practitioners (scientists) are the product of that culture. Science, it follows, affects and is affected by the various elements and intellectual spheres of the culture in which it is embedded. These elements include, but are not limited to: social fabric, power structures, politics, socioeconomic factors, philosophy, and religion. An example may help to illustrate how social and cultural factors impact scientific knowledge. Telling the story of the evolution of humans (*Homo sapiens*) over the course of the past 7 million years is central to the biosocial sciences. Scientists have formulated several elaborate and differing story lines about this evolution. Until recently, the dominant story was centered about "the man-hunter" and *his* crucial role in the evolution of humans to the form we now know (Lovejoy, 1981). This scenario was consistent with the white-male culture that dominated scientific circles up to the 1960s and early 1970s. As the feminist movement grew stronger and women were able to claim recognition in the various scientific disciplines, the story about hominid evolution started to change. One story that is more consistent with a feminist approach is centered about "the female-gatherer" and *her* central role in the evolution of humans (Hrdy, 1986). It is noteworthy that both story lines are consistent with the available evidence.

Sixth, it follows from the previous discussions that scientific knowledge is never absolute or certain. This knowledge, including "facts," theories, and laws, is tentative and subject to change. Scientific claims change as new evidence, made possible through advances in *theory* and technology, is brought to bear on existing theories or laws, or as old evidence is reinterpreted in the light of new theoretical advances or shifts in the directions of established research programs. It should be emphasized that tentativeness in science does not only arise from the fact that scientific knowledge is inferential, creative, and socially and culturally embedded. There are also compelling logical arguments that lend credence to the notion of tentativeness in science. Indeed, contrary to common belief, scientific hypotheses, theories, and laws can *never* be absolutely "proven." This holds irrespective of the amount of empirical evidence gathered in support of one of these ideas or the other (Popper, 1963, 1988). For example, to be "proven," a certain scientific law should account for *every single instance* of the phenomenon it purports to describe *at all times*. It can logically be argued that one such future instance, of which we have no knowledge whatsoever, may behave in a manner contrary to what the law states. As such, the law can never acquire an absolutely "proven" status. This equally holds in the case of hypotheses and theories.

There are compelling logical arguments that lend credence to the notion of tentativeness in science.

Finally, before considering approaches that can be used to facilitate student learning of the NOS and their relative effectiveness, it is important to note that individuals often conflate the NOS with science processes. Although these aspects of science overlap and interact in important ways, it is nonetheless important to distinguish the two. Scientific processes are activities related to collecting and analyzing data and drawing conclusions (AAAS, 1990, 1993; NRC, 1996). For example, observing and inferring are scientific processes. On the other hand, the NOS refers to the epistemological underpinnings of the activities of science. As such, realizing that observations are necessarily theory-laden and are constrained by our perceptual apparatus belongs within the realm of the NOS.

Professional development efforts must not conclude, as they have in the past, with the development of adequate teacher understandings. The research is quite clear that teachers' understandings do not automatically translate into classroom practice. Certainly, teachers must have an in-depth understanding of what they are expected to teach. However, professional development efforts must also emphasize how teachers can successfully facilitate the development of students' understandings of the NOS. In the following pages, we present a series of classroom-tested activities/approaches that facilitate the development of students' conceptions. Presentation of these activities/approaches is preceded by a short discussion of two widely advocated approaches that, although intuitive, consistently lack supportive empirical evidence of success.

Communicating Functional Understandings of the NOS

Three general approaches have been used to enhance students' and teachers' understandings of the NOS. The first approach—labeled here as an *implicit* approach—suggests that by "doing science" students will also come to understand the NOS (Lawson, 1982; Rowe, 1974). This approach was adopted by most of the curricula of the 1960s and 1970s that emphasized hands-on, inquiry-based activities and/or process-skills instruction. Research studies have indicated that the implicit approach was not effective in enhancing students' and teachers' understandings of the NOS (e.g., Durkee, 1974; Haukoos & Penick, 1985; Riley, 1979; Spears & Zollman, 1977; Trent, 1965; Troxel, 1968). It should be noted that two interrelated assumptions underlie the implicit approach and compromise its effectiveness. The first depicts attaining an understanding of the NOS to be an "affective" (as compared to a cognitive) learning outcome. This first assumption entails the second assumption; the assumption that learning about the NOS would result as a by-product of "doing science."

The second approach—the *historical* approach—suggests that incorporating the history of science (HOS) in science teaching can serve to enhance students' views of the NOS. *History of Science Cases for High Schools* (Klopfer & Watson, 1957) and *Harvard Project Physics* (Rutherford, Holton, & Watson, 1970) were two notable curriculum development efforts that included substantial attention to the HOS at the high school level. However, a review of the efforts that aimed to assess the influence of incorporating the HOS in science teaching (Klopfer & Cooley, 1963; Solomon, Duveen, Scot, & McCarthy, 1992; Welch & Walberg, 1972; Yager & Wick, 1966) indicates that evidence concerning the effectiveness of the historical approach is, at best, inconclusive.

The third approach suggests that the goal of improving students' views of the scientific endeavor "should be planned for instead of being anticipated as a side effect or secondary product" of varying approaches to science teaching (Akindehin, 1988, p. 73). This *explicit* approach uses instruction geared toward various aspects of the NOS and utilizes *elements* from the history and philosophy of science to improve learners' views of the NOS. In general, relative to the implicit and historical approaches, the explicit approach has been more effective in helping learners achieve enhanced understandings of the NOS (e.g., Akindehin, 1988; Billeh & Hasan, 1975; Carey & Stauss, 1968, 1970; Jones, 1969; Lavach, 1969; Ogunniyi, 1983; Olstad, 1969).

We strongly believe that a functional understanding of the NOS can be best facilitated through an explicit reflective approach. We have developed a set of activities that we use in our own teaching to explicitly teach certain aspects of the NOS. These activities have also been used with students at the elementary, middle, and high school levels. It is our experience that such activities, coupled with the use of specific historical episodes and elements from the philosophy of science, have been effective in enhancing K–12 students' and preservice/inservice science teachers' views of the NOS. Although it is not possible to provide a description of all these activities here (see Lederman & Abd-El-Khalick, 1998), in what follows we present a few examples. The first example relates to a class of "generic" activities referred to as black box activities. The second example, "Real Fossils, Real Science" (Luchessa & Lederman, 1992), is a content-embedded activity. The final example depicts the use of perceptual Gestalts to help learners develop adequate conceptions of some important aspects of the NOS.

Black Box Activities

In black box activities, students examine "phenomena" and attempt to explain how they work. Without actually "seeing" what is inside the black box, students make observations, collect data, draw inferences, and suggest hypotheses to explain their data. Next, based on those hypotheses, students make predictions and devise "ways" to test them. Based on their tests, they judge whether their hypotheses are appropriate or not. Students finally construct models to explain the "phenomena" investigated and test whether their models "work" in mimicking the "behavior" of the original phenomenon. Such activities are followed by discussions that explicitly focus on the distinction between observations and inferences, the role of models and theoretical constructs in science, the tentative nature of scientific knowledge, and the role of creativity in devising scientific explanations.

The pGLO activity is a 'black box' activity?

The "Cans" is an example of a black box activity (see Figure 1). The materials needed to prepare the setup include two ditto-master fluid or Coleman fuel cans (if not available use two 500-mL Erlenmeyer flasks wrapped with aluminum foil), two rubber stoppers, rubber tubing, one thistle tube or funnel, and glass tubing. (Optional: ethyl alcohol, iodine, and food coloring.)

We start the activity with the "Cans" demonstration that supposedly represents a natural "phenomenon." The initial levels of liquid in Cans A and B appear in Figure 1. Using a beaker, we pour enough water into the thistle tube or funnel until water starts pouring into the funnel from the glass tubing above. The water will now flow for a long period of time. The "Cans" will appear to be a self-perpetuated or closed system in which the liquid seems to cycle by itself! (Optional: Instead of clear water in Can B, we fill half of the can with water colored with blue food coloring and

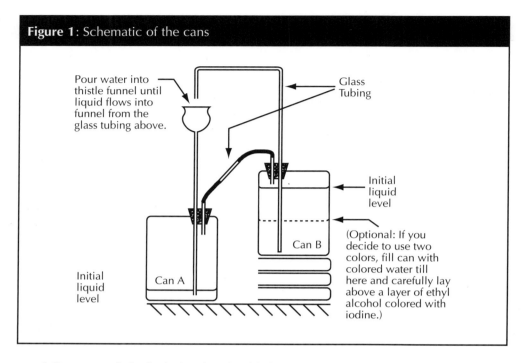

Figure 1: Schematic of the cans

Pour water into thistle funnel until liquid flows into funnel from the glass tubing above.

Glass Tubing

Initial liquid level

Can B

(Optional: If you decide to use two colors, fill can with colored water till here and carefully lay above a layer of ethyl alcohol colored with iodine.)

Initial liquid level

Can A

carefully pour ethyl alcohol colored with iodine above the colored water. A more complex pattern of color changes will now be apparent.)

Note that, as with the "Cans," a black box activity demonstration should present students with an open-ended situation. The answer as to how the demonstration works should not be readily available to students. This will ensure that students are faced with a genuine problem. In the present example, students are often perplexed as to how the "Cans" demonstration works. Their answers usually range from there being a small pump inside the cans, all the way to very complex chemical reactions. Moreover, a black box activity demonstration should be *black!* Students should not be able to "see" what is going on "inside." Most phenomena that scientists investigate are "black" in the sense that they cannot be "directly" observed (e.g., atoms, black holes, reaction dynamics, gravity, etc.). The teacher may elect at the conclusion of the activity to let students see how the demonstration is set up. However, not doing that is more consistent with the way science is conducted. Scientists do not have the luxury to open an atom and "see" what it is all about. Despite that, scientists are able to produce relatively reliable bodies of knowledge about the phenomena they investigate.

While the liquid flows, we ask students to make observations. We examine students' responses and help them to differentiate observations from inferences. For example, "water is cycling between the two cans" and "gaseous pressure from a chemical reaction pushes the water" are inferences. Possible observations would be more like, "no water is passing through the glass tube piece between the rubber tubes" and "there was a change in color from blue to red." We also discuss with students the extent to which their inferences are consistent with the observations they make.

Based on their observations and inferences, we ask students to suggest hypotheses to explain how the "Cans" work. We ask them to judge whether their hypotheses are consistent with the data that they have collected. We discuss with them how these data can support or weaken their hypotheses. We emphasize that scientists' hypotheses should be *consistent* with the evidence available to them. Scientific knowledge is, eventually, based on *empirical* evidence. For instance, students may hypothesize that a chemical reaction produces a gas that pushes the water from one can to the other. We ask them whether such a hypothesis is consistent with the evidence. For instance, a change in temperature and/or the production of a gas are possible indications of chemical change. Students can feel the cans and observe whether gas fumes pass through the small piece of glass tubing. We discuss how these data can support or weaken their hypotheses. For example, many, but not all, chemical reactions are accompanied by a change in color. We ask students whether they can infer with confidence that the change in color in the demonstration (in case colored water and ethyl alcohol were used) is the result of a chemical reaction.

After making their initial hypotheses, we ask students to design tests to see whether their hypotheses are supported by evidence. Based on a hypothesis, a student can make a prediction and then test this prediction by collecting more evidence or data. We ask students whether they can, through testing, prove their hypotheses. The idea is to communicate to students that through testing (and experimentation) we can never prove a hypothesis for certain. Tests can only add support to a certain hypothesis. Irrespective of the amount of evidence collected, a hypothesis can never be proven with absolute certainty. However, when sufficient supportive evidence is collected, a certain hypothesis gains more acceptance as a plausible explanation. This serves as an opportunity to discuss the tentativeness of science.

Based on their hypotheses, student groups can now design actual models of the "Cans." The only criterion to judge a model is its workability: A model is acceptable as long as it "behaves" like the phenomenon it is supposed to represent. Now that students have a working model of the phenomenon, we ask them whether they know what *is* inside the "Cans" (which represents a natural phenomenon). If we can never "open" the cans and look inside, can we ever tell whether our model is an exact copy of what is inside? Can we ever be certain how the phenomenon "actually" works? As such, scientific models are never exact copies of natural phenomena. These models are, rather, inferred or hypothesized from the behavior of the phenomenon. They are workable representations of those phenomena. Scientific knowledge, in this sense, is never certain. It is a product of human inference, even though it is based on empirical evidence.

Real Fossils, Real Science

This activity aims to help learners realize that scientific knowledge is partly a product of human inference, imagination, and creativity. The advantage of this activity is that students work with the same artifacts and data (fossil fragments) as paleobiologists. The materials needed for this activity are fossil fragments (not complete fossils), construction paper, and scissors.

We give each student (or pair of students) a fossil fragment and ask them to make a detailed diagram of it. The diagrams may be larger than the actual fragments. The students, however, must include the appropriate scale with their diagrams. We usually obtain sets of similar or identical fossil fragments so that different students may get similar or identical fragments. We ask students to trace the outer perimeter of their fossil fragment diagrams on a separate sheet of colored construction paper. This tracing is cut out and discarded to form a window so that when the construction paper border is placed over the paper containing the fossil fragment diagram, only the diagram appears. Using a different color pencil we instruct students to complete their fossil drawing (to scale) on the construction paper containing the fossil fragment diagram. (Figure 2) Students should end up with a drawing of an organism from which, they believe, the fossil fragment has come. Each student ends up with a complete fossil drawing having two parts: the original fossil fragment drawing in one color and the inferred drawing of a complete organism in another color. We ask students to staple together the construction paper with the previously cut window and the paper with the complete drawing (Figure 3) The papers should be stapled on one side such that they can be flipped open. Moreover, the fossil fragment diagram should only show through the construction paper window. This format enhances the presentation of original (fossil fragment) and completed diagrams to other student.

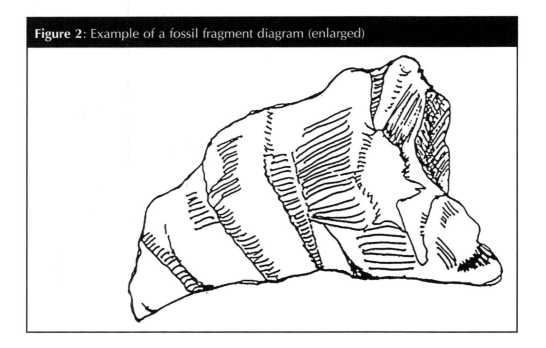

Figure 2: Example of a fossil fragment diagram (enlarged)

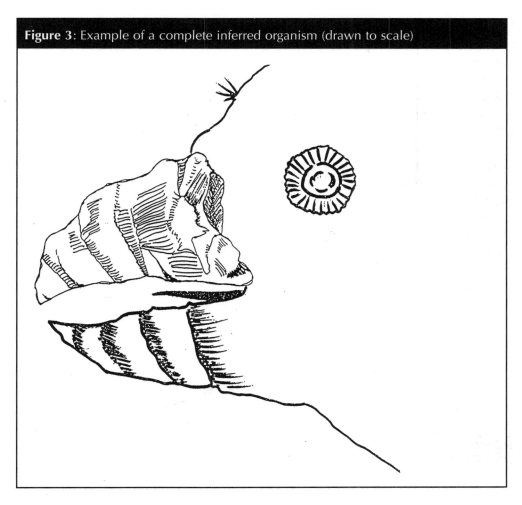

Figure 3: Example of a complete inferred organism (drawn to scale)

Next, we ask students to make oral presentations in which they describe the habitat, diet, behavior, and other characteristics of the organisms they have extrapolated from the fossil fragments. At this point, we ask whether some students knew in advance what organism their fossil fragment came from (e.g., coral). We ask those students, if any, whether that knowledge affected the inferences they made about the habitat, diet, etc., of the complete organism that they inferred from the fossil fragment. We take the time to explain to students that scientists' prior knowledge often influences their interpretations of the data and affect their conclusions. It is usually interesting to compare those organisms that different students have inferred from similar or identical fossil fragments. If those organisms were different, we ask our students whether they can tell for sure from which organism the original fossil-fragment originated. We explain to students that we might not be able to give a definite answer. We continue by asking whether it is possible that scientists face a similar situation and whether scientists can differ in the inferences they derive from evidence. We explicate that all too often scientists may reach differing conclusions based on the same evidence, just as the students have done in this activity. Scientists also often hold their views strongly and do not give them up easily.

We make explicit to students that what they have done is very similar to what paleobiologists and other scientists that investigate fossils often do. We point out that much creativity is involved in extrapolating or inferring from fossils the kind, habitat, and lifestyle of the organisms whose fossils or fossil-fragments are investigated. From this point, the discussion can be carried further to introduce older students and preservice or inservice teachers to the notion that scientific knowledge is affected, to varying extents, by the social and cultural context in which it is produced. The aforementioned case about hominid evolution serves as one example that can be used to link this discussion to scientific practice.

Young? Old?

In this activity, a perceptual Gestalt (see Figure 4) is used to help learners realize that scientists' beliefs, prior knowledge, training, experiences, and expectations actually influence their work. All these background factors form a mind-set that affects what scientists observe (and don't observe) and how they make sense of or interpret their observations. It is this individuality or (sometimes collective) mind-set that accounts for the role of subjectivity in the production of scientific knowledge.

We place Figure 4 on the overhead and ask students what they see. Students usually first recognize the face of an old lady. A few usually see the profile of an attractive young woman. If students cannot see the young lady, we insist that it shows in the drawing and that they can see it if they look hard enough. We do not at this stage point at the drawing to help students "see" one image or the other. Next, we point out, for example, how the nose of the old lady forms the cheek and chin of the young women to help students recognize the image. Many students will still not be able to see one or the other image. We ask students: How come you are looking at the very same drawing and are seeing two different things? We continue by asking: How come that some of you see only one face and not the other? Is it possible that some scientists may look at the same piece of evidence or set of data and see different things? At this point, we discuss with our students how a scientist's training, previous knowledge, and experiences dispose him/her to "see" a certain set of evidence from a certain perspective. In the same manner that students were not able to see the face of the young lady in the drawing, scientists sometimes fail to "see" (or perceive of) a certain set of evidence as relevant to their questions. Scientists sometimes tend to infer different things from the same set of data in the same manner that the students inferred totally different things from the same piece of evidence: the drawing.

To help students see both images, we show them Figure 5 of the old lady and Figure 6 of the young woman. Now students can look at Figure 4 and, with some effort, see both faces. Students can now shift from one face to the other. They, however, can never see both faces at the same time. Next, we make explicit connections to the practice of science. The

Figure 4: Gestalt figure of old/young woman

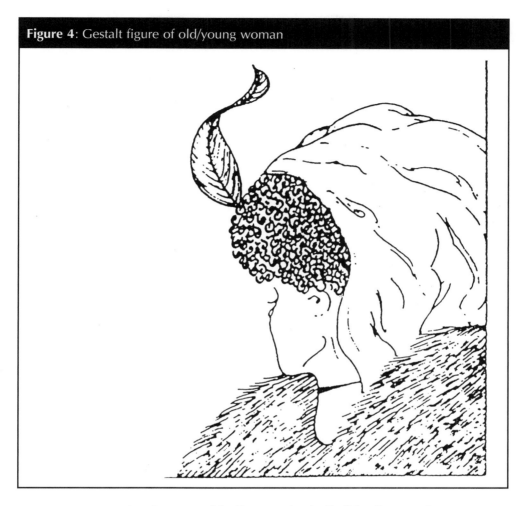

controversy concerning the cause of the "mass extinction" of the dinosaurs is a recent case in which scientists suggested different hypotheses to account for the same evidence. This controversy lingers on and is not quite settled yet. For a summary of the controversy, see Glen (1990).

It is believed that about 60 million years ago, toward the end of the Cretaceous period (geological symbol: K) and the beginning of the Tertiary period (geological symbol: T), the dinosaurs, which during the Cretaceous period reigned the lands, became extinct. (Whether there truly was a "mass extinction" or not is another interesting question. For a view on the issue, see Raup [1991].) For many years, scientists have speculated about the probable cause for that extinction. New and breaking evidence was uncovered in the early 1980s and since then more evidence has been accumulated by literally hundreds of scientists. The major evidence was an anomalous and unearthly concentration of the element iridium in the geological record at the boundary between the Cretaceous and the Tertiary periods (referred to as the K-T boundary).

Figure 5: Gestalt figure emphasizing old woman

Anomalous shocked quartz, stishovite (a mineral derived from quartz under extremely high pressures) and other pieces of evidence were also investigated. Based on the accumulated evidence, scientists have formulated many hypotheses to explain the extinction, two of which gained wide acceptance. The two hypotheses were advanced by two groups of scientists. The first group, known as the impactors, suggested that a huge meteorite (10 kilometers in diameter) hit the earth at the end of the Cretaceous period and led to a series of events that caused the extinction (Alvarez & Asaro, 1990). Another group, referred to as the volcanists, claimed that massive and violent volcanic eruptions were responsible for the extinction (Courtillot, 1990). Each group insisted that their hypothesis explained the evidence better. The controversy went on for several years and is not quite over yet. This is an interesting case of starting from the same evidence and reaching differing conclusions when scientists approach a question from different perspectives (or paradigms). In this case, these two perspectives can gener-

Figure 6: Gestalt figure emphasizing young woman

ally be referred to as "Catastrophism" (the belief that drastic, large-scale, and abrupt events have shaped the face of the earth in rather short periods of time) espoused by the impactors, and "Uniformitarianism" or "Gradualism" (the belief that natural elements of the same type and vigor have gradually shaped, and continue to shape, the earth's surface formations over extended periods of time) espoused by the volcanists.

We cannot overemphasize the importance of taking the time at the conclusion of any activity to *explicitly* point out to students the aspects of the NOS that the activity highlighted. To encourage reflection, we discuss with students the implications of such aspects of the NOS on the way they view scientists, scientific knowledge, and the practice of science.

Conclusion

In conclusion, it is important to emphasize that we should no longer assume that students will come to understand the NOS as a by-product of "doing" science-based or inquiry

We cannot overemphasize the importance of taking the time at the conclusion of any activity to explicitly point out to students the aspects of the NOS that the activity highlighted.

activities. Nor should we assume that if teachers understand the NOS, they will automatically teach in a manner "consistent" with those understandings. The NOS should be thought of as a "cognitive" rather than as an "affective" instructional outcome. If K–12 students are expected to develop more adequate conceptions of the NOS, then, as any cognitive objective, this outcome should be planned for, explicitly taught, and assessed. All this can be facilitated through concerted and continued professional development efforts designed to promote science teachers' understanding of the NOS, provide approaches teachers can use to facilitate students' conceptions, and foster commitment to the idea that the NOS is a curriculum objective of primary importance that permeates all aspects of curriculum and instruction.

References

Aikenhead, G. 1973. The measurement of high school students' knowledge about science and scientists. *Science Education* 57(4):359–349.

Akindehin, F. 1988. Effect of an instructional package on preservice science teachers' understanding of the nature of science and acquisition of science-related attitudes. *Science Education,* 72(1):73–82.

Alvarez, W., and F. Asaro. 1990. An extraterrestrial impact. *Scientific American,* Oct., 78–84.

American Association for the Advancement of Science (AAAS). 1990. *Science for all Americans.* New York: Oxford University Press.

———. 1993. *Benchmarks for science literacy: A Project 2061 report.* New York: Oxford University Press.

Bady, R. A. 1979. Students' understanding of the logic of hypothesis testing. *Journal of Research in Science Teaching* 16(1):61–65.

Billeh, V. Y., and O. E. Hasan. 1975. Factors influencing teachers' gain in understanding the nature of science. *Journal of Research in Science Teaching* 12(3):209–219.

Broadhurst, N. A. 1970. A study of selected learning outcomes of graduating high school students in South Australian schools. *Science Education* 54(1):17–21.

Carey, R. L., and N. G. Stauss. 1968. An analysis of the understanding of the nature of science by prospective secondary science teachers. *Science Education* 52(4):358–363.

Carey, R. L., and N. G. Stauss. 1970. An analysis of experienced science teachers' understanding of the nature of science. *School Science and Mathematics* 70(5):366–376.

Central Association of Science and Mathematics Teachers. 1907. A consideration of the principles that should determine the courses in biology in the secondary schools. *School Science and Mathematics* 7:241–247.

Chalmers, A. F. 1982. *What is this thing called science?* 2nd ed. Queensland, Australia: University of Queensland Press.

Courtillot, V. 1990. A volcanic eruption. *Scientific American,* Oct., 85–92

Durkee, P. 1974. An analysis of the appropriateness and utilization of TOUS with special reference to high-ability students studying physics. *Science Education* 58(3):343–356.

Glen, W. 1990. What killed the dinosaurs? *American Scientist* 78:354–370

Haukoos, G. D., and J. E. Penick. 1985. The effects of classroom climate on college science students: A replication study. *Journal of Research in Science Teaching* 22(2):163–168.

Hrdy, S. B. 1986. Empathy, polyandry, and the myth of the coy female. In *Feminist approaches to science*, ed. R. Bleier, 119–146. Pergamon Publishers.

Jones, K. M. 1969. The attainment of understandings about the scientific enterprise, scientists, and the aims and methods of science by students in a college physical science course. *Journal of Research in Science Teaching* 6(1):47–49.

Kimball, M. E. 1967–68. Understanding the nature of science: A comparison of scientists and science teachers. *Journal of Research in Science Teaching* 5:110–120.

Klopfer, L. E. 1969. The teaching of science and the history of science. *Journal of Research for Science Teaching* 6:87–95.

Klopfer, L. E., and W. W. Cooley. 1963. The history of science cases for high schools in the development of student understanding of science and scientists. *Journal of Research for Science Teaching* 1(1):33–47.

Klopfer, L. E., and F. G. Watson. 1957. Historical materials and high school science teaching. *The Science Teacher* 24(6):264–293.

Lavach, J. F. 1969. Organization and evaluation of an inservice program in the history of science. *Journal of Research in Science Teaching* 6:166–170.

Lawson, A. E. 1982. The nature of advanced reasoning and science instruction. *Journal of Research in Science Teaching* 19: 743–760.

Lederman, N. G. 1992. Students' and teachers' conceptions of the nature of science: A review of the research. *Journal of Research in Science Teaching* 29(4):331–359.

Lederman, N. G., and F. Abd-El-Khalick. 1988. Avoiding de-natured science: Activities that promote understandings of the nature of science. In *The nature of science in science education: Rationales and strategies,* ed. W. McComas. The Netherlands: Kluwer Academic Publishers.

Lederman, N. G., and M. Niess. 1997. The nature of science: Naturally? *School Science and Mathematics* 97(1):1–2.

Lederman, N. G., and M. O'Malley. 1990. Students' perceptions of tentativeness in science: Development, use, and sources of change. *Science Education* 74(2):225–239.

Lovejoy, C. O. 1981. The origin of man. *Science* 211:341–350.

Luchessa, K., and N. G. Lederman. 1992. Real fossils, real science. *The Science Teacher* 59:68–92.

Mackay, L. D. 1971. Development of understanding about the nature of science. *Journal of Research in Science Teaching* 8(1):57–66.

Mead, M., and R. Metraux. 1957. Image of the scientist among high school students. *Science* 126:384–390.

National Research Council. 1996. *National science education standards.* Washington, DC: National Academic Press.

National Science Teachers Association. 1982. *Science-technology-society: Science education for the 1980s.* (An NSTA position statement). Washington, DC: Author.

Ogunniyi, M. B. 1983. Relative effects of a history/philosophy of science course on student teachers' performance on two models of science. *Research in Science & Technological Education* 1(2):193–199.

Olstad, R. G. 1969. The effect of science teaching methods on the understanding of science. *Science Education* 53(1):9–11.

Popper, K. R. 1963. *Conjectures and refutations: The growth of scientific knowledge.* London: Routledge.

———. 1988. *The open universe: An argument for indeterminism.* London: Routledge.

Raup, D. 1991. *Extinction: Bad genes or bad luck?* New York: W W Norton & Co.

Riley, J. P. II, 1979. The influence of hands-on science process training on preservice teachers' acquisition of process skills and attitude toward science and science teaching. *Journal of Research in Science Teaching* 16(5):373–384.

Rowe, M. B. 1974. A humanistic intent: The program of preservice elementary education at the University of Florida. *Science Education* 58:369–376.

Rubba, P. A., and H. Andersen. 1978. Development of an instrument to assess secondary school students' understanding of the nature of scientific knowledge. *Science Education* 62(4):449–459.

Rutherford, F. J., G. Holton, and F. G. Watson. 1970. *The project physics course.* New York: Holt, Rinehart & Winston.

Solomon, J., J. Duveen, L. Scot, and S. McCarthy. 1992. Teaching about the nature of science through history: Action research in the classroom. *Journal of Research in Science Teaching* 29(4):409–421.

Spears, J., and D. Zollman. 1977. The influence of structured versus unstructured laboratory on students' understanding the process of science. *Journal of Research in Science Teaching* 4(1):33–38.

Tamir, P., and A. Zohar. 1991. Anthropomorphism and teleology in reasoning about biological phenomena. *Science Education* 75(1):57–68.

Trent, J. 1965. The attainment of the concept "understanding science" using contrasting physics courses. *Journal of Research in Science Teaching* 3(3):224–229.

Troxel, V. A. 1968. *Analysis of instructional outcomes of students involved with three sources in high school chemistry.* Washington, DC: US Department of Health, Education, and Welfare, Office of Education.

Welch, W. W., and H. J. Walberg. 1972. A national experiment in curriculum evaluation. *American Educational Research Journal* 9(3):373–383.

Wilson, L. 1954. A study of opinions related to the nature of science and its purpose in society. *Science Education* 38(2):236–242.

Yager, R. E., and J. W. Wick. 1966. Three emphases in teaching biology: A statistical comparison of results. *Journal of Research in Science Teaching* 4:16–20.

What is the status of this now? 2007

A Continuum of Standards for Science Teachers and Teaching

Steven W. Gilbert
Indiana University Kokomo

Steven W. Gilbert is an associate professor and chair of education at Indiana University Kokomo. In addition to teaching and writing on science teacher education, the author has coordinated the review of science teacher education programs for NCATE for ten years and chaired the development of NSTA's new performance-based standards for science teacher preparation.

Professional standards are such an important part of the reform of teacher education that it is almost impossible to practice in science education without encountering them. Nearly all states have content standards or curriculum frameworks for mathematics and science (Council of Chief State School Officers, 1998). Many either have or are developing standards-based science assessments. Over the last decade, the Benchmarks for Science Literacy (American Association for the Advancement of Science, 1993) and the *National Science Education Standards* (NSES; National Research Council, 1996) have emerged as a national professional framework for science education. Standards for science teaching and teacher education are as important to this reform effort as the science standards for what children should know and be able to do.

This chapter will not deal directly with the NSES for science teaching and teacher preparation. Instead, it will focus on an emerging continuum of science teaching standards for accreditation, licensure, and certification that is part of the New Professional Teacher Project (NPTP). The potential impact of this continuum on teacher education is hard to overestimate: It promises to move preparation and professional development away from the fragmented, credit-driven systems that now exist toward a more unified approach based on evidence of teaching competency. By doing so, it will also help to raise teaching from the quasi-professional status it now enjoys to the status of a true profession.

The New Professional Teacher Project

The NPTP was initiated in the early 1990s by the National Council for the Accreditation of Teacher Education (NCATE) in cooperation with the Interstate New Teachers Assessment and Support Consortium (INTASC) and the National Board for Professional Teaching Standards (NBPTS). The major purpose of this project is to develop a continuum of national professional standards for teacher education (Wise, 1994)—in particular, to develop and apply internally consistent, performance-based standards to the education of teachers of science at different stages in their careers.

The NPTP proposes a pattern for preparation of teachers similar to professional preparation in fields such as law, architecture, and medicine. At the core of the project is an articulated system of individual performance standards for professional teacher development *written by the profession* and recognized by state licensing agencies. Figure 1 provides an overview of the NPTP system (adapted from NCATE, 1994).

Three sets of quality assurance standards—for accreditation, licensure, and professional certification—underlie the NPTP model. Accreditation standards are designed to ensure the quality of professional *programs* based on the performance of their graduates. The National Science Teachers Association (NSTA), a constituent member of NCATE, prepares the standards for science teacher education and conducts institutional reviews, when required.

In most professions, accreditation is granted as the result of an independent review by a recognized professional association. States support such review by requiring accreditation before approving the operation of a professional program. The separation of these two processes helps to shield professional practices from political influences. This shield is not present in education. Even in states with professional standards boards, such boards may operate as state functionaries rather than as independent professional groups. This is one reason some critics do not regard education as a true profession.

Under the NPTP model, all new teachers are prepared only by professionally accredited institutions. Following graduation, each teacher candidate is issued a provisional teaching license and proceeds into a paid, mentored, clinical internship lasting from one to three years. During this period, a certified mentor works closely with each novice as he or she develops teaching skills defined by the INTASC standards for initial licensure in science teaching. Only interns who successfully complete this experience receive a regular teaching license.

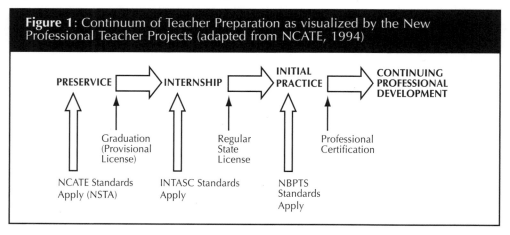

Figure 1: Continuum of Teacher Preparation as visualized by the New Professional Teacher Projects (adapted from NCATE, 1994)

This is not the end of the process though. Teachers holding a regular license continue to work toward professional certification by the NBPTS. Although no state currently requires it, professional certification by NBPTS may become a desirable, even necessary, goal for teachers in the future. The standards-based system for teacher education envisioned by the NPTP raises the prospect of a tiered system of rewards based on demonstrated competency rather than on degrees, courses, and workshops. Under this system, districts or states might preferentially link demonstrations of competency to such things as desirable service options, salary adjustments, promotions, grants, awards, or reciprocal transfer of teaching licenses among states.

Although no state currently requires it, professional certification by NBPTS may become a desirable, even necessary, goal for teachers in the future.

Characteristics of the National Standards

The standards in the NPTP are competency-based rather than prescriptive—that is, they identify desired knowledge, performance, or dispositional outcomes but do not prescribe ways to achieve those ends. The NSTA Standards for Science Teacher Preparation (Appendix A), for example, identify individual student competencies that *programs* should ensure for the initial preparation of teachers. The full text of the NSTA standards, available from the NSTA on the World Wide Web, also provides (a) examples of performance indicators for preservice, induction, and advanced levels of practice; (b) a rationale and discussion for each standard; and (c) recommendations for practices in programs.

INTASC's draft standards for initial licensure of science teachers (Appendix B) differ in scope and emphasis from the NSTA standards, in part because they are adapted from 10 predefined core principles intended to describe postgraduate competencies associated with effective teaching across fields. The complete INTASC documents contain indicators of knowledge, performances, and dispositions for each principle.

As of this writing, the NBPTS standards for advanced certification in science teaching for lower grade levels are still in development. The recently adopted standards for teachers of science for adolescents and young adults (high school) are in Appendix C. These standards are more overtly science-specific than the INTASC standards.

Table 1 compares the content of the standards in this continuum and the NSES. They are clearly consistent and mutually reinforcing. All of these standards were written with strong representation of the science education community and reflect the content and spirit of the Benchmarks and, especially, the NSES.

A particular concern expressed often by science educators is the lack of specificity in these three sets of standards concerning science content preparation. This is a recurring and problematic issue when standards for science are discussed. The number of possible permutations of content that could underlie science programs is so large that

Table 1: Comparison of NSES, NSTA/NCATE, INTASC, and NBPTS

NSES	NSTA/NCATE	INTASC**	NBPTS ***
*Content B, C, D	Content	Content	Knowledge of Science
Teaching B	Pedagogy	Student Development	Understanding Students
Teaching B	Pedagogy	Student Diversity	Understanding Students Equitable Participation
Teaching B	Pedagogy	Instructional Variety	Engagement Conceptual Understandings
Teaching D	Environment for Learning	Learning Environment	Learning Environment
Not directly addressed	Not directly addressed	Communication	Not directly addressed
Teaching A, F	Science Curriculum	Curriculum Decisions	Instructional Resources
Teaching C Assessment A–E	Assessment	Assessment	Assessment
Teaching A, F	Professional Practice	Reflective Practitioners	Collegiality and Leadership Reflection
Content F	Social Context	Community Membership	Family/Community Outreach
Content G	Nature of Science	Not directly addressed	Knowledge of Science
Teaching A, B, E Content A	Inquiry	Not directly addressed	Science Inquiry
Content E, F, G	Context of Science	Not directly addressed	Contexts of Science

* These standards are for what children at various levels should learn, and thus have strong, if indirect, relevance to competencies of teachers ** Draft standards *** Adolescent and young adult standards1996:70

prescriptive standards for content are difficult to write. Both the NSES and Bench-marks provide an overarching framework for content preparation, but neither prescribe specific content to be delivered. NSTA/NCATE standards specifically require teacher preparation in content that *supports student learning as defined by state or national standards developed by the science education community.* They, thus, point toward the NSES and Benchmarks but leave the door open for innovation.

Potential Impact of National Standards on Teachers and Teaching

Any impact of national standards is tempered by the fact that education in the United States is a state responsibility. Control of education is closely guarded in part because of the political nature of education, because most K–12 education is paid for by state and local governments, and because states in some cases are constitutionally required to maintain such control. Even so, a majority of the states are working with NCATE, INTASC, and the NBPTS to develop more professional systems for accreditation, licensure, and certification similar to that described by the NPTP. The impact of these efforts at reform will become most apparent to teachers through changes in licensure and professional development requirements and consequent changes in the nature of acceptable inservice programs.

To begin with, certifying and licensing agencies increasingly will expect teachers at all levels to engage in professional development that fosters long-term, demonstrable growth. Experiences that do not have any apparent impact on student learning or welfare will be less acceptable than in the past. In addition, teachers will be under increasing pressure to document positive changes in their work in order to receive credit for professional development, which will require systematic assessment of teaching and learning.

Apart from this immediate effect on teachers, professional standards for teachers and teaching may help to remove educational practice from the political arena—a development that would be undoubtedly welcome in many states. Legislatures, agencies, and school boards could find themselves under increasing pressure to justify to the public policies and practices that deviate from the recommendations and standards of the professional associations. If they subsequently relinquish control to educators, the latter will be held accountable for demonstrating positive results. Given pressure to account for their performance, schools may find it increasingly difficult to allow teachers to close the classroom door and practice as they choose.

Standards-based performance assessment raises fear among some teachers that they may not be able to meet high standards. Other teachers question at the control and documentation such a system requires. Even among supporters of *Standards*-based reform there remains the problem of how to assess the performances of individual teachers in a fair and unbiased way. McDonnell (1989) asserts that the question of evaluation may be the biggest obstacle in the way of teacher education reform.

While these concerns may be justified to some extent, the potential for abuse exists in any assessment system and the alternative—no meaningful assessment or accountability—is increasingly unacceptable to the community. One way to allay these fears is to ensure that genuine accountability becomes part of the professional culture, and that such accountability is based upon acceptable standards for performance. Because teaching is a complex activity with often ephemeral outcomes, teachers must necessarily

Legislatures, agencies, and school boards could find themselves under increasing pressure to justify to the public policies and practices that deviate from the recommendations and standards of the professional associations.

take more responsibility for exhibiting and explaining the results of their work than practitioners in other profession, where the criteria for acceptable performance may be more obvious. Standards help to eliminate uncertainty by providing teachers with a framework for measuring and explaining their success.

They also move teacher education away from reliance on credit hours or continuing renewal units toward truer measures of professional attainment. Most school systems provide salary increases primarily for years of service and formal coursework (or continuing renewal units), but they require no evidence that either of these factors have influenced student learning and achievement. In a performance-based system, on the other hand, experiences are less important than outcomes. It is, therefore, feasible for teachers to undertake professional development on their own and receive credit for doing so—something not possible in most school districts today.

For example, suppose a new biology teacher wishes to improve her performance in relation to the NSES by more closely linking classroom activities to resources in the community. Through inquiry, she identifies several ways to achieve her goal, and sets out to revise her curriculum accordingly. Upon assessing her work, she finds she has made demonstrably positive gains in relation to her goals—which are fully consistent with district, state, and national science education standards. This is professional development in its truest sense, and it is rewarded under a performance-based system.

Standards should provide teachers with a framework for professional development. Within this framework, teachers should have broad latitude in making appropriate curriculum decisions and undertaking necessary professional development. It is entirely appropriate, however, for policymakers to require teachers to justify their choices, even if the impact of professional development is not always immediate and clear-cut. For example, a biology teacher from Illinois who lands a teaching job on the Mississippi coast would probably be justified in claiming that taking a course in marine biology is appropriate professional development. However, the teacher should ultimately be called upon to demonstrate how he has incorporated the experience into his curriculum to make it more relevant to his students' needs.

The cycle of professional development for teachers shown in Figure 2 underlies the new approach to performance-based development. During the evaluation phase, the practitioner identifies areas of need in relation to the professional standards. Once the teacher has decided on the most important need(s) to address, she moves on to considering how to deal with them. She develops a plan for improvement, including actions she will take and assessments she will collect to show that the goals of the professional development effort are met. Once this cycle is completed, a new one begins that builds on the successes (or, in some cases, failures) of the past to create a spiral of quality development.

Teachers should receive credit for any professional development initiatives they can reasonably link to improvements in student learning, achievement, or welfare either (a) directly, in or out of the classroom; (b) through work with student teachers, colleagues, administrators, or others in the school system; or (c) through parents, the community, and other institutions.

Portfolios

The NPTP model does not reject testing as part of the assessment process, particularly before regular licensing. Tests of content knowledge and skills in writing and reading, for example, are likely to continue to be a part of the overall teacher preparation system. Such testing, however, weeds out people rather than helps them to improve. Besides, the ability to pass tests does not prove one's ability to teach. Beyond the minimal competencies defined by tests are the more complex and varied skills that underlie good practice. These skills can be demonstrated only through multiple assessments in authentic contexts (for students) or in the classroom (for teachers).

Most school systems provide salary increases primarily for years of service and formal coursework (or continuing renewal units), but they require no evidence that either of these factors have influenced student learning and achievement.

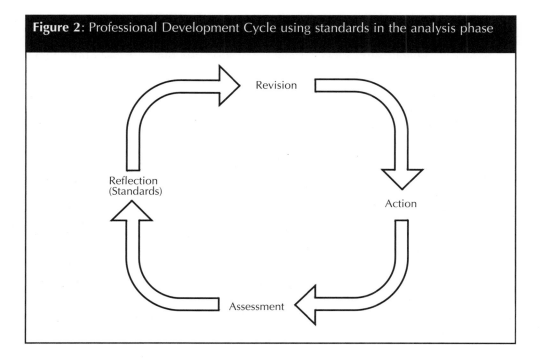

Figure 2: Professional Development Cycle using standards in the analysis phase

Revision

Reflection (Standards)

Action

Assessment

In a performance-based system, teachers often present evidence of effectiveness in a portfolio: a collection of artifacts representing final accomplishment, development, or both. Portfolios representing final accomplishment contain examples of one's best work. Developmental portfolios document changes in the quality of practice defined by goals or standards of the profession. By definition, portfolios for professional development are primarily developmental.

The sources of data for a portfolio are as many and varied as the competencies they define.

The sources of data for a portfolio are as many and varied as the competencies they define. These may include, but are not limited to: in-basket exercises, evidence of impact on students, success of students, artifacts produced by the teacher, attestations of teaching accomplishment, artifacts produced by students, observations, videos of talks to various audiences, visuals, parent communications, surveys, photographs of activities, text materials, case studies, records of professional activities, summative evaluations, awards, and evidence of recognition (NCATE, 1998).

Professional assessment of this kind is new to most K–12 educators but not to those in higher education. University faculty routinely collect and present evidence of their work for merit review, promotion, and tenure. At most institutions, committees of colleagues review a faculty member's work at several levels (typically department, school, and university) before making recommendations for tenure or promotion. Departments generally conduct merit reviews. While the current university system is by no means ideal, it more closely resembles professional practice than most K–12 systems.

Standards for Professional Teacher Education Programs

Accreditation standards for science teacher education programs are part of the NPTP continuum. In order to be consistent with INTASC and NBPTS standards for science teachers, the newest NSTA Standards for Science Teacher Preparation, adopted in 1998, differ sharply from the more prescriptive NSTA standards they replace. Adopted by NCATE as national accreditation guidelines in the same year, they provide for the assessment of a science teacher education program on the basis of the performances of its graduates. They are more flexible than past standards in terms of program content, but require institutions to demonstrate the alignment of their programs with the NSES or other recognized standards for science education developed and recognized by the professional science education community. The goal of the NSTA is to promote a process of self-study similar to the self-study paradigm proposed by the Teacher Education Accreditation Council (TEAC, 1998; see Figure 3).

The TEAC model values the role played by the institution in its own development. Rather than imposing practices, it assesses institutional commitment to assessment of quality and subsequent change. It is facilitative, a characteristic of the NSTA/NCATE model as well. Under the NSTA/NCATE program standards, institutions preparing teachers are expected to have:

◆ A clear, defensible rationale for the goals and practices of the program in relation to professionally developed standards and needs of students.
◆ Practices and indicators aligned with goals, on one end, and authentic assessments, on the other end.
◆ Multiple assessments providing evidence of performance and teaching competency.
◆ Evidence the program uses student assessment to evaluate its own performance and to improve the quality of its services.

These review criteria should apply to any program, preservice, or inservice, providing professional development experiences to persons in teaching, including alternative certification programs.

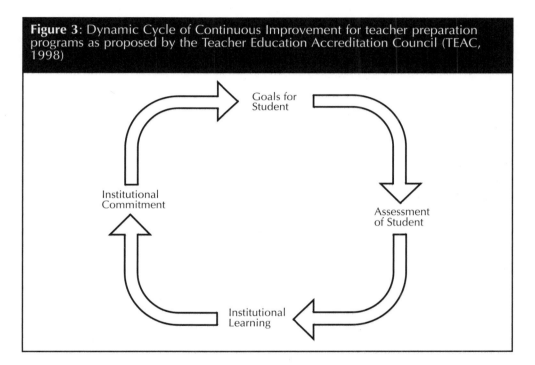

Figure 3: Dynamic Cycle of Continuous Improvement for teacher preparation programs as proposed by the Teacher Education Accreditation Council (TEAC, 1998)

Conclusion

Darling-Hammond (1991) has noted that the weight of the research shows that fully prepared teachers are generally more successful with students than teachers without full preparation for licensure. This being the case, there is good reason to believe that professional preparation and development models based on a continuum of rigorous professional standards could revolutionize teaching as a profession and an activity. There are obstacles to reform, however.

Because education is more political than most professions, many states have been reluctant to cede control to professional associations and are sometimes constitutionally restricted from doing so. In addition, teacher shortages have occasionally forced policymakers to develop shortcuts to licensure that defeat efforts to raise standards for entry into the profession. Also obstructing reform is a belief that persists among some members of the community, including policymakers, that (a) teacher preparation is of limited value, (b) content is of paramount importance, (c) teaching requires few special skills, and (d) anyone with a baccalaureate degree can be a teacher.

It is interesting to note that the similar sentiments against formal education and professionalization were expressed by some medical practitioners more than a hundred years ago, as medicine was evolving into a modern profession. Perhaps the belief that anyone can be a teacher persists because we have not set our standards high enough, and because we lack a shared vision of what education can be. At its best, the continuum of standards discussed in this chapter will translate such a vision into real professional practice.

Appendix A:
Abbreviated NSTA Standards for Science Teacher Preparation

1.0 Standards for Science Teacher Preparation: Content
The program prepares candidates to structure and interpret the concepts, ideas, and relationships in science that are needed to advance student learning in the area of licensure as defined by state and national standards developed by the science education community. Content refers to:

♦ Concepts and principles understood through science.
♦ Concepts and relationships unifying science domains.
♦ Processes of investigation in a science discipline.
♦ Applications of mathematics in science research.

2.0 Standards for Science Teacher Preparation: Nature of Science
The program prepares teachers to engage students in activities to define the values, beliefs, and assumptions inherent to the creation of scientific knowledge within the scientific community and contrast science to other ways of knowing. Nature of science refers to:

♦ Characteristics distinguishing science from other ways of knowing.
♦ Characteristics distinguishing basic science, applied science, and technology.
♦ Processes and conventions of science as a professional activity.
♦ Standards defining acceptable evidence and scientific explanation.

3.0 Standards for Science Teacher Preparation: Inquiry
The program prepares candidates to engage students regularly and effectively in science inquiry and facilitate understanding of the role that inquiry plays in the development of scientific knowledge. Inquiry refers to:

◆ Questioning and formulating solvable problems.
◆ Reflecting on and constructing knowledge from data.
◆ Collaborating and exchanging information while seeking solutions.
◆ Developing concepts and relationships from empirical experience.

4.0 Standards for Science Teacher Preparation: Context of Science
The program prepares candidates to relate science to the daily lives and interests of students and to a larger framework of human endeavor and understanding. The context of science refers to:

◆ Relationships among systems of human endeavor, including science and technology.
◆ Relationships among scientific, technological, personal, social, and cultural values.
◆ Relevance and importance of science to the personal lives of students.

5.0 Standards for Science Teacher Preparation: Skills of Teaching
The program prepares candidates to create a community of diverse student learners who can construct meaning from science experiences and possess a disposition for further inquiry and learning. Pedagogy refers to:

◆ Science teaching actions, strategies, and methodologies.
◆ Interactions with students that promote learning and achievement.
◆ Effective organization of classroom experiences.
◆ Use of advanced technology to extend and enhance learning.
◆ Use of prior conceptions and student interests to promote new learning.

6.0 Standards for Science Teacher Preparation: Curriculum
The program prepares candidates to develop and apply a coherent, focused science curriculum that is consistent with state and national standards for science education and appropriate for addressing the needs, abilities, and interests of students. Science curriculum refers to:

◆ An extended framework of goals, plans, materials, and resources for instruction.
◆ The instructional context, both in and out of school, within which pedagogy is embedded.

7.0 Standards for Science Teacher Preparation: Social Context

The program prepares candidates to relate science to the community and to use human and institutional resources in the community to advance the education of their students in science. The social context of science teaching refers to:

◆ Social and community support network within which occur science teaching and learning.
◆ Relationship of science teaching and learning to the needs and values of the community.
◆ Involvement of people and institutions from the community in the teaching of science.

8.0 Standards for Science Teacher Preparation: Assessment

The program prepares candidates to use a variety of contemporary assessment strategies to evaluate the intellectual, social, and personal development of the learner in all aspects of science. Assessment refers to:

◆ Alignment of goals, instruction, and outcomes.
◆ Measurement and evaluation of student learning in a variety of dimensions.
◆ Use of outcome data to guide and change instruction.

9.0 Standards for Science Teacher Preparation: Environment for Learning

The program prepares candidates to design and manage safe and supportive learning environments reflecting high expectations for the success of all students. Learning environments refers to:

◆ Physical spaces within which learning of science occurs.
◆ Psychological and social environment of the student engaged in learning science.
◆ Treatment and ethical use of living organisms.
◆ Safety in all areas related to science instruction.

10.0 Standards for Science Teacher Preparation: Professional Practice

The program prepares candidates to participate in the professional community, improving practice through their personal actions, education, and development. Professional practice refers to:

◆ Knowledge of and participation in the activities of the professional community.
◆ Ethical behavior consistent with the best interests of students and the community.
◆ Reflection on professional practices and continuous efforts to ensure the highest quality of science instruction.
◆ Willingness to work with students and new colleagues as they enter the profession.

Appendix B: Draft INTASC Model Standards in Science for Beginning Teacher Licensing and Development (Council of Chief State School Officers, 1998)

Principle 1: Content

The teacher of science understands the central concepts, tools of inquiry, applications, and structures of science and of the science disciplines he or she teaches and can create learning experiences that make these aspects of content meaningful to students.

Principle 2: Student Development

The teacher of science understands how children learn and develop and can provide learning opportunities that support their intellectual, social, and personal development.

Principle 3: Student Diversity

The teacher of science understands how students differ in their approaches to learning and creates instructional opportunities that are adapted to diverse learners.

Principle 4: Instructional Variety

The teacher of science understands and uses a variety of instructional strategies to encourage students' development of critical thinking, problem solving, and performance skills.

Principle 5: Learning Environment

The teacher of science uses an understanding of individual and group motivation and behavior to create a learning environment that encourages positive social interaction, active engagement in learning, and self-motivation.

Principle 6: Communication

The teacher of science uses knowledge of effective verbal, nonverbal, and media communication techniques to foster active inquiry, collaboration, and supportive interaction in the classroom.

Principle 7: Curriculum Decisions

The teacher of science plans instruction based upon knowledge of subject matter, students, the community, and curriculum goals.

Principle 8: Assessment

The teacher of science understands and uses formal and informal assessment strategies to evaluate and ensure the continuous intellectual, social, and physical development of the learner.

Principle 9: Reflective Practitioners
The teacher of science is a reflective practitioner who continually evaluates the effects of his/her choices and actions on others (students, parents, and other professionals in the learning community) and who actively seeks out opportunities to grow professionally.

Principle 10: Community Membership
The teacher of science fosters relationships with school colleagues, parents, and agencies in the larger community to support students' learning and well-being.

Appendix C: NBPTS Science Standards for Adolescents and Young Adults (14–18+)

I. Understanding Students:
Accomplished science teachers know how students learn; actively come to know their students as individuals; and determine students' understandings of science, as well as their individual learning backgrounds.

II. Knowledge of Science:
Accomplished science teachers have a broad and current knowledge of science and science education, along with in-depth knowledge of one of the subfields of science, which they use to set important learning goals.

III. Instructional Resources:
Accomplished science teachers select and adapt instructional resources, including technology, and laboratory and community resources, and create their own to support active student explorations of science.

IV. Engagement:
Accomplished science teachers stimulate interest in science and technology and elicit all their students' sustained participation in learning activities.

V. Learning Environment:
Accomplished science teachers create safe and supportive learning environments that foster high expectations for the success of all students and in which students experience the values inherent in the practice of science.

VI. Equitable Participation:
Accomplished science teachers take steps to ensure that all students, including those from groups which have historically not been encouraged to enter the world of science, participate in the study of science.

VII. Science Inquiry:
Accomplished science teachers develop in students the mental operations, habits of mind, and attitudes that characterize the process of scientific inquiry.

VIII. Conceptual Understandings:
Accomplished science teachers use a variety of instructional strategies to expand students' understandings of the major ideas of science.

IX. Contexts of Science:
Accomplished science teachers create opportunities for students to examine the human contexts of science, including its history, reciprocal relationship with technology, ties to mathematics, and impacts on society, so that students make connections across the disciplines of science and into other subject areas.

X. Assessment:
Accomplished science teachers assess student learning through a variety of means that align with stated learning goals.

XI. Family and Community Outreach:
Accomplished science teachers proactively work with families and communities to serve the best interests of each student.

XII. Collegiality and Leadership:
Accomplished science teachers contribute to the quality of the practice of their colleagues, to the instructional program of the school, and to the work of the larger professional community.

XIII. Reflection:
Accomplished science teachers constantly analyze, evaluate, and strengthen their practice in order to improve the quality of their students' learning experiences.

Notes
[1] INTASC is a working group of the Council of Chief State School Officers (CCSSO).

[2] In professional parlance, "accreditation" refers to review and recognition by an independent professional group, while "program approval" is granted by a state regulatory agency.

[3] As with accreditation, "certification" is recognition of professional ability by an independent professional group, whereas licensing is the granting of a permit to practice by the state.

References
American Academy for the Advancement of Science. 1993. *Benchmarks for science literacy*. New York: Oxford University Press.

Council of Chief State School Officers. 1997. *Model standards in science for beginning teacher licensing and development: A resource for state dialogue.* [Draft for Comment]. Washington, DC: Council of Chief State School Officers.

Council of Chief State School Officers. 1998. State mathematics and science standards, frameworks and student assessments: What is the status of development in the 50 states? [Online]. Available: http://www.ccsso.org/frmwkweb.html.

Darling-Hammond, L. 1991. Are our teachers ready to teach? *Quality Teaching* 1(1):6–7,10.

McDonnell, L. M. 1989. *The dilemma of teacher policy.* Santa Monica, CA: RAND Corporation.

National Council for the Accreditation of Teacher Education. 1994. *Teacher preparation: A continuum.* [Brochure]. Washington, DC: NCATE.

National Council for the Accreditation of Teacher Education. 1998. *Accreditation standards for candidates in elementary teacher programs.* [Working Paper for use of the drafting committee].

National Research Council. 1996. *National science education standards.* Washington, DC: National Academy Press.

Teacher Education Accreditation Council. 1998. *Foundations for an innovative accreditation system.* [Draft]. Washington, DC: Teacher Education Accreditation Council.

Wise, A. 1994. The coming revolution in teacher licensure: Redefining teacher preparation. *Action in Teacher Education* 16(2):1–13.

Alphabet Soup for Science Teachers: Making Sense of Current National Science Education Reform Initiatives

Angelo Collins
Vanderbilt University

Angelo Collins is the executive director of the Janet and Harry Knowles Foundation, which is dedicated to improving the quality and quantity of high school science teachers. Author of numerous articles, she has held leadership positions in the Teacher Assessment Project, the National Committee on Science Education Standards and Achievement, ScienceFEAT, and the Science Performance Assessment Project of the Interstate New Teacher Assessment and Support Consortium. Honors include NABT Outstanding Biology Teacher Award, the Distinguished Alumni Award of the College of Education of the University of Wisconsin, and being elected as a fellow of AAAS.

Recently, while I was attending a panel at the National Science Foundation (NSF), the scientist who was involved in the review of proposals for funding science education research commented that he had never heard of the National Science Education Leadership Association (NSELA). More recently, working with a group of science teachers who had done action research in their classrooms, I suggested they submit their work to the National Association for Research in Science Teaching (NARST). They responded by asking about the difference between NARST and the National Science Teachers Association (NSTA). Later, I reminisced about the acronyms and abbreviations, such as BSCS for the Biological Science Curriculum Study, that had challenged my early days as a science teacher. In this chapter, I will highlight four current science education reform initiatives, each of which is frequently identified by an acronym or abbreviation. Then, I will reflect on why studying, supporting, and participating in these reform efforts advances the profession of science teaching. Finally, I will briefly review a sampling of other reform initiatives that are further removed from the science classroom but that have an impact on science education policy and practice.

AAAS

While there can always be debate about when an initiative began, I propose that the current reform initiatives in science education began with the publication in 1983 of *A Nation at Risk* (National Commission on Excellence in Education, 1983). Shortly thereafter, the American Association for the Advancement of Science (AAAS) initiated Project 2061. The first product of Project 2061, *Science for All Americans* (Rutherford & Ahlgren, 1989), was published after many cycles of writing, review, and revision. *Science for All Americans* (SFAA) introduces key ideas about teaching and learning science that today are taken for granted, such as scientific literacy. SFAA describes a scientifically literate person as "one who is aware that science, mathematics, and technology are interdependent human enterprises with strengths and limitations; understands key concepts and principles of science; is familiar with the natural world and recognizes both its diversity and unity; and uses scientific knowledge and scientific ways of thinking for individual and social purposes" (p. ix). SFAA includes a clarion call that science is for all students, "regardless of their social circumstances and career aspirations" (p. x). The current rallying cry that "less is more" is foreshadowed in SFAA when it states: "The schools do not need to be asked to teach more and more content, but to teach less in order to teach it better. By concentrating on fewer topics…students will end up with richer insights and deeper understandings than they can hope to gain from superficial exposure to more topics (p. xi)." SFAA delineates important topics in science, mathematics, and technology, including concepts and principles, habits of mind, and applications, and it suggests effective approaches to learning, teaching, and policy. SFAA defines contemporary science education reform when it describes the goal that all students attain deep understanding of selected science topics that are useful in making personal and social decisions.

> *Project 2061 has maintained a program to promote scientific literacy for all students, steadfastly producing materials to meet the continuously emerging demands of the science education reform movement.*

In the 10 years since SFAA was published, Project 2061 has produced a series of documents that supported teaching and learning for scientific literacy. *Benchmarks for Science Literacy* (AAAS, 1993) distributes the science topics identified in SFAA to appropriate grade levels, providing a reference for evaluating and designing curriculum materials. *Resources for Science Literacy: Professional Development* (AAAS, 1997) provides a list of tradebooks that teachers, parents, and others can use to update science understanding, a report of the cognitive research that underlies the Benchmarks, syllabi for selected college courses that are aligned with SFAA, a comparison of the Benchmarks and the *National Science Education Standards* (National Research Council, 1996), and materials used to design and conduct a workshop on implementing science education reform. Most recently, Project 2061 released *Blueprints for Reform* (AAAS, 1998), which includes a discussion of 12 critical areas in science education reform. Soon to be released are three additional publications: The *Atlas of Scientific Literacy* will contain a set of strand maps—two-dimensional drawings that illustrate how topics presented at different grade levels inform and influence one another in the development of curriculum and of student understanding.

Does Uncle Chor Kam have this?

google this

Designs for Science Literacy and *Resources for Scientific Literacy: Curriculum Materials Evaluation* are also forthcoming. Finally, Project 2061 recently initiated the Professional Development Program, which will provide custom-tailored workshops for a variety of audiences.

I believe that Project 2061 is characterized by the term constancy; throughout 10 years of reform, Project 2061 has maintained a program to promote scientific literacy for all students, steadfastly producing materials to meet the continuously emerging demands of the science education reform movement.

NSES

In 1991, the National Council on Educational Standards and Testing was established by Congress to promote world-class educational standards in the United States. Early in 1992, in response to a request from the president of NSTA, the National Academy of Sciences (NAS), with its operating arm, the National Resource Council (NRC), agreed to coordinate the development of standards for science education. In 1996, the *National Science Education Standards* (NSES), describing both a vision and criteria for science education reform, were published. NSES includes standards for science content, teaching, and assessment, developed simultaneously and presented in mutually reinforcing ways. NSES also acknowledges that the science education reform agenda, which envisions all students attaining understanding of essential and useful ideas in science through inquiry, cannot be realized without support. Therefore, NSES includes standards for professional development, for science programs, and for educational systems.

NSES presents a comprehensive vision of science education reform, bringing together in one place in nontechnical language the current best knowledge of teaching and learning in order to promote scientific literacy.

A frequently-asked-question (FAQ) about science education is: "Why are there two documents (*Benchmarks* and NSES) that describe what all students should understand and be able to do in science?" There is no simple answer to this question. Different agencies prepared these publications at slightly different periods of recent history, in response to different political pressures and under different constraints, including time. One teacher was pleased that science had two documents, because she was able to convince her administrator of the need for change when she pointed out that two national agencies had described a similar vision. Although grouped differently and presented with different levels of detail, there is more than 90 percent agreement in the *Benchmarks* and NSES about the important science content that all students should understand (AAAS, 1997).

> *Although grouped differently and presented with different levels of detail, there is more than 90 percent agreement in the* Benchmarks *and* NSES *about the important science content that all students should understand.*

Both Project 2061 and NSES recognize the systemic nature of reform in science education. Both address concerns about teaching, about assessment, and about policy and support. Both identify a limited number of important science topics and emphasize reasoning, history, and application in science. Both describe a vision of what all students should understand and be able to do.

Recognizing that teaching is contextual, NBPTS determined to offer certification to teachers in different school subjects and at different age levels.

NBPTS

The next two reform initiatives will focus on what a teacher of science should know and be able to do. Founded in 1987, the National Board for Professional Teaching Standards (NBPTS) set high standards for the teaching profession and designed an assessment system that both has a high fidelity to teaching and allows teachers to demonstrate they meet these high standards. In 1989, the NBPTS presented the five core propositions that defined what an accomplished teacher should know and be able to do:

- Teachers are committed to students and their learning.
- Teachers know the subjects they teach and how to teach those subjects to students.
- Teachers are responsible for managing and monitoring student learning.
- Teachers think systematically about their practice and learn from experience.
- Teachers are members of learning communities

Recognizing that teaching is contextual, NBPTS determined to offer certification to teachers in different school subjects and at different age levels. *Adolescence and Young Adulthood /Science, Standards for National Board Certification* (NBPTS, 1997) for teachers of students ages 14–18 and over were released in November 1997, and in 1998 *Early Adolescence/Science Standards* (NBPTS, 1998) for teachers of students ages 11-15. The five core principles are expanded into 13 standards for science teachers: (a) understanding students, (b) knowledge of science, (c) instructional resources, (d) engagement, (e) learning environment, (f) equitable participation, (g) science inquiry, (h) conceptual understandings, (i) contexts of science, (j) assessment, (k) family and community outreach, (l) collegiality and leadership, and (m) reflection.

Beginning in the 1997–98 academic year, experienced high school science teachers were able to apply for National Board Certification by completing a portfolio and a set of assessment center exercises. The portfolio has six entries: (a) Teaching Major Ideas over Time, (b) Assessing Student Work, (c) Hands-On Science, (d) Discussions about Science, and (e) two entries on Documented Accomplishments. In this portfolio, the teacher uses artifacts, such as student work samples and lesson plans, with productions, such as videotapes and reflections, to provide evidence of accomplished practice. The assessment center exercises allow the teacher to demonstrate understanding of science and science pedagogy in a series of essays. During academic year 1998–99, teachers of middle-grades science were able to seek NBPTS certification for the first time.

NBPTS is in no way separate from other reform movements in science education. For example, when a high school science teacher applies to participate in the portfolio process for NBPTS, the introductory information includes the NSES Content Standards. Further, the NBPTS Standards for Science Teaching are very similar to the NSES Teaching Standards that envision science teachers who plan an inquiry-based science program for their students; engage in ongoing assessment of their teaching and of student learning; design and manage learning environments that provide students with the time, space, and resources needed for learning science; and develop communities of science learners that reflect the intellectual rigor of scientific inquiry and the attitudes and social values conducive to science learning (NRC, 1996).

INTASC

Shortly after NBPTS introduced the five core propositions of teaching, a consortium of state school officers began to discuss how the certification of accomplished teachers by NBPTS would influence the licensure of beginning teachers. In 1992, Interstate New Teacher Assessment and Support Consortium (INTASC), a consortium that now includes over 30 states, released the *Model Standards for Beginning Teacher Licensing and Development: A Resource for State Dialogue* (INTASC, 1992). These 10 principles are aligned with the five core propositions of NBPTS. The themes of the 10 INTASC Standards are that teachers:

- understand the central concepts, tools of inquiry, and structure of the disciplines they teach;
- understand how children learn and develop;
- understand how students differ in their approaches to learning;
- use a variety of instructional strategies;
- understand individual and group motivation;
- use knowledge of effective verbal and nonverbal communication;
- plan effective science instruction;
- understand and use formal and informal assessment strategies;
- are reflective practitioners; and
- foster relationships within and beyond the school community.

In 1998, INTASC released the *Model Standards for Science for Beginning Teacher Licensing and Development: A Resource for State Dialogue* (1998). The principles remain the same but explain how they apply to science teaching. Also, each principle is cross-referenced to a significant passage in NSES. INTASC proposes a four-stage assessment process for beginning teachers: a test of general knowledge; a test of subject matter knowledge; a test of general teaching knowledge; and, during the second or third year of teaching, the development of a portfolio. INTASC is conducting the field test of the science teacher portfolio process during the 1998-99 academic year. This portfolio, also relying on videotapes, student work samples, reflections, and explanations, is organized into three entries. The first, "Setting the Stage," includes information on the teaching context and the instructional focus. Entry two, "Instructional Design and Implementation," includes a record of daily instruction, videotapes of lessons on scientific inquiry and on teaching for understanding, and student work samples. The final entry focuses on "Analysis for Action and Relationships to Learning Communities."

Across these four reform initiatives—AAAS, NSES, NBPTS, and INTASC—here are several common themes. One is the emphasis on students—all students—that they attain deep understanding of important science ideas. Another is that understanding science includes understanding and being able to engage in scientific inquiry. A third is that science is important in daily contexts, as well as in classrooms and laboratories. All of these reform initiatives assume that professional science teachers have a store of both theoretical and practical knowledge that enables them to design instruction appropriate to the context in which they are teaching. Further, they all assume that both teachers and students demonstrate their accomplishments through performance of complex assessment tasks. Finally, all assume that participation in a variety of learning communities is a life-long task that fosters deep understanding and shapes policy.

> *There is a myth that teaching is a solitary activity. In reality, when science teachers enter a classroom they bring with them parents, educational psychologists, curriculum designers, assessment experts, scientists, policymakers, and other teachers.*

There is a myth that teaching is a solitary activity. In reality, when science teachers enter a classroom they bring with them parents, educational psychologists, curriculum designers, assessment experts, scientists, policymakers, and other teachers, to name a few. These four reform initiatives that inform current and future science teaching represent the efforts of many of these individuals and organizations concerned about students and teachers of science. All have and have had classroom teachers involved in design, development, review, and implementation. All assume that learning to teach is a lifelong process of professional development. All envision teaching tomorrow as very different from teaching today. Science teachers, aware of the demands of the profession, use these reform initiatives to inform their practice, to plan their own professional development, and to effect change in education policy. In supporting and participating in reform efforts, they demonstrate that teachers do have specialized knowledge and skills.

Other Science Education Reform Efforts

AAAS, NSES, NBPTS, and INTASC represent only a small number of the reform initiatives that influence the life of a classroom teacher. When work began on NSES, there was a commitment to engage all the professional organizations that were stakeholders in the process of review and revision. The project began with an advisory board that included a representative from a number of key professional organizations of teachers: AAAS; NSTA; the American Association of Physics Teachers (AAPT); the American Chemical Society (ACS); the National Association of Biology Teachers (NABT); the Earth Sciences Education Coalition (ESEC); the Council of State Science Supervisors (CSSS), which has become the National Science Education Leadership Association (NSELA); and the National Science Resources Council (NSRC). After the first review was released, literally hundreds of other organizations demanded to participate. It is with that event in mind that I hesitantly list nine other projects that I believe will directly or indirectly impact science education reform in the United States. This list is by no means complete.

Science teachers, aware of the demands of the profession, use these reform initiatives to inform their practice, to plan their own professional development, and to effect change in education policy.

Certification and Accreditation in Science Education (CASE), not surprisingly, adopted standards as a way to influence undergraduate and graduate programs that prepare science teachers. In cooperation with NSTA, the Association for the Education of Teachers of Science (AETS), and the National Council for the Accreditation of Teacher Education (NCATE), CASE defines 10 standards that focus on content, nature of science, inquiry, context of science, pedagogy, science curriculum, social contexts, professional practice, learning environments, and assessment (Gilbert, 1997).

AETS has proposed standards for college and university faculty who prepare science teachers. The standards are identified as knowledge of science; science pedagogy; curriculum, instruction, and assessment; knowledge of learning and cognition; research/scholarly activity; and professional development activities (AETS, 1997).

The Third International Mathematics and Science Study (TIMSS) was administered to over a half million students at five grade levels from 41 countries in 1995. In the United States, this study was supported by the National Center for Educational Statistics (NCES). The results were released in 1997-98. The relatively poor performance of U.S. students on TIMSS renewed interest in mathematics and science education reform. TIMSS-Revisited (TIMSS-R), planned for 1998–2001, is designed to again test the science and mathematics knowledge and skill of students in the United States in order to track changes in student performance over time (Third International Mathematics and Science Study, 1998).

The Program for International Student Assessment (PISA) is organized to produce policy-oriented indicators of students' achievement on a regular basis in an efficient, timely, cost-efficient manner. PISA's intention is to design indicators that not only test knowledge and skill but also indicate the student's ability to be a life-long learner and to analyze, reason, and communicate. PISA is supported by the Organisation for Economic Co-operation and Development (OECD; Program for International Student Assessment, 1998).

The National Center for Improving Science Education (NCISE) was formed to

"promote changes in state and local policies and practices in science curriculum, science teaching, and the assessment of student learning in science. The Center synthesizes and translates recent and forthcoming studies and reports and develops practical resources for policymakers and practitioners. Bridging the gap between research, practice, and policy, the Center's work promotes cooperation and collaboration among organizations, institutions, and individuals committed to the improvement of science education (NCISE, n.d.)."

The National Institute for Science Education (NISE) was formed to

"address the totality of the education enterprise, to assess its effectiveness and examine what activities need to be established, what activities are no longer needed and what approaches will enhance science education. The NISE vision is that all students leave the educational system with an ability to make informed decisions about the SMET (Science. Mathematics, Engineering and Technology)-related matters they encounter in their daily lives (NISE, 1998)."

The National Center for Improving Student Learning and Achievement in Mathematics and Science (NCISLA) is a collaborative of researchers concerned with designing instruction and assessment based on sound cognitive and social principles that lead to student achievement (Romberg, 1997).

Finally, two current reform initiatives, not directly related to science but likely to influence teaching of all school subjects, are the National Commission on Teaching and America's Future (NCTAF) and the National Partnership for Excellence and Accountability in Teaching (NPEAT). NCTAF, in its report *What Matters Most: Teaching for America's Future*, proposes an:

"audacious goal that . . . by the year 2006, America will provide all students in the country with what should be their educational birthright: access to competent, caring, and qualified teachers. This commission recommends five changes:
- *Get serious about standards, for both students and teachers.*
- *Reinvent teacher preparation and professional development.*
- *Overhaul teacher recruitment and put qualified teachers in every classroom.*
- *Encourage and reward teacher knowledge and skill.*

◆ *Create schools that are organized for student and teacher success"* (National Commission on Teaching and America's Future, 1996, pp. 5–7).

NPEAT is a collaborative of researchers, teachers, and policymakers committed to making progress on the five NCTAF recommendations.

ABC, XYZ! While it is probably not realistic to keep track of all the reform initiatives, let alone participate in all of them, especially not while being responsible for the well-being and achievement of students, individually and collectively, these reform initiatives influence life in classrooms. These reform initiatives provide teachers with opportunities and guidance for professional development. All encourage teachers to learn more science, more about students, more about learning, and more about teaching and assessment. They provide reasons for teachers to participate in education policy decisions at the school, district, state, and national levels. They provide the mandate, design, and warrant for the professional development of science teachers into the next century.

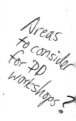

Areas to consider for PD workshops?

References

American Association for the Advancement of Science (AAAS). 1993. *Benchmarks for science literacy.* New York: Oxford University Press.

———. 1997. *Resources for science literacy: Professional development.* New York: Oxford University Press.

———. 1998. *Blueprints for reform.* Washington, DC: AAAS.

Association for the Education of Teachers of Science. 1997. *Position statement: Professional knowledge standards for science teacher educators.* AETS Newsletter, 31(3), (Suppl.), 1-6.

Gilbert, S. 1997. Status report on certification and accreditation in science education. *AETS Newsletter, 31(3)*, 6-10.

Interstate New Teacher Assessment and Support Consortium (INTASC). 1992. *Model standards for beginning teacher licensing and development: A resource for state dialogue.* Washington, DC: INTASC.

———. 1998. *Model standards for science for beginning teacher licensing and development: A resource for state dialogue.* Washington, DC: INTASC.

National Board for Professional Teaching Standards (NBPTS). 1991. *Toward high and rigorous standards for the teaching profession, 3rd Edition.* Detroit, MI: NBPTS.

———. 1997. *Adolescence and young adulthood/science, standards for national board certification.* Detroit: NBPTS.

———. 1998. *Early adolescence/science standards.* Detroit: NBPTS.

National Center for Improving Science Education (NCISE). n.d. [Mission statement, back or front cover of all publications]. Washington, DC: NCISE.

National Commission on Teaching & America's Future (NCTAF). (September, 1997). *What matters most: Teaching for America's future. The summary report.* New York: NCTAF.

National Commission on Excellence in Education. 1983. *A nation at risk: The imperative for educational reform.* Washington, DC: U.S. Government Printing Office.

National Institute for Science Education (NISE). http://www.wcer.wis.edu/nise/

National Research Council. 1996. *National science education standards.* Washington, DC: National Academy Press.

Program for International Student Assessment. 1998. *Monitoring knowledge and skills in the new millennium.* Advertising brochure. (Available from PISA International, 19 Prospect Hill Road, Camberwell, Victoria 3124, Australia.)

Romberg, T. 1997. Center Mission. *Principled Practice in Mathematics & Science Education.* 1(1), 15

Rutherford, F. J., & Ahlgren, A. 1989. *Science for all Americans.* New York: Oxford University Press.

Third International Mathematics and Science Study (TIMSS). (Available from 463 Erickson Hall, College of Education, Michigan State University. East Lansing, MI. 48824)

Using ENC and ERIC to Plan for Professional Development

Thomas Gadsden, Jr., and Kimberly S. Roempler
Eisenhower National Clearinghouse for Mathematics and Science Education
The Ohio State University

Thomas Gadsden, Jr., is associate director for collaboration at the Eisenhower National Clear-inghouse for Mathematics and Science Education at The Ohio State University. During his career as teacher, professor, district supervisor, informal educator, and officer of professional organiza-tions, he has led and facilitated numerous professional development efforts and made presenta-tions throughout the United States and in Europe and Africa on topics ranging from elementary science to high energy physics to effective use of the World Wide Web.

Kimberly S. Roempler is associate director for instructional resources for the Eisenhower Na-tional Clearinghouse for Mathematics and Science Education at The Ohio State University. She is involved in both preservice and inservice science teacher education, and is the acting science resource specialist at ENC and author of numerous articles and papers. She continues to teach introductory-level science classes at Columbus State Community College.

No longer can we describe good teaching as the one-way transmission of informa-tion from one person to another. Similarly, significant professional development can no longer be seen as something done by one party to another. All participants in a professional development effort (the initiators, facilitators, information sources, teach-ers, community, parents, evaluators, students) must become learners and take part in the inquiry. Consequently, it is important that each participant also plays a role in plan-ning so that the planning itself becomes the beginning of professional growth and systemic improvement.

Where can facilitators and planning teams find the information and examples that they each will need in order to plan and begin the inquiry? Certainly, the traditional sources of such information are as valid today as they have ever been. Libraries, professional journals, consultants, and the experiences of colleagues provide much of great value. Now, however, the newest source of information, the World Wide Web, makes available resources unimaginable just a decade ago. Yet the explosive growth of this virtual megalibrary and vehicle for asynchronous teaching and com-munication has left many feeling confused, overwhelmed, and lost as they try to locate the resources that will be of value for their specific needs and interests. Where can one find the guidance, the resources, the insights, and the ideas necessary for successful professional development?

Online Resources for Planning: ENC and ERIC

Two of the richest online resources for science and mathematics education are the Eisenhower National Clearinghouse for Mathematics and Science Education (ENC) and the Educational Resources Information Centers (ERIC).

The mission of ENC is to "identify effective curriculum resources, create high-quality professional development materials, and disseminate useful information and products to improve K–12 mathematics and science teaching and learning" (Eisenhower National Clearinghouse for Mathematics and Science Education [ENC], 1998a, p. 1).

ENC's World Wide Web site, ENC Online <http://www.enc.org>, provides searchable online access to information (the ENC Resource Finder) about the great majority of K–12 mathematics and science curriculum resources that are currently available. The ENC National Repository now contains more than 14,000 mathematics and science instructional and professional resources. Catalog records describing each of these resources include appropriate grade levels, subjects covered, abstracts, tables of contents, physical descriptions, evaluative information, and information about vendors and suppliers. A variety of search tools helps teachers find the most appropriate curriculum materials for specific grade levels, subject areas, topics, resource types, cost ranges, and other criteria.

> *The mission of ENC is to identify effective curriculum resources, create high-quality professional development materials, and disseminate useful information and products to improve K–12 mathematics and science teaching and learning.*

In addition to this extensive database, ENC also creates topical and timely online publications that are also available in print or CD-ROM. For example, each issue of *ENC Focus* provides information about a special topic in math and science education, articles about innovative educators and programs, and catalog records from the ENC Resource Finder for selected curriculum materials that exemplify the topic. Recent topics have included children's literature in math and science, professional development, multicultural teaching, and informal science education. Future topics will address innovative curricula, inquiry and problem solving, and educational technology. In the annually published *The Guidebook of Federal Resources for K–12 Mathematics and Science*, ENC provides listings of resources and opportunities available to teachers in each state from each federal agency (ENC, 1998b).

ENC recently compiled the results of two in-depth projects, one that focused on the Third International Mathematics and Science Study (TIMSS) and the other on equity in the math and science classroom. The resulting Web sites are rich with teacher stories, journal articles, professional development activities, additional relevant Web sites, and information about curriculum materials. Each one is available on CD-ROM, as well as online at <http://timss.enc.org>, and <http://equity.enc.org>, respectively.

ENC Online also contains carefully organized and selected links to over 900 other outstanding mathematics and science Web resources that provide up-to-date content information, lessons and activities, and extensive professional resources. Educators who are planning professional development can quickly reach existing resources, such as the North Central Regional Educational Laboratory's (NCREL) *Pathways to School Improvement* (1999), the WestEd Eisenhower Regional Consortium for Science and Mathematics Education's *Tales from the Electronic Frontier* (Shinohara, Wenn, and Sussman, 1996), and the publications and products of the U.S. Department of Education. Soon they will also have access to resources that are currently under development, such as the Teacher Materials Project (TMAT), a database of evaluated science professional development materials created by Horizon Research, Inc. (1998), and the reports of the National Staff Development Council (NSDC) initiative, *What Works in the Middle: Results-Based Staff Development* (1999).

> *ERIC is the primary source for abstracts of educational research and scholarly writings.*

While ENC concentrates more on curriculum materials, ERIC is the primary source for abstracts of educational research and scholarly writings. The main ERIC Web site <http://www.accesseric.org:81> leads to the virtual homes of ERIC's network of 18 clearinghouses and 13 adjuncts and affiliates. Each one focuses on a separate specialty, many of particular value to the professional developer, including

◆ Information and Technology
◆ Assessment and Evaluation
◆ Elementary and Early Childhood
◆ Parent Information
◆ Teaching and Teacher Education
◆ Rural Education and Small Schools
◆ Urban Education
◆ Science, Mathematics, and Environmental Education (Educational Resources Information Center [ERIC], Access ERIC, 1998a).

Educators can reach the online resources of ERIC Clearinghouse for Science, Mathematics, and Environmental Education (CSMEE) at <http://www.ericse.org>.

From each of the ERIC Web sites one can search the ERIC Database of nearly one million abstracts of documents and journal articles on education research and practice. Users have a choice of several search engines of varying sophistication. One of the search engines, for example, includes a "wizard" that will guide the user to interactively develop search strategies and identify the correct descriptors (ERIC, Access ERIC, 1998b).

In addition to pointing to a wealth of other valuable educational Web sites, ERIC creates and maintains a substantial number of their own online resources. For example, AskERIC <http://ericir.syr.edu> responds to questions concerning "educational research, education issues, or the practice of education" (ERIC, Clearinghouse on Information & Technology [ERIC/IT], 1999a, par. 1). ERIC publishes an outstanding series of short reports (*ERIC Digests*—also online) on topics of current interest in education. *ERIC Bulletins* and *Curriculum Files*, 4- to 12-page articles that treat specific topics in greater depth, are also available in print and online. Other ERIC publications include monographs and education resource books. Plus, ERIC collects and makes available online thousands of lesson plans at <http://ericir.syr.edu/Virtual/Lessons>.

In addition to pointing to a wealth of other valuable educational Web sites, ERIC creates and maintains a substantial number of their own online resources.

The U.S. Department of Education funds both ENC and the ERIC network. ENC and ERIC/CSMEE share their physical location and the ENC/ERIC Resource Center at The Ohio State University, in Columbus, Ohio.

The best way to become familiar with the kinds of assistance each of these World Wide Web resources can provide teams that are planning for professional development is to electronically explore the resources they contain. The remainder of this chapter will provide specific suggestions to guide that exploration within the context of systematic planning for professional development and framed within Loucks-Horsley's planning sequence for the professional development design process (Loucks-Horsley, 1998).

Setting Goals

As the planning begins, professional developers face a host of questions:

◆ What are the purposes and goals of this professional development project?
◆ Who should participate in the professional development?
◆ What strategies will be used to accomplish the goals?
◆ How can one know that there is progress?
◆ How can the learnings be internalized and improvements be sustained?
◆ How will schoolchildren benefit?

Once the organizers of a professional development endeavor have formed a planning team representative of all participants, including administrators, parents, community leaders, and others, the first steps in planning for professional development require the setting of goals. Even though all team members are convinced that improvement of science teaching and learning is essential, a planning group composed of individuals with varying backgrounds, experiences, and investments in education is likely to encounter differences in their perceptions of those needs. Thus, to build consensus and formulate goals that draw the education community together, the planning team must first create a common understanding of the needs for change. Then, they can become advocates for change and work together to secure the necessary commitment and support of the district administration and the community. The planners for professional development facilitate the team's efforts by developing familiarity with the vast array of resources that address questions like those above. The following are examples of resources helpful in various stages of planning and implementing a professional development project.

Research concerning what is happening in science education locally, nationally, and globally can help place a district's needs in perspective and suggest promising directions for change. The ENC Web site, *Tools for discussion: Attaining excellence through TIMSS*, provides educators, parents, and business and community leaders with information and tools they can use to examine science performance in the United States in relation to other nations. Tables show comparative results along with data about curriculum, textbooks, and teaching practices (ENC, 1997). The "Executive Summary of A Splintered Vision: An Investigation of U.S. Science and Mathematics Education," can stimulate discussions that lead to new insights concerning the strengths and weaknesses of a district's science curriculum (McNeely, 1997). *Pathways to School Improvement* provides another source for research-based information on science teaching and professional development (NCREL, 1999).

Once the organizers of a professional development endeavor have formed a planning team representative of all participants, including administrators, parents, community leaders, and others, the first steps in planning for professional development require the setting of goals.

Through ERIC, a planning team can learn about important educational trends using the National Center for Educational Statistics (NCES, U.S. Department of Education). For example, *The Condition of Education, 1998* reports on 60 indicators grouped in categories including access, participation, achievement, curriculum, and diversity in education. Planners also can learn about proficiency trends among 9-, 13-, and 17-year-olds and welfare participation as related to educational attainment (Snyder & Wirt, 1998). From NCES's *Digest of Education Statistics* (a massive report with over 400 tables of statistics like educational attainment by state and by metropolitan area, state education regulations, income and poverty levels by state, and enrollment by school district), the planning team can obtain information to help in the development of understanding of the relative status of education in their community (Snyder, Hoffman, & Geddes, 1998).

National standards and frameworks, found through ENC Online, exemplify key professional movements to improve teaching and learning. The full-text electronic versions of the *National Science Education Standards* (National Academy of Sciences [NAS], 1998), the *Benchmarks for Science Literacy* (Project 2061, 1997), and several state frameworks provide a national context and vision for formulating the goals and objectives for local reform initiatives. Another one of the reform sites located on ENC Online, the Annenberg/CPB Projects' searchable database, *The Online Guide to Math and Science Reform,* contains concise information on strategies, impact, funding, and other details for about 250 science professional enhancement initiatives (1999). Updated twice each month, the information can provide welcome insights and ideas as well as contacts for those beginning similar projects.

Planning: Designing the Professional Development Plan

With project goals established and sufficient support secured, the professional development facilitator will work with the planning team to create a plan for sustainable professional development. The group can find guidance in an online monograph by McKean and Nelsen (1997), "Short-Term Professional Development Programs," that defines criteria for successful interventions and discusses a variety of such projects and their evaluations by expert panels.

As we recognize that all children can learn, equity cannot remain a sidebar issue.

Professional development must also address local issues and societal transitions affecting education. For example, concerns about the changing demographics of a district and the need to adjust for these changes may be critical to the success of a professional development project. As we recognize that all children can learn, equity cannot remain a sidebar issue. *Making Schools Work for Every Child* brings this issue to the forefront. This Web site provides stories, vignettes, an equity guide, and Web resources for community building and self assessment, as well as articles concerning bias and diversity issues (ENC, 1998c). An Equity Tool Kit activity called "Survey Says..." located on this site can help educators assess their own positions and actions using an awareness survey (Michigan Department of Education, North Central Regional Educational Laboratory, and The Math Science Consortia, 1997b).

For guidance in constructing and orchestrating successful professional development, a search on ENC's listing of professional organizations will locate The National Staff Development Council (NSDC). NSDC's *Standards for Staff Development* provides needed guidance for context, process, and content for professional development (1999). The *National Science Education Standards* also include standards for professional development that are specific for science teaching (NAS, 1998).

As a planning team considers the overall structure of a professional development endeavor, they might search the ERIC Database and uncover an *ERIC Digest* article from June, 1995, "Reconceptualizing Professional Teacher Development," that helps to clarify an appropriate paradigm for professional development, one that will "shift teachers away from dependency on external sources for the solution to their problems and toward professional growth and self-reliance in instructional decision making" (ERIC, Clearinghouse on Teaching and Teacher Education [ERIC/TTE], 1995, par. 4). ENC's *Ideas that Work* on ENC Online offers the information and the insights needed to select effective professional development strategies for the project (Loucks-Horsley, 1998). Together all of these resources will help the professional development planning team create a common vision and plan consistent with national standards that will shape the professional development experience.

Doing: Planning for Action

For each component of a professional development endeavor (such as institutes, follow-up workshops and conferences, online discussions, etc.), facilitators must structure activities that will help participants identify successful practices and challenge outdated ones. Activities must stimulate inquiry and discussion and foster internalization and competence with new skills and understandings as well as encouraging ongoing dialog and continual evidence-based improvement of teaching. To identify teaching materials to serve as examples for study in professional development activities, facilitators can conduct searches on ENC Online by going to "Search" and selecting a search tool. For example, an educator might conduct a search to identify instructional materials for the middle level (grades 6, 7, 8) for teaching *life sciences* (subject)—in particular, *populations*—using *manipulatives* (resource type). The search results identify 17 possibilities and include detailed descriptions of each (ENC, 1999b). Reading through the catalog record and abstract for the very first one on the list, a kit, *Survival Strategies, Module 2*, by Project WIZE (Wildlife Inquiry through Zoo Education; Falk, 1984) shows that it's a good match with the criteria. The ENC catalog record for *Survival Strategies* (and all other instructional materials) includes the exact contents, the cost, and how to obtain the materials.

Another search might locate *Tales of the Electronic Frontier,* which describes classroom experiences in using the Internet for teaching K–12 science and mathematics (Shinohara et al., 1996). By clicking on the Web address (URL) in the catalog record, one can go directly to the online version. The cases described can serve as excellent stimuli for participant reflection and discussion.

ENC and ERIC can also provide much of the context and content for improving subject matter knowledge, as well as information about assessment, leadership, technology, curriculum materials, research, etc. Planning for activities in which participants can learn how to conduct their own searches to find, examine, and evaluate Web sites can open the door for continuing self-directed online learning. Having participants create lesson plans that incorporate technology can help increase their understanding and confidence in classroom application of the Internet.

From both ERIC and ENC Web sites professional developers and participants can reach the Gateway to Educational Materials (GEM) and can locate nearly 4,000 valuable Web sites by searching multiple databases at the same time (ERIC/IT, 1999b). One of the records retrieved, described, and linked to is the Tramline Virtual Field Trip, which features *The Desert Web Tour*, among others (Tramline, Inc., 1998). ERIC/IT is also home to the Virtual Reference Desk and its AskA+ Locator service that helps students, teachers, and parents locate experts like those at Ask a Volcanologist or Ask Shamu who will answer their questions (1998). At ERIC-CSMEE virtual visitors (those electronically visiting the Web site) can find extensive information on teaching science outside the classroom (1999).

Professional development is not just for teachers and administrators. At the Web site, *Equity@ENC: Making Schools Work for Every Child,* one can find "Community

Building," a section containing resources to help educators build relationships with parents and other members of diverse school communities. Among these resources, the "Partnering with Families and the Community" activities can help show parents and community members how to take a more active role in their children's science education, especially in removing barriers that may inhibit learning among women, minorities, and those with disabilities (Michigan Department of Education et al., 1997a).

ENC and ERIC can provide much of the context and content for improving subject matter knowledge, as well as information about assessment, leadership, technology, curriculum materials, and research.

Reflecting: Extending the Professional Growth

Planning for effective professional development also means planning for the extension, institutionalization, evaluation, reflection, and continuing improvement of teaching and of the professional development itself. One goal of any professional development must be that participants learn how to sustain and continue their own learning. The best indicator of the success of professional developers may be that they are no longer needed.

By searching ENC's Digital Dozen (the monthly selection of exemplary Web sites), participants may locate "Live to Learn," an in-print, video, and online professional development package created by the George Lucas Educational Foundation. One part, for example, Jan Hawkin's "The World at Your Fingertips," may elicit discussion among participants about the uses of educational technology (1997).

For continuation of learning and reform activity, much long-term professional development can occur over the Internet. ENC Online's listing of reform sites includes "Online Professional Development Opportunities" (ENC, 1999a). For example, *The Biology Project* at the University of Arizona shows a comprehensive program of multiple-choice problem sets with linked tutorials and graphics for improving understanding (Grimes & Hallick, 1999). Another, *World Builders*, a distance education course at California State University, Los Angeles, uses problem-based constructivist activities to teach what it takes to create a livable world (Viau, 1999).

As participants use the Web site, TIMSS@ENC, they find additional tools to help them connect with online communities discussing and working with the TIMSS findings. *TIMSS Forum*, for example, offered by the Mid-Atlantic Eisenhower Consortium, is an electronic discussion forum that encourages online teacher interaction concerning the TIMSS results and their implications for practice (Mid-Atlantic Eisenhower Consortium for Mathematics and Science Education, 1997).

Through ENC's list of partners, one will find that each of the Eisenhower Regional Consortia has identified a wealth of education resources, services, and opportunities available in each region. Many of the Consortia have also created excellent online products. For example, WestEd Eisenhower Consortium maintains *Science*

Adventures (Eisenhower Regional Consortia for Mathematics and Science Education, 1997), which provides a way to locate informal education resources and opportunities across the United States.

Through ENC and ERIC, a participant team would be able to locate most of the online resources and guidance they need to continue their own learning and to expand their discussions and investigations to include others around their community and the nation. For example, ERIC is a good source of information about assessments and surveys to evaluate the success of a workshop or institute and advise ongoing improvements. ERIC resources can help participants understand how to conduct their own action research as a way to obtain useful feedback on their own application of learnings gained through the professional development program. Continuing professional growth coupled with sound evaluation and data-driven improvements provide the foundations for sustainable and valuable education reform.

Bringing It All Together

ENC and ERIC open doors for the planning and accomplishment of sustainable, ongoing, standards-based professional development that can significantly enhance the lives of children. Professional development is not a single event, but a continuing process that can take place in highly varied forms and situations, from an individual seeking self-improvement, to a school district seeking to correct deficiencies or to help their best scholars achieve their maximum potentials, to a professional organization attempting to revitalize and reform education in response to dramatic societal changes. Now, thanks to electronic technologies, careful planning and rich professional development experiences can occur nearly anywhere and involve nearly anyone in the nation. Using ENC and ERIC as gateways to resources for professional development planning allows accomplishment of high-quality professional development in the relative isolation of rural and remote communities, within the milieu of inner cities, at the great scientific and learning centers of the nation, and even in the midst of the natural world.

ERIC resources can help participants understand how to conduct their own action research as a way to obtain useful feedback on their own application of learnings gained through the professional development program.

The Eisenhower National Clearinghouse is supported through a contract with the U.S. Department of Education.

References

The Annenberg/CPB Projects. 1999. *The online guide to math & science reform* [Online database, January 29]. Available WWW: http://www.learner.org/theguide.

Educational Resources Information Center, Access ERIC. 1998a. *ERIC sites* [WWW document, November 24]. Available WWW: http://www.accesseric.org:81/sites/barak.html

————. 1998b. *ERIC-sponsored internet access to the ERIC database* [WWW document, November 24]. Available WWW: http://www.accesseric.org:81/searchdb/dbchart.html

Educational Resources Information Center, Clearinghouse for Science, Mathematics, and Environmental Education. 1999. *Science education resources* [WWW document]. Available WWW: http://www.ericse.org/sciindex.html

Educational Resources Information Center, Clearinghouse on Information & Technology. 1998. *About the Virtual Reference Desk* [WWW document]. Available WWW: http://www.vrd.org/Networker2.html

————. 1999a. *About AskERIC* [WWW document, February]. Available WWW: http://ericir.syr.edu/Qa/Kind_Question.html

————. 1999b. *The gateway to educational materials* [Online meta-database, February]. Available WWW: http://www.thegateway.org

Educational Resources Information Center, Clearinghouse on Teaching and Teacher Education. 1995. Reconceptualizing professional teacher development. *ERIC Digest, ED383695* [WWW document]. Available WWW: http://www.ed.gov/databases/ERIC_Digests/ed383695.html

Eisenhower National Clearinghouse for Mathematics and Science Education. 1997. *Tools for discussion: Attaining excellence through TIMSS* [WWW document]. Available WWW: http://timss.enc.org

————. 1998a. ENC [Special Issue]. *ENC Update, 5* (3).

————. 1998b. *The guidebook of federal resources for K–12 mathematics and science* [WWW document]. Available WWW: http://www.enc.org/partners/index.htm

————. 1998c. *Making schools work for every child* [WWW document]. Available WWW: http://equity.enc.org

————. 1999a. *Ideas for reform* [WWW document, February 5]. Available WWW: http://www.enc.org/reform/index.htm

————. 1999b. *Resource finder* [Online database, search results, February 5]. Available WWW: http://watt.enc.org/main2.html

Eisenhower Regional Consortia for Mathematics and Science Education. 1997. *Science adventures* [Online database]. Available WWW: http://www.scienceadventures.org

Falk, D. 1984. Survival strategies, Module 2. In *Wildlife inquiry through zoo education*, ed. D. Falk [Series]. New York: New York Zoological Society.

Grimes, B. and R. Hallick. 1999. *The biology project* [WWW document]. Available WWW: http://www.biology.arizona.edu/the_biology_project/the_biology_project.html

Hawkins, J. 1997. The world at your fingertips. In Burness, P. (Ed.), *Learn & live* [WWW document]. Available WWW: http://www.glef.org/learnlive/book/technology/hawkins1.html

Horizon Research, Inc. 1998. The teaching materials (TMAT) project: Increasing the availability of materials for the professional development of science and mathematics teachers [Brochure]. Chapel Hill, NC: Author.

Killion, J. 1999. *Results-based staff development: What works in the middle grades*. Oxford, OH: National Staff Development Council.

Loucks-Horsley, S. 1998. Effective professional development for teachers of mathematics. In Eisenhower National Clearinghouse for Mathematics and Science Education, *Ideas that work: Mathematics professional development* [WWW document]. Available WWW: http://www.enc.org/reform/ideas/133273/3273_5.htm

McKean, K. E. and R. T. Nelsen. 1997. *Columbia Education Center presents: Short-term professional development programs* [WWW document]. Available WWW: http://www.mcrel.org/resources/articles/prodev-intro.asp

McNeely, M. E., ed. 1997. Executive summary of a splintered vision: An investigation of U.S. science and mathematics education. In Eisenhower National Clearinghouse for Mathematics and Science Education, *TIMSS resource kit: Guidebook to examine school curricula* [WWW document]. Available WWW: http://timss.enc.org/TIMSS/timss/curicula/125448/5448_161.htm

Michigan Department of Education, North Central Regional Educational Laboratory, and The Math Science Consortia. 1997a. Partnering with families and the community. In Eisenhower National Clearinghouse for Mathematics and Science Education, *Equity@ENC: Community building* [WWW document; reprinted from *Connecting with the learner: An equity toolkit*]. Available WWW: http://equity.enc.org/equity/combuild/index2.htm

———. 1997b. Survey says.... In Eisenhower National Clearinghouse for Mathematics and Science Education, *Equity@ENC: Self-assessment* [WWW document; reprinted from *Connecting with the learner: An equity toolkit*]. Available WWW: http://equity.enc.org/equity/selfeval/index2.htm

Mid-Atlantic Eisenhower Consortium for Mathematics and Science Education. 1997. *TIMSS forum* [Online discussion forum; Donahoe, P. (Admin.)]. Available WWW: http://timss.enc.org/TIMSS/addtools/lists/index.htm#2

National Academy of Sciences. 1998. *National science education standards* [WWW document]. Available WWW: http://www.nap.edu/readingroom/books/nses/html

National Staff Development Council. 1999. *Standards for staff development* [WWW document, February 5]. Available WWW: http://www.nsdc.org/standards.html

North Central Regional Educational Laboratory. 1999. *Pathways to school improvement* [WWW Document, February 8]. Available WWW: http://www.ncrel.org/sdrs/pathwayg.htm

Project 2061. 1997. *Benchmarks on-line* [WWW document]. Available WWW: http://project2061.aaas.org/tools/benchol/bolframe.html

Shinohara, M., R. Wenn, and A. Sussman. 1996. *Tales from the electronic frontier* [WWW document]. Available WWW: http://www.wested.org/werc/portfolio8.html

Snyder, T., C. Hoffman, and C. Geddes. 1998. *Digest of education statistics 1997* [WWW document]. Available WWW: http://nces.ed.gov/pubs/digest97/index.html

Snyder, T., and J. Wirt. 1998. *The condition of education, 1998* [WWW document]. Available WWW: http://nces.ed.gov/pubs98/condition98/index.html

Tramline, Inc. 1998. *Deserts field trip* [WWW document]. Available WWW http://www.field-guides.com/desert/desert.htm

Viau, E. A. 1999. *World builders* [WWW document]. Available WWW: http://curriculum.calstatela.edu/courses/builders/index.html

Pathways to the Science *Standards*

Juliana Texley

Juliana Texley is retired and acts as a consultant on testing and curriculum. She was superintendent of anchor Bay School District, New Baltimore, Michigan for 10 years. She taught science at
all levels for 25 years. Her Ph.D. is in science education, and she serves on the adjunct faculty of
Central Michigan University and St. Clair Community College. She was awarded a Presidential
Award for Science Teaching.

From the headline-making publications of *A Nation at Risk* (National Commission on Excellence in Education, 1983.) and *Science For All Americans* (AAAS, 1989), to the final publication of the *National Science Education Standards* (NSES) in 1996, 13 eventful years passed in science education. To the public, to legislators, and to the press, some 300 reports on the state of school science created the impression that the profession lacked a common focus for reform—a "fibrillating heart" sending powerful but mixed messages. But from the perspective of the American classroom teacher, the waiting years were productive ones.

The NSES authors described the waiting years with classic understatement: "Some outstanding things happen in science classrooms today, even without national standards" (p. 12). In fact, in the 1980s and 1990s innovation was widespread. Hundreds of projects were initiated to explore pathways to change—some by national organizations like the American Association for the Advancement of Science (AAAS) and the National Science Teachers Association (NSTA), some by consortia of publishers and researchers with funding from the National Science Foundation (NSF), some by business and industry programs (like Toyota's TAPESTRY), and still others by teacher teams in site-based reform efforts (including NSF's Systemic Initiative.) Using the capacity of the nation's universities and teacher-training institutions, these projects were usually evaluated empirically and compared to the growing body of common wisdom that was ultimately codified into the NSES. So, despite the impatient antici-pation of classroom teachers for definitive national standards, the development years were productive ones.

Science educators were aware of the diminishing scientific literacy of Americans long before *A Nation at Risk*. To a great extent, a consensus was reached on solutions long before the *Standards* clarified it to the public at large. The profession agreed: Good teaching involves guided and structured inquiry, with an emphasis on opportu-nity to learn among communities of learners; good assessment provides valid and usable data throughout the learning process; content must be less broad with greater depth; programs and systems must be coherent, integrated, and focused on support of learning, equity, and good teaching; and, perhaps most importantly, persistent, effective change must be supported with a professional development system that is both authentic to and embraced by America's science teachers.

Despite this consensus, it took precedent-setting cooperation among professionals in science, business, industry, government, and the professions to produce a document with the influence of the NSES. Without this coherent and powerful voice, the financial and legislative support needed to embed the standards into the structure of American education would never occur. And without active acceptance by classroom teachers, the landmark document would be destined for the library shelf.

It took precedent-setting cooperation among professionals in science, business, industry, government, and the professions to produce a document with the influence of the NSES.

The publicity that accompanied the final release of the NSES in 1996 was not universally positive. The headlines that proclaimed the standards new and revolutionary implied rejection of existing practice. So it was with mixed emotion that classroom teachers received copies of the *Standards*. They celebrated, because the unprecedented collaboration among scientists, educators, and business leaders had validated a visionary document and provided them with ammunition to support change. But they also confessed confusion: Where should they begin? What place would the work of the last 13 years play? How could the standards be imbedded into practice in a manner that would make this round of change sustainable? In some ways, the excitement that accompanied the standards had the potential of becoming a barrier to further change for veterans who had been working toward change for over a decade and who had seen other initiatives come and go over their careers.

It was in that context that NSTA convened a large, representative group of members to evaluate current practice in the context of the NSES and to create a comprehensive professional development package that would move the vision into practice. Current research provided a clear set of guidelines for the implementation effort: learning occurs best when it begins on familiar ground, *inservice* programs are most effective when they are long-term, and instruction changes only when practicioners embrace change not only intellectually but also emotionally (Holmes Group, 1990). From a base of research and best practice, NSTA proposed to develop professional development for elementary, middle, and secondary teachers which would relate the best of current work to the standards and link today's classrooms with tomorrow's high ideals.

The NSTA Pathways project was underway. The first phase involved the development of three publications (one for each level) that would provide convenient access to familiar current resources. In order to achieve not only intellectual but also emotional commitment to change, a project team sought to recognize that some elements of best practice in every classroom in America. Believing that change is easiest when personal choices are supported by positive reinforcement, three Pathways books (Texley & Wild, 1996) emphasized that elements of the standards existed in every school. The project sought to bring easily-accessible tools to those classrooms so that the teacher could move forward with support from the profession. Phase II would involve accumulating resources for easy access on CD-ROM, and ultimately the series would be part of aggressive professional development.

The Pathways team quickly reached consensus on its goals:

◆ Change in professional practice would be effective only if it was generated by teachers; therefore, the Pathways project would be based upon those standards-compatible efforts that have been used effectively in classrooms.

◆ The standards are models, not formulas. There is no single route toward an ideal program or system; the most appropriate first steps would be those chosen by each community.

◆ To achieve sustainable change in classroom practice, Pathways would first help teachers recognize their preconceptions and those elements of their own programs that were most compatible with best practice.

◆ The program would encourage teachers to apply new standards to existing practice and to value small steps toward more effective science education rather than totally reject their own current methods.

◆ The public, including parents and community leaders, would need to become more aware of existing and newly adopted practices that move their systems toward the standards, in order to provide reinforcement and affirmation to teachers who are moving toward change. Therefore, teachers would have to include in their own agenda a commitment to working with outside stakeholders on the realization of the standards.

The Phase I Pathways books were devoted to support of classroom teachers. In order to link current practice to the standards, the editors surveyed over 700 existing projects and programs which had been evaluated as effective. For each level (elementary, middle, high school) and for each area of the NSES, connections were defined to accessible resources and effective practices. Consider these examples from the secondary Pathways:

Teaching Standard A: "…planning inquiry-based science…"
◆ Concept mapping and (Gowan's) vee diagrams

- Prereading strategies for comprehension
- Assessing preconceptions

Teaching Standard B: "...guiding and facilitating learning..."
- Constructivist research on preconceptions
- Open-ended inquiry
- New approaches to traditional labs

Teaching Standard C: "...engaging in ongoing assessment..."
- Constructivist questioning
- Research on wait time and effective classroom dialogue

Teaching Standard D: "...designing and managing the learning environment..."
- Block and other innovative approaches to scheduling
- Management techniques to maximize time on task

Teaching Standard E: "...developing communities of learners..."
- Sensitivity to multicultural differences
- Cooperative learning techniques
- Increasing accessibility for handicapped students and opportunity to learn

Teaching Standard F: "...Teachers...actively participating in...program development..."
- *Scope, Sequence, and Coordination* (NSTA, 1992) models from the National Science Teachers Association
- *Project 2061* models from the American Association for the Advancement of Science
- Model "Triad" projects from the National Science Foundation

The publications linked the professional development standards to research on the need for content knowledge in science teachers, models for peer collaboration and research and internship experiences through business and industry. The authors illustrated the Assessment Standards with examples of successful projects in performance assessment, interviewing and group tests, portfolios, and assessments of programs and systems. Case studies in outcomes-based education, Science/Technology/Society projects, event-based science, and programs directed toward increasing opportunity to learn in underrepresented groups provided pathways to achieving the Program Standards. Using the System standards, Pathways referenced projects that addressed the barriers to reform in state and federal systems, as well as models for working with parents, business/industry, and school boards.

For each familiar project, model, or plan, the Pathways program would provide easy-access document references from the professional journals most commonly available to classroom teachers, Web sites, and a companion CD-ROM. By putting the work of fellow professionals at arm's reach, the authors hoped to reaffirm that the keys to reaching the newly defined standards were no farther than the closest professional library.

At the outset, the Pathways publication team struggled not only with the volume of material available—almost two decades of work—but also with the structure which would make the content most recognizable to teachers. To see themselves changing, teachers must first see themselves. They did not need a restatement of the NSES: In order to link current practice to the standards most effectively, the Pathways publications looked at a number of issues:

1. Voice. The reforms which the NSES demand can never be achieved without a strong, new level of shared understanding and mission among all of the stakeholders in education—community leaders, parents, business and industry, and education. But to the extent that the NSES publication attempted to address all of these audiences, the book failed to reach any of them most effectively. Agreeing with the standards and research (ERIC, 1995) that longstanding change must begin with teachers, the Pathways project would limit its voice and focus *only* on classroom teachers.

2. Grade structure. After considerable debate, the NSES chose to use a grade structure which was loosely based upon the most common divisions in state assessment projects: Elementary (K–4), Middle (5–8), and Secondary (9–12). The Pathways publications recognized that American schools vary greatly in grade configurations, and that the most effective vehicle for change would affirm the grade levels in each community. So the NSTA publications included an overlap—Elementary (K–6) and Middle (5–8).

3. Secondary certification and assignments. One of the most difficult issues faced by the Pathways project was how to effect change in secondary classrooms. Ultimately, there was consensus that in order to achieve the essential emotional commitment among secondary teachers, they must first recognize themselves and their own best practice. Since secondary staffs identify themselves not as science teachers but as biology, chemistry, physics, or earth science teachers, the Pathways secondary publication chose that structure and integrated standards information on the cross-disciplinary issues of inquiry, history and nature of science, and integrated content within each of those four certification areas.

4. Cross-level references. Realizing that the emerging discipline of middle-level education often finds itself sandwiched between long-established bodies of secondary and elementary practice, the middle-level Pathways provides unique tables that cross-reference the standards and skill levels which progress from elementary through secondary levels.

5. Content. Recognizing that secondary teachers invariably have content majors, but that the norm for teacher preparation in the content area weakens in the middle and elementary areas, the Pathways publications for the latter two teacher groups include brief, concise summaries of the hard science upon which the standards are based. They do not to teach the science; the scope of the publications could never allow that depth of coverage, and simply reading the science could never convey it effectively. The content summaries defined not only what should be taught, but in the "less is more" spirit of the standards they delimited what is not included in the core content expected of students by the standards.

6. Student materials. Within the context of the project's goal to be immediately useful to teachers, the project team considered the issue of whether to include actual (photocopyable) student activities. Ultimately, the team rejected the idea. Rather than affirming the project philosophy that teachers should build upon their existing curriculum (their current texts and materials), photocopyable materials might create the impression that existing programs must be replaced in their entirety. Thus, new student exercises might be more limiting for teachers than vignette-models of teachers who made small but significant improvements in their own existing methodology.

7. Evaluation. Another intense debate among the Pathways team was the issue of the use of the standards and the Pathways project in particular, for teacher evaluation. Although the authors and reviewers clearly understood that the project was a professional development effort and not a tool for those outside the classroom (i.e., administrators) to judge progress, the team was very conscious of the potential for abuse of any measurement scales that might be included. For that reason, a very sound series of charts on which a teacher might measure his/her progress toward the standards was ultimately rejected. But the project did devote attention to NSTA's system.

8. Learning Theory. Recognizing that the most significant contributions to the profession in the past decades have emerged from our growing understanding of neuroscience and how children learn, the Pathways project devoted significant text to describing the nature of the learner as associated with each content area. This strand is particularly strong in the elementary edition, where the close association between developmental level and developmentally appropriate content is constantly emphasized.

Pathways, thus, addressed its primary audience with an approach that was designed to achieve professional growth through an emotional and intellectual commitment that could only begin on familiar ground. The sources that were included in the Phase I publications (chiefly references and CD-ROM access) were almost exclusively those that would be easily accessed in school and educational resource center libraries. For example, a project that might have been described both in the *Journal of Research in Science Teaching* (JRST) and *The Science Teacher* (TST) would have been referenced in the latter. (Where research data was needed, the secondary reference to JRST would be available in TST.) The structure of the references, like that of the entire document, was built upon not what might be a future ideal but what exists today. Secondary references were divided into (and often repeated for) each certification area; elementary and middle school areas were consciously overlapped so that teachers could find the programs most applicable to their entire school structure in one volume.

As a vehicle for professional development, the Pathways project may be unique in its emphasis on empowerment. A consistent message throughout the publications is that the information provided should be used not only as a tool, but also as a weapon. "Take this to your administrator...or to your school board." Recognizing that change will be awkward, uncomfortable, and inevitably expensive, the text provided many tools for teachers to use in justifying their efforts to the stakeholders who affect their professional lives.

> As a vehicle for professional development, the Pathways project may be unique in its emphasis on empowerment.

Also unique is the series' recognition of the systemic barriers that may face teachers as they move toward the standards. Inquiry-based instruction is highly effective, but it is also messy, expensive, and occasionally unreliable. Will the administrator understand? New forms of assessment may increase validity, but when the grading standards change, how will the parents of high-performing students react? When a teacher works toward an outcomes-based curriculum, how will the administration react to possible attacks from opponents? When the system makes a commitment to equal opportunity to learn, will the necessary support in the form of compensatory education follow? Where previous university-generated professional development programs have often been criticized as being unrealistic or "ivory-tower," Pathways sought to increase its effectiveness by imbedding a constant recognition of the systemic barriers to reform that exist in American schools.

As the project explored standards and barriers, it became apparent that several areas of the standards had few or dated links within the current literature. A revision of the NSTA program for science program evaluation was one of the first associated projects that was a result of the impetus created by the Pathways project. The revised program assessment instrument will not only be a publication but a computer-based system in which a group of staff members can compare their perceptions and measurements to those of others and to the ideal represented by the standards in a process authentic to site-based professional development.

Another area of the standards that the Pathways team found almost ignored in the science education literature was the topic of the physical facilities that must support good science education programs. A 1998 study by the U.S. General Accounting Office found that 40 percent of American schools had serious structural problems, many of which limited the nature of instruction in areas like science. Data supporting ideal science education facilities were conspicuously absent from the literature of the profession, and what did exist was dated and impractical. The team first solicited a brief, coherent summary of the physical requirements of good science classrooms and then moved to support a new publication and professional development package that would bring together best practice in architecture and school construction. This publication is expected from NSTA in 1999.

The Pathways appendix addressing science facilities and the NSTA Facilities Book that would follow are good examples of the difference between the project's approach to professional development and advocacy and that common to previous projects. Classroom teachers cite physical plant limitations as the single greatest barrier to reform within their schools. Inquiry, however desirable, becomes impossible or unsafe within crowded, ill-equipped, unventilated classrooms. Pathways would not stop at simply recommending good facilities, but would provide a vital tool for advocacy by science teachers by succinctly defining the space, ventilation, storage, and schedules that must be present for progress to occur. Secondary students would need a minimum of 60 square feet in a laboratory facility (up from the current 15 or 10, due to both the new equipment standards and the greater size of today's teens). Ventilation should exceed 20 cubic feet/minute. Large deep sinks with hot and cold water would be required in all science programs, along with deep shelving and lockable cabinets. Fire and earthquake protection should be built in, and all facilities should be accessible to all students (Appendix C, Texley & Wild, 1996). Written as such a guide, the facilities appendix and the publication that would follow become not only tools but also a source of ammunition for the new teacher-advocate.

> *Pathways would not stop at simply recommending good facilities, but would provide a vital tool for advocacy by science teachers by succinctly defining the space, ventilation, storage, and schedules that must be present for progress to occur.*

Pathways publications are an essential but very basic first step toward implementation of the *National Standards*. As their goals, approach, and unique voice reach the classroom teachers of the United States, the need for followup support in many areas becomes more apparent. The revised Program Evaluation Modules and the Facilities Book are two examples of responses to the initiative. It is also clear that in order to fulfill the promise of teacher advocacy, short but very practical professional development efforts will have to be developed which speak directly to administrators and parent groups in language they can understand. School board programs may also follow. At the same time, a natural outgrowth for teachers will be program-specific projects which take existing curricular materials and help staff make the necessary alterations to bring those programs closer to the vision of the standards.

Pathways is, therefore, not only a project but also a unique, grassroots approach to professional development generated by teachers themselves through the voice of their NSTA affiliation as a response to the vision of the NSES. With the enthusiasm which characterizes the most highly motivated of their students, teachers have answered the role call of the National Academy with a spirited: "Yes, we are here...and ready to move forward from our own classrooms on our individual pathway to the standards."

References

American Association for the Advancement of Science. 1989. *Science for All Americans.* New York: Oxford University Press.

ERIC, U.S. Department of Education. Professional Development. 1995. Theme issue. *ERIC Review* 3(3):1–32.

Holmes Group. 1990. *Tomorrow's schools: Principles for the Design of Professional Development in Schools.* East Lansing, MI.:Holmes Group.

National Academy of Sciences. 1996. *National science education standards.* Washington, DC. National Academy Press.

National Commission on Excellence in Education. 1983. *A Nation at Risk:The Imperative for Educational Reform.* Washington, DC.

National Science Teachers Association. 1992. *Scope, Sequence and Coordination of Secondary School Science.* Arlington, Virginia: NSTA.

Texley, J., and A. Wild. 1996. *Pathways to the Science Standards.* High School Edition. Arlington, Virginia: National Science Teachers Association.

The Professional Development of Science Teachers for Science Education Reform: A Review of the Research

Julie Gess-Newsome
University of Utah

Julie Gess-Newsome is the J. Lawrence Walkup Distinguished Professor of Science Education and the Director of the Science and Mathematics Learning Center at Northern Arizona University. Prior to receiving her Ph.D. from Oregon State University in 1992, Dr. Gess-Newsome taught high school biology and general science for 8 years in Wyoming and South Dakota. Her research interests include teacher cognition and development with an emphasis on teachers' understanding of content as it relates to instruction. Recent work has focused on the knowledge and beliefs of college science faculty. Dr. Gess-Newsome is currently the president of the Association for the Education of Teachers of Science, the former editor of the Science Teacher Education section of Science Education, and the co-editor of a recent book on pedagogical content knowledge published by Kluwer.

The *National Science Education Standards* (National Research Council, 1996, herein called the *Standards*) represent both an accomplishment of and challenge to the science teaching community. On one hand, they encourage the integration of content through unifying concepts and processes, articulate classroom practices that accurately portray the nature and history of science, and sustain efforts to provide equitable science education for all students. On the other hand, the *Standards* ask teachers to implement teaching practices that they have had limited opportunities to experience. How can teachers move from tried-and-true practices of "teaching as telling" to "teacher as guide and facilitator?" How can teachers make explicit content connections for students that are personally unclear? How can teachers create communities of learners when they lead professional lives in isolated classrooms? One answer exists in the opportunities teachers have to continue to learn, grow, and develop throughout their professional careers. The *Standards* clearly provide a direction and goal for this professional development.

What does it mean to develop professionally? Defining teaching as a profession implies that, similar to other professions, it is a complex activity guided by a knowledge base that has evolved through formal research and personal classroom experience. As a professional, a teacher is both a user and creator of knowledge when making planned and spontaneous instructional decisions (Fueyo & Koorland, 1997).

Development implies change: Obviously, everyone changes during his or her career, but development is "drawn from that subclass of changes that are desirable and positive in quality as opposed to negative. Thus increases in ability, skill, power, strength, wisdom, insight, virtue, happiness, and so forth would certainly qualify as development" (Jackson, 1992, p. 62). Professional development, then, includes opportunities for continuous skill and knowledge acquisition in an effort to create effective learning opportunities for students. Development, however, is personal and can be only stimulated by, but not forced through, outside agents (Clark, 1992; McLaughlin, 1990). As science teachers select development goals, the *Standards* can provide a source of external stimulus and direction for continuing professional growth.

This chapter provides an overview of what is known about the professional knowledge base needed to implement the *Standards* and the ways that teachers acquire and use this knowledge to impact teaching practices across their career. This chapter concludes with the identification of characteristics that are common to successful professional development programs and the implications of professional development for science education reform.

> *Professional development includes opportunities for continuous skill and knowledge acquisition in an effort to create effective learning opportunities for students.*

Professional Knowledge and Teaching Practices that Support the *Standards*

The *Standards* set clear expectations for student learning: students should have a firm and integrated understanding of the underlying concepts and processes of science, as well as a grasp of the nature and structure of the discipline. Past educational practices, however, have not always been successful in delivering these student outcomes. Fortunately, research has revealed teaching strategies that support these goals and complement the teaching strategies outlined in the *Standards*. Such practices include using inquiry-oriented and problem solving lessons, active student participation, and frequent teacher-student interactions; creating social environments where risk is supported and where there is open discussion and use of student ideas; implementing lessons that provide an accurate portrayal of disciplinary knowledge, nature, and structure; recognizing and challenging student misconceptions; and using alternative representations or discrepant events to facilitate student learning (Gess-Newsome, 1999; Hollon, Roth, & Anderson, 1991; Lederman, 1992; Smith & Neale, 1991). To incorporate instructional strategies of this nature, teachers will need well-developed knowledge of both pedagogy and content. The challenge of science education reform then is to assist teachers in moving from current teaching practices to those identified above.

Instructional practice is based in teacher knowledge and belief. Early public school memories shape teachers' views about what it means to learn and the best ways to organize and represent content for teaching. Often the lessons learned include "teaching is telling," "to learn is to memorize," and "content is disconnected" (Ball, 1990; Gess-Newsome & Lederman, 1993). University science classrooms often reinforce these early lessons. As a result, most secondary teachers enter the classroom confident in their subject matter knowledge (Brookhart & Freeman, 1992), though the fragmented, superficial, and disconnected nature of their knowledge limits their ability to teach in the manner specified by the *Standards* (Ball, 1990; Gess-Newsome, 1999). Early efforts to learn content are often suppressed by the overwhelming task of establishing classroom routines and navigating the choppy waters of classroom instruction and student interaction. Thus, teaching experiences assist new science teachers in gaining general pedagogical skills but rarely help them integrate and deepen the limited subject matter knowledge they possess.

There are several unfortunate consequences of superficial content understanding. First, teachers resort to teaching as they were taught, emphasizing the memorization of isolated facts and algorithms. Second, fragmented knowledge limits a teacher's ability to teach in creative and innovative manners—making them pedagogical prisoners of their own poor content understanding—afraid to introduce lessons that may encourage students to move beyond the realm of the teacher's knowledge. Finally, limited subject matter knowledge results in an overreliance on the textbook rather than student understanding as the basis for lesson planning, the dominance of lower level questions and rule-constrained classroom activities, limited use of student questions or comments in classroom discourse, limited development of conceptual connections, and the misrepresentation of the nature and structure of the discipline (Carlsen, 1991; Dobey & Schafer, 1984; Gess-Newsome, 1999; Mosenthal & Ball, 1992; Talbert, McLaughlin, & Rowan, 1993). These classroom practices are in direct contrast to those recommended by the *Standards*.

Instructional practice is based in teacher knowledge and belief.

Early career classroom trial and error eventually gives way to mid-career mastery of classroom routines, increased content understanding, and refinement and personalization of the curriculum and instructional repertoire (Huberman, 1992). Teachers in this stage have achieved a level of self-acceptance and teaching confidence that places them in an ideal position to take on new challenges. Though teachers in mid-career vacillate between periods of positive action and emotion (i.e., experimentation, excitement, and serenity) and periods of self-doubt, career questioning, and innovation resistance, professional development can make the difference between lingering in positive or negative career stages (Huberman, 1992). It is during this midcareer stage that teachers are most likely to possess the skills, knowledge, and classroom practices identified with exemplary practice.

In terms of science education reform, the intersection of a teacher's understanding of content and pedagogy directly impacts classroom practice. Inservice efforts to help motivated midcareer teachers adopt constructivist classroom practices make *ι* without adequate content knowledge, changes in pedagogical practices sustained. And it is not only the amount of knowledge that is important, but manner in which it is organized (Knapp, 1997; Hollon et al., 1991; Smith & Neale, 1991). Therefore, in order to support the professional development of science teachers, changes in beliefs and knowledge about content and pedagogy are needed.

Characteristics of Successful Professional Development
The portrait of teacher knowledge, practice, and development presented in the preceding section creates a backdrop on which one can position the elements of successful professional development programs. The characteristics outlined below are among those that appear consistently in the literature and positively impact teachers' professional development efforts.

Effective Professional Development Includes <u>Sustained Support</u>
Perry (1975) is cited as asking the question: "If development is so good, why doesn't everyone just grow?" (Sprinthall, Reiman, & Thies-Sprinthall, 1996, p. 693). A reasonable question, with an equally reasonable answer. Change is exhilarating, providing feelings of empowerment and personal efficacy. But development and growth are also difficult processes, fraught with cognitive challenges, requiring the restructuring of knowledge and beliefs. Change often involves choosing to relinquish safe and familiar practices for the new and uncertain. Therefore, change efforts need sustained cognitive and emotional support if they are to succeed.

> *The intersection of a teacher's understanding of content and pedagogy directly impacts classroom practice.*

What constitutes sustained support? While it is clear that single-day workshops are too short and fragmented and have limited follow-through (Bullough, Kauchak, Crow, Hobbs, & Stokes, 1997; McLaughlin, 1990), how long professional support for change should last is unclear. While some researchers have suggested a two-year period of support (Gibbons, Kimmel, & O'Shea, 1997; Reys, B., Reys, R., Barnes, Beem, & Papick, 1997), it seems that if a lifetime of development is expected, a career lifetime of professional support must be provided. At minimum, teachers need support while confronting the personal challenges associated with change until they move into the reward stage of personal classroom reform (Hollon et al., 1991; Smith & Neale, 1991).

What constitutes support? Though the following list is not exhaustive and does not take into consideration individual or site-specific needs, it provides a general orientation to forms of support often mentioned in the literature: leadership that nurtures individual development, a limited number of course preparations, opportunities to modify classroom practices in low-stakes settings, a chance of achieving significant student outcomes, regular feedback about teaching performance, access to collegial expertise and external stimulation, time, and opportunities to be involved with a critical mass of others who support change (Adams & Krockover, 1997; Gess-Newsome & Lederman, 1995; Knapp, 1997; Huberman, 1992; McLaughlin, 1990).

Effective Professional Development Is Designed by and for Individuals

Because each teacher is unique, designing a single professional development program for all teachers is unrealistic (Clark, 1992). For professional development to be effective, it must meet the perceived needs of individuals at their career stage. Early career teachers can benefit most from assistance in classroom management, designing subject-specific lessons, establishing conceptual connections within and across lessons, using student comments and questions, monitoring student understanding, and meeting the needs of individual students (Gess-Newsome, 1999; Reynolds, 1992). Opportunities for professional renewal at the midcareer stage may include shifting roles (i.e., mentor, peer coach, department leadership) or designing classroom experiments in an effort to develop more effective instructional practices (Huberman, 1992; Sprinthall et al., 1996). Teachers late in their careers, while less likely candidates for new innovations, can be excellent resources for imparting the wisdom of practice developed over a career. Allowing teachers to select the content of and path to their own professional development is, therefore, a critical component of successful support programs.

> *Change often involves choosing to relinquish safe and familiar practices for the new and uncertain.*

Effective Professional Development Is Connected to Classroom Practice

Policy statements, such as those found in the *Standards* and state curricula, are important for large-scale decision making but have limited interest for individual teachers as they plan for classroom instruction (Cohen, 1995). Issues that are relevant to teachers include the more immediate concerns of classroom life, such as students, issues of instruction, and working with colleagues (Clark & Peterson, 1986; McLaughlin, 1990), while working with students from differing ability and motivation groups is cited as the greatest continuing challenge for teachers across their career (Huberman, 1992). In fact, increased student learning constitutes the single largest motivator of change in classroom practices (Sprinthall et al., 1996).

When assessing available sources of professional learning, teachers consistently rank learning from their own classroom as the most important, while learning from outside experts rates as the least important (Smylie, 1989). Professional development, then, should work from the concerns, interests, and motivations of teachers. Professional development programs that are clearly connected to the classroom, that model appropriate classroom teaching practices, and that result in significant increases of student learning will clearly be more effective than those that do not (Reys et al., 1997; Thiessen, 1992). Studying and learning from one's classroom experi-

Professional development programs that are clearly connected to the classroom, model appropriate classroom teaching practices, and result in significant increases of student learning will clearly be more effective than those that do not.

ence, in turn, adds to the context-specific professional knowledge valued by teachers and directly improves classroom practice—the ultimate site of reform efforts.

Effective Professional Development Helps Teachers Learn Science Content in New Ways

How teachers understand their content has obvious implications for how they teach. One challenge presented by reform efforts is to help teachers move beyond the fragmented knowledge they possess to the deep, connected knowledge required for teaching for understanding. In addition to learning their content in new ways, teachers also need to experience the process of learning from activities that are based on integrated content and process understandings. The use of content learning and hands-on experiences similar to those intended for students results in increased teacher content confidence and pedagogical understanding (Radford, 1998). Learning from exemplary science lessons that include the time to develop connections among science ideas through discourse with peers fosters changes in content knowledge, pedagogical practices, and beliefs in what it means to know and learn science. As a result, learning science as it should be taught gives teachers the opportunity to reorganize and refine their content understandings that support teaching practices outlined by the *Standards*.

Effective Professional Development Challenges Pedagogical Beliefs and Practices

Some experienced teachers, through years of effort, master many of the teaching practices outlined by the *Standards* while others do not. Why? Though teaching experience is a critical aspect of learning to teach, changes in classroom practice often must be accompanied by changes in beliefs (Reynolds, 1992). Teachers' beliefs about student learning, their lack of confidence in subject matter understanding, or their perceptions of the potential pedagogical challenges of reform will foil attempts to implement new curriculum or significantly change classroom practice (Cronin-Jones, 1991). Professional development then involves the examination of pedagogical beliefs and practices for compatibility and usefulness. Core beliefs need to be retained and reinforced while inconsistent beliefs need to be modified or discarded in order to allow for the adoption of new teaching practices.

It has been traditionally assumed that changes in instructional practice must be preceded by changes in belief. Recent findings, however, suggest that when teachers are encouraged to try innovative lessons that result in increased student understanding, they often will modify their beliefs after the fact (Guskey, 1986; McLaughlin, 1990). Therefore, imitating practices that model the ideals of science education reform may encourage teachers to adopt reform practices when they see improved student learning. However, the adoption of isolated practices may also result in piecemeal instructional practices, threatening curricular coherence and subverting reform efforts (Knapp, 1997). The complex relationship between teacher belief and instructional practice needs to be further clarified by research.

Tools for reflection often act as the conduit between classroom practice and research. Formal reflection activities, such as action research, can assist teachers in gathering data concerning the effectiveness of instruction and direct future development efforts (Henson, 1996). Informal reflection, such as recording teaching beliefs or content knowledge structures, makes explicit what teachers know and allows for the evaluation of the congruence between beliefs, knowledge, and instructional practice. Professional development activities should provide teachers with a variety of tools for reflection so that they can be drawn upon as needed throughout their careers.

Effective Professional Development *Promotes Incremental Change*

Teachers who are ultimately the most satisfied with their careers assume responsibility for student learning and engage in classroom-based experiments aimed at improving their practice (Huberman, 1992; Louis, Marks, & Kruse, 1996). In contrast, those teachers who are heavily involved in school or districtwide reform experience less career satisfaction. Although fundamental or large-scale change is often needed for systemwide reform, it is less likely to be sustained or achieved than incremental change. This finding suggests that professional development efforts should help foster incremental classroom-based change: Teachers can make important changes to some aspects of their teaching without a complete abandonment of their instructional repertoire. The affective advantage of incremental change is the retention of effective existing practices, the maintenance of a sense of pedagogical security, and the increased potential of positively impacting student learning (Knapp, 1997; McLaughlin, 1990).

Effective Professional Development Provides for *Collaboration*

Teachers face an interesting dichotomy. Though they appreciate and see the advantages of opportunities to work together in professional communities (Bullough et al., 1997), the nature of the teaching profession offers few opportunities to collaborate in meaningful ways (Raymond, Butts, & Townsend, 1992). Even while many teachers desire to work collaboratively, they have few concrete ideas on how to reach this goal (Book, 1996). Additionally, schools are rarely composed of only one teaching culture. In fact, departmental cultures within a secondary school are more varied in pedagogical beliefs and content conceptions than are science departments across school settings (Grossman & Stodolsky, 1995; Siskin, 1994). As a result, despite many attempts to incorporate school- or systemwide change, research has repeatedly shown that change occurs either individually or, at best, in small pockets within schools (Bullough, et al., 1997). In general, efforts to encourage professional development are best aimed at individuals, but when collaboration efforts are needed or desired, professional networks (such as state, local, and national chapters of the National Science Teachers Association) may offer a promising avenue for creating a critical mass of teachers who can support and encourage one another in their change efforts (Knapp, 97; Talbert, et al., 1993).

Even while many teachers desire to work collaboratively, they have few concrete ideas on how to reach this goal.

Implications of Professional Development for Science Education Reform

In the past, the public blamed teachers for many of the perceived shortcomings of the educational system. Staff developers introduced teacher-proof curricula and training in educational innovations to passive teaching audiences only to have the materials disregarded or substantially modified. Today, teachers are recognized as the core of reform efforts, for without a change in individual teaching practice there can be no change in education nationally (Cohen, 1995). The *Standards* acknowledged this view by characterizing teachers as reflective practitioners, producers of knowledge, members of a collegial profession, and both the sources and facilitators of change. Repeated examinations of restructuring efforts have produced similar results. Though change efforts introduced from the top down or by outside sources stimulate change, changes that are not championed by individual teachers and implemented within the confines of their own classroom rarely succeed (Cohen, 1995; McLaughlin, 1990; Sprinthall et al., 1996). Therefore, helping teachers design or select their own programs of professional development represents the greatest hope of reaching the teaching practices idealized in the *Standards*. Professional development efforts should connect to classroom practice, help teachers learn their content in new ways, challenge pedagogical beliefs and practices, promote incremental change, provide for collaboration, and exist in a climate of sustained support. Despite this conclusion, it is critical that larger efforts to assist teachers in their professional development continue (Cohen, 1995). As stated in the *Standards*: "Teachers are central to education, but they must not be placed in a position of being solely responsible for reform. Teachers will need to work within a collegial, organizational, and policy context that is supportive of good science teaching (NRC, 1996, p. 27)."

References

Adams, P. E., and G. H. Krockover. 1997. Concerns and perceptions of beginning secondary science and mathematics teachers. *Science Education* 81:29–50.

Ball, D. L. 1990. The mathematical understandings that preservice teachers bring to teacher education. *Elementary School Journal* 90:449–466.

Book, C. L. 1996. Professional development schools. In *Handbook of research on teacher* education. 2d ed., ed. J. Sikula, T. J. Buttery, & E. Guyton, 194–212. New York: Macmillan.

Brookhart, S. M., and D. J. Freeman. 1992. Characteristics of entering teacher candidates. *Review of Educational Research* 62:37–60.

Bullough, R. V. Jr., D. Kauchak, N. A. Crow, S. Hobbs, and D. Stokes. 1997. Professional development schools: Catalysts for teacher and school change. *Teaching and Teacher Education* 13:153–169.

Carlsen, W. S. 1991. Effects of new biology teachers' subject-matter knowledge on curricular planning. *Science Education* 75:631–647.

Clark, C. M. 1992. Teachers as designers in self-directed professional development. In *Understanding teacher development*, ed. A. Hargreaves & M. G. Fullan, 75–84. New York: Teachers College Press.

Clark, C., and P. L. Peterson. 1986. Teachers' thought processes. In *Handbook of research on teaching*. 3d ed., ed, M. C. Wittrock, 255–296. New York: Macmillian.

Cohen, D. K. 1995. What is the system in systemic reform? *Educational Researcher* 24(9):11–17, 31.

Cronin-Jones, L. L. 1991. Science teacher beliefs and their influence on curriculum implementations: Two case studies. *Journal of Research in Science Teaching* 28:235–250.

Dobey, D. C., and L. E. Schafer. 1984. The effects of knowledge on elementary science inquiry teaching. *Science Education* 68:39–51.

Fueyo, V., and M. A. Koorland. 1997. Teacher as researcher: A synonym for professionalism. *Journal of Teacher Education* 48:336–344.

Gess-Newsome, J. 1999. Secondary teachers' knowledge and beliefs about subject matter and its impact on instruction. In *Examining pedagogical content knowledge: The construct and its implications for science education*, ed. J. Gess-Newsome & N. G. Lederman. Kluwer Publishing: Dordrecht, The Netherlands.

Gess-Newsome, J., and N. G. Lederman. 1993. Preservice biology teachers' knowledge structures as a function of professional teacher education: A year-long assessment. *Science Education* 77:25–45.

Gess-Newsome, J., and N. G. Lederman. 1995. Biology teachers' perceptions of subject matter structure and its relationship to classroom practice. *Journal of Research in Science Teaching* 32:301–325.

Gibbons, S., H. Kimmel, and M. O'Shea. 1997. Changing teacher behavior through staff development: Implementing the teaching and content standards in science. *School Science and Mathematics* 97:302–309.

Grossman, P. L. and S. S. Stodolsky. 1995. Content as context: The role of school subjects in secondary school teaching. *Educational Researcher* 24(8):5–11.

Guskey, T. R. 1986. Staff development and the process of teacher change. *Educational Researcher* 15:5–12.

Henson, K. T. 1996. Teachers as researchers. In *Handbook of research on teacher education*. 2nd ed., ed. J. Sikula, T. J. Buttery, & E. Guyton, 53–66. New York: Macmillan.

Hollon, R. E., K. J. Roth, and C. W. Anderson. 1991. Science teachers' conceptions of teaching and learning. In *Advances in research on teaching*, vol. 2, ed., J. Brophy, 145–186. Greenwich, CT: JAI.

Huberman, M. 1992. Teacher development and instructional mastery. In *Understanding teacher development*, ed. A. Hargreaves & M. G. Fullan, 122–142. New York: Teachers College Press.

Jackson, P. W. 1992. Helping teachers develop. In *Understanding teacher development*, ed. A. Hargreaves & M. G. Fullan, 62–74). New York: Teachers College Press.

Knapp, M. S. 1997. Between systemic reforms and the mathematics and science classroom: The dynamics of innovation, implementation, and professional learning. *Review of Educational Research* 67:227–266.

Lederman, N. G. 1992. Students and teachers' conceptions of the nature of science: A review of the research. *Journal of Research in Science Teaching* 29:331–359.

Louis, K. S., H. M. Marks, and S. Kruse. 1996. Teachers' professional community in restructuring schools. *American Educational Research Journal* 33:757–798.

McLaughlin, M. W. 1990. The Rand Change Agent Study revisited: Macro perspective and micro realities. *Educational Researcher* 19:11–16.

Mosenthal, J. H., and D. L. Ball. 1992. Constructing new forms of teaching: Subject matter knowledge in in-service teacher education. *Journal of Teacher Education* 43:347–356.

National Research Council. 1996. *National science education standards.* Washington, DC: National Academy Press.

Perry, W. G. 1975. Sharing in the costs of growth. In *Encouraging development in college students*, ed., C. Parker, 267–276. Minneapolis: University of Minnesota Press.

Radford, D. L. 1998. Transferring theory into practice: A model for professional development for science education reform. *Journal of Research in Science Teaching* 35:73–88.

Raymond, D., Butts, R., and D. Townsend. 1992. Contexts for teacher development: Insights from teachers' stories. In *Understanding teacher development*, ed. A. Hargreaves & M. G. Fullan, 143–161. New York: Teachers College Press.

Reynolds, A. 1992. What is competent beginning teaching? A review of the literature. *Review of Educational Research* 62:1–35.

Reys, B. J., R. E. Reys, D. Barnes, J. Beem, and I. Papick. 1997. Collaborative curriculum investigation as a vehicle for teacher enhancement and mathematics curriculum reform. *School Science and Mathematics* 97:253–259.

Siskin, L. S. 1994. *Realms of knowledge: Academic departments in secondary schools.* Washington, DC: Falmer Press.

Smith, D. C., and D. C. Neale. 1991. The construction of subject-matter knowledge in primary science teaching. In *Advances in Research on Teaching*, vol. 2, ed. J. Brophy, 187–244. Greenwich, CT: JAI.

Smylie, M. A. 1989. Teachers' views of the effectiveness of sources of learning to teach. *The Elementary School Journal* 89:543–558.

Sprinthall, N., A. J. Reiman, and L. Thies-Sprinthall. 1996. Teacher professional development. In *Handbook of research on teacher education.* 2d ed., ed. J. Sikula, T. J. Buttery, & E. Guyton, 666–703. New York: Macmillan.

Talbert, J. E., M. W. McLaughlin, and B. Rowan. 1993. Understanding context effects on secondary school teaching. *Teachers College Record* 95:45–68.

Thiessen, D. 1992. Classroom-based teacher development. In *Understanding teacher development*, ed. A. Hargreaves & M. G. Fullan, 85–109. New York: Teachers College Press.

Science Teacher Professional Development: A Researcher's Perspective[1]

Jane Butler Kahle and Mary Kay Kelly
Miami University

Jane Butler Kahle is Condit Professor of Science Education, Miami University. As principal investigator of Ohio's Systemic Initiative, *Discovery*, she has led Ohio's systemic reform of science and mathematics education for the past nine years. Dr. Kahle received the Distinguished Contributions to Science Education Through Research Award from the National Association of Research in Science Teaching in April, 2000. Currently, she is serving as division director, for elementary, secondary and informal education at the National Science Foundation.

Mary Kay Kelly is a doctoral candidate in the Department of Educational Leadership at Miami University. She holds an M.Ed. in Curriculum and Teacher Leadership from Miami University, a BS in life science and middle level science education from the University of Minnesota, and a BA in biology from the College of St. Benedict. A former science teacher, she is a research assistant for Ohio's SSI.

The theory of systemic reform rests on some assumptions that should be examined and tested. First, systemic reform seeks greater coherence, an alignment of policies, but the education system is fragmented by design—50 states, 15,000 districts, countless other agencies impacting the schools—and this fragmentation is intended to permit variation. The agencies of government responsible for the schools are divided from each other by the federal structure and by the separation of powers. They are further divided by powerful traditions of local control and parental rights. On top of that, within any given jurisdiction there are a variety of stakeholders each with their own views about standards, assessment, locus of authority, etc. (Corcoran, 1997).

The Systemic Initiatives and Professional Development

In 1990, the Education and Human Resource Directorate of the National Science Foundation (NSF) began a new program intended to systemically reform science and mathematics education. Building upon a bipartisan acceptance of national goals and standards, NSF first invited states (Statewide Systemic Initiatives—SSIs), then cities (Urban Systemic Initiatives—USIs), and finally culturally or geographically similar rural areas (Rural Systemic Initiatives—RSIs), to submit proposals addressing both the policies and the practices of science and mathematics education from kindergarten through college. The systemic initiatives (SIs) differed from other NSF programs and projects in that they were longer (five years possible) and larger

($2–3 million/year). Most importantly, they differed in the way in which they were managed—that is, awards were made through annual cooperative agreements with NSF, rather than through grants. Therefore, these initiatives have been closely monitored and assessed both internally (to document progress for each renewal) and externally (to assess the efficacy of the program in improving the teaching and learning of science and mathematics for all students). In this chapter, we explore what has been learned from a national perspective (based upon the more complete assessment of the state initiatives) and from one state that has invested heavily in professional development and in assessing the progress of its SSI, three USIs, and one RSI.

Although researchers have defined systemic reform as reform that is focused in two arenas—(a) creating new policy instruments to enact systemic reform and (b) reducing impediments to systemic reform (inherited tangles of regulation, bureaucracy, and policy) (Cohen, 1995; Smith & O'Day, 1993)—NSF has articulated a vision that goes beyond policy to embrace practice. The Foundation has defined systemic reform in the following way:

> *"Systemic reform" is a process of educational reform based on the premise that achieving excellence and equity requires alignment of critical activities and components. It involves a change in infrastructure as well as outcomes. Central elements include: (a) high standards for learning expected from all students; (b) alignment among all the parts of the system—policies, practices, and accountability mechanisms; (c) a change in governance that includes greater school site flexibility; (d) greater involvement of the public and the community; (e) a closer link between formal and informal learning experiences; (f) enhanced attention to professional development; and (g) increased articulation between the precollege and postsecondary educational institutions* (NSF, 1996, p. 5).

Generally, only in their later years have the SIs addressed policy (points b and c above). Most SIs began with the reform of practice, specifically, by focusing on changing science and mathematics teaching through teacher professional development (point f above). The professional development programs, established by the 24 states and the Commonwealth of Puerto Rico, focused on one or more of the following activities.

1. Human resource development through summer institutes, academic-year follow-up and support, brief seminars, workshops and/or conferences, leadership training, curriculum development, and dissemination of existing standards-based curriculum.
2. System capacity building through demonstration sites, partnerships and infrastructure development, and Internet and/or telecommunication support.
3. Some combination of system capacity building and human resource development (Shields, Corcoran, & Zucker, 1994; Corcoran, Shields, & Zucker, 1998).

Indeed, professional development for teachers was the primary strategy for reform in 18 states and a secondary strategy in the remaining seven initiatives. The various components of professional development, listed above, were used in different combinations in each state. In Ohio, the SSI focused on system capacity and human resource development by building a regional infrastructure to provide continuous support for teachers who had completed a six-week summer institute in science or mathematics that was followed by a series of six academic-year seminars on pedagogy, assessment, and equity.

The SIs and Research and Evaluation

Initially, NSF funded external agencies to both monitor (describe the process of reform) and assess the progress (describe measurable outcomes) of the SSIs. As a result of the early descriptions and evaluations, NSF identified components that drive systemic reform and requested grantees to assess progress against them. The components, called drivers, included (a) implementation of comprehensive, standards-based curricula, instruction, and assessment in every classroom, laboratory, or other learning experience; (b) development of a coherent, consistent set of policies that supports high quality science and mathematics education for all students, continuing education for all teachers of science and mathematics, and administrative support; (c) convergence of all resources used to support science and mathematics education into a unitary program to upgrade science and mathematics education for all students; (d) collaboration and broad-based support from parents, policymakers, institutions of higher education, business and industry, foundations, and other segments of the community; (e) accumulation of a broad and deep array of evidence that the program is enhancing student achievement; and (f) improvement in the achievement of all students, including those historically underserved. In a measurement sense, the drivers served as indicators of progress toward reform. Therefore, annually each SI provided concrete evidence that it was addressing successfully each driver.

In addition, many initiatives have conducted comprehensive research and evaluation studies on elements and programs specific to their reform. Because Ohio's SI was based on a design/research/redesign model, it has used evaluation in both a formative (redirecting programs, reallocating funds, etc.) and summative (identifying and reporting outcomes) sense. Through this process, it has learned not only what was working, but what was not, and why. Further, it has been able to garner public support to continue the reform beyond its period of NSF funding.

Briefly, during the last seven years, assessments of the SSIs across states and within one state indicate the following:

◆ Most states, including Ohio, have directed the majority of their NSF dollars toward the professional development of teachers of science and mathematics.
◆ Many states, including Ohio, have built new, or strengthened the existing, educational infrastructure, resulting in regionalization of services and support.

- Only three states have stressed curriculum development, because of the time and effort needed to produce research-validated materials. Other states, including Ohio, have chosen to disseminate information about curricula.

- All states have allocated the least amount of energy and dollars to postsecondary education with little attention paid to preservice teacher education across the states, including Ohio.

- All states concur with the goal of promoting conceptual understanding and problem solving in the teaching and learning of science and mathematics. This goal is the cornerstone of the reform in Ohio. Most states, including Ohio, have embarked on aligning state-level policies with the goals of systemic reform; few states have addressed policy alignment at the local level (Kahle, 1996).

As reform in Ohio has expanded to include multiple local, state, and national initiatives, its SSI needed to build upon what had been learned both nationally and within the state. Therefore, for the past five years, progress has been assessed and reported annually (Kahle, 1997). From a researcher's perspective, the issues faced in designing a multilayer study, in assessing multiple components of a complex system, in comparing responses and achievement scores from cohorts of students, teachers, and principals, and in assigning attribution are the core of research issues facing long-term, multifaceted reforms.

A Researcher's Perspective: Foibles and Follies in the Evaluation of Systemic Reform

The underlying assumption…is that systemic reform is a proven strategy and that we know how to do it, and therefore the only important question is "are they doing it right?" (Corcoran, 1997)

As the above quote suggests, the issues surrounding any assessment of systemic reform are complicated, because researchers are trying to learn how to do systemic reform while simultaneously learning how to evaluate it. From a researcher's perspective, the first hurdle is the development of the necessary skills and strategies to do large-scale assessments across a period of time.

What have we learned about evaluating systemic reform through the assessment of Ohio SSI? First, simply obtaining reliable and valid data across a state, urban district, or large geographical region (Appalachia or Native American reservations, for example) is complex. We have had to carefully weigh quality of data needed against cost of obtaining the data. Therefore, data on school climates or classroom practices are mainly collected by questionnaires, because observations of schools and classes are too expensive and labor-intensive to collect samples that are representative of the systemic reform. But data such as the kind collected by questionnaires is subject to self-report bias. We have attempted to deal with these problems in Ohio by developing a multilevel, nested research design in which smaller subsets of the large random sample of principals and teachers who respond to our surveys are observed and interviewed. Second, by asking multiple audiences (principals, teachers, students, and parents) to respond to similar questions, each group's response can be validated, and we can partially control for the bias inherent in self-reported data.

Research and evaluation issues become even more complex with student outcome data. In many states and districts, privacy laws protect individual teacher and student data. In addition, scores on high-stake tests (e.g., the Ohio Proficiency Test, which must be passed for high school graduation) are reported publicly only by pass/fail, not by mean score, limiting their usefulness in documenting student improvement across years. Further, there is considerable argument about the appropriateness of existing standardized tests. Ohio's SSI developed its own tests in order to assess student ability to interpret, analyze, and synthesize scientific and mathematical information. Then, test validity and reliability had to be established. Although these carefully designed paper-and-pencil tests provided a very useful measure of student achievement, several different types of achievement measures may be necessary to assess all students fairly. Therefore, in 1998, student learning was assessed in selected schools using the Third International Mathematics and Science Study's (TIMSS) performance tasks[2]. In addition, multiple-choice versions of selected TIMSS' tasks were added to the SSI's written test. Initial analysis of the data suggests

The issues surrounding any assessment of systemic reform are complicated, because researchers are trying to learn how to do systemic reform while simultaneously learning how to evaluate it.

that paper-and-pencil tasks alone inadequately measure student understanding, particularly the understanding of urban, African American students (Harmon, 1991; Kelly & Kahle, 1999). However, expense, as well as unresolved technical problems in both delivery and scoring, limit the use of performance assessments in large-scale reforms. The same issues affect the use of portfolios and journals.

Another concern is collecting, analyzing, and reporting data by disaggregated groups. Currently, reports from large national and international databases (National Assessment of Educational Progress—NAEP, TIMSS, and the National Educational Longitudinal Study, 1988—NELS-88) report results by either race or sex. One cannot find information about how African American girls achieve in science in comparison to Latinas, for example. The issue of disaggregated data in research and evaluation of systemic reform is so critical that NSF has published a *Brief* to guide researchers and/or evaluators of systemic reform in the collection and use of disaggregated data (NSF, no date). It advises, at a minimum, that disaggregating the following kinds of data is necessary in order to assess student participation and performance:

◆ enrollment in specific courses, such as algebra and physics;
◆ successful completion (grade of C or better) of specific courses;

- participation in special programs, such as gifted and talented classes, special education classes, honor societies, and internships; and
- performance on standardized assessments, including criterion-referenced tests, performance assessments, portfolios, and norm-referenced tests (p. 9).

Psychometricians have also identified a variety of issues that affect evaluation and research about systemic reform. For example, in order to compare scores of cohorts of students, tests and questionnaires must include items that are identical across years (Boone, 1998). Likewise, researchers must take into account experiences among students in different educational settings when comparing student achievement. Webb (1998) proposed the use of conditional metrics in evaluating students involved in larg-scale reforms. Further, Boone's (1998) analysis of nonresponse patterns on a science achievement test by sex and race suggests that sophisticated statistics, such as item response theory, should be used in order to estimate a student's true achievement level. In addition, Witte (1996) suggests that trend data, data that acknowledge the long-term aspect of systemic reform and that provide accurate estimates of achievement growth, are particularly needed.

One of the most perplexing problems that a researcher involved with systemic reform has to face is the gradual loss of any control group.

However, from a researcher's perspective, the most serious concern in research and evaluation of systemic reform is attribution. Policymakers and funding agencies want to know what is working and why, yet assigning attribution to any one part of a complex system is difficult at best. Although differences in teaching practices were identified between teachers who had, and who had not, participated in the SSI's professional development in Ohio, those differences could not be directly attributed to the SSI's intervention strategies (six-week summer content courses, followed by seminars in pedagogy, assessment, and equity). Other things were going on in the state and in the schools. Students varied from year to year. Or, perhaps, in spite of efforts to develop a matched-pair research design, SSI teachers were fundamentally different from non-SSI teachers. In any case, well-designed, longitudinal, cross-jurisdictional studies are needed to evaluate complex systems and to assign attribution to any one part of the system (Corcoran, 1997), and these designs are just beginning to emerge.

One of the most perplexing problems that a researcher involved with systemic reform has to face is the gradual loss of any control group. If the reform is systemic (and working), participants infect their colleagues with their enthusiasm and ideas. Redesign is constant to cope with the changing nature of the sample. In Ohio, we have stopped trying to compare teachers who have had the SSI's professional development with those who have not. With multiple state and local reform projects, as well as one SSI, three USIs, and one RSI, we are primarily trying to document and understand change.

What We Have Learned

Corcoran, Shields, and Zucker (1998) provided a national snapshot of what has been learned from the SSIs concerning teacher professional development, while Ohio's research and evaluation provides a detailed portrait of one state's reform. Nationally, the SSIs invested heavily in professional development. Professional development was the single largest category of expenditures across the SSIs, averaging about a third of all of the SSI dollars expended. The national reasons for this investment were mirrored in Ohio. They included (a) the inadequate preparation of elementary and middle school teachers in science and mathematics; (b) the poor quality of professional development offered by local districts, usually through their Eisenhower programs; (c) the need to change the culture of professional development (e.g., teacher demand for high quality programs); (d) the need to provide high-profile, successful programs that would help "sell" the reform; and (e) the experience and expertise of many SSI leaders and staff in the design and delivery of professional development, making this a comfortable approach to reform (Corcoran, Shields, & Zucker, 1998). All of these were factors in Ohio, with equity as an additional

In Ohio, we have stopped trying to compare teachers who have had the SSI's professional development with those who have not.

factor. Ohio's SSI initially focused on the professional development of middle school teachers, not only because of content weakness at that level, but also because it wanted to involve teachers at grade levels where all children are enrolled in similar mathematics and science courses (e.g., grades four through nine).

The goal of Ohio's SSI was not only to change teaching practice but also to affect student outcomes. It invested heavily (and wisely) in formative evaluation, and the findings indicated the need for redesign of its professional development programs in several areas. First, in order to reach more teachers, shorter, but rigorous, content courses introducing science and mathematics at the level to be taught were needed. Research-validated curricula were identified and Cascade programs were developed. SSI-trained teacher leaders and resource teachers taught the Cascade programs in local districts. Further, the six-week institutes were moved from university campuses to schools, and different formats (four weeks, three weeks for two summers, three weeks followed by Saturday sessions during the school year) were tested. In addition, the institutes were modified to meet the needs of elementary and high school teachers. As Ohio's reform moved from a teacher focus to a school focus, the SSI introduced institutes to help principals understand how to evaluate standards-based science and mathematics teaching.

Three years into Ohio's reform, the SSI began to assess progress and outcomes through summative evaluation. It used a nested research design, which yielded different, yet important, data at each of three levels. At the state level, questionnaires were used with a broad random sample of teachers and administrators to provide evidence of changes in teaching practice, in administrative support, and in teacher

Professional development was the single largest category of expenditures across the SSIs, averaging about a third of all SSI dollars expended.

expectations. At the district level, approximately 12 schools that were part of the larger random sample were visited annually. The observations over several days validated questionnaire responses, as well as provided information to redesign the questionnaires. In addition, student achievement and attitudinal data were collected in the schools visited. Currently, intensive case studies in 5 of the 12 schools are being conducted. The case studies focus on how systemic reform works in schools that are at different stages of readiness for reform, and they are providing information about opportunities to learn as well as about catalysts and barriers to reform.

We have learned that both teaching practices and student learning have changed. In addition, we know that the changes in teaching practices

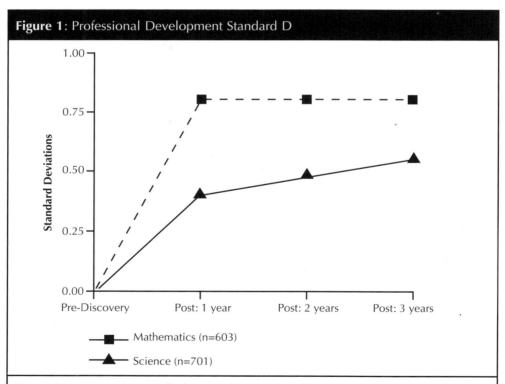

Figure 1: Professional Development Standard D

Reported increase in the use of reform teaching practices by SSI participants. It is convenient to show mathematics and science results on the same axes because units are common. However, they should not be directly compared. From "The Impact Over Time of Project Discovery on Teachers' Attitudes, Preparation, and Teaching Practice, Final Report," by J. Supovitz, December 1996, Chapel Hill, NC: Horizon Research, Inc. Adapted with permission.

are sustained over time. Teachers were surveyed regarding the nature of their teaching before they began their summer professional development and in the spring of the following year for three years. The items reflect a range of reform practices (e.g., *having students work in small groups*, *doing inquiry activities*, *making conjectures*, *and exploring possible methods to solve a problem*). As Figure 1 shows, the average participant, in both mathematics and science, reports an increase in the use of standards-based teaching practices after participation in the SSI's professional development programs. Further, in the second and third years after the professional development, teachers sustain the use of the reform practices. We have learned that sustained professional development, focused on content, affects teaching practice and that the changes are retained.

We also addressed issues in research and evaluation by collecting student achievement data in two ways. In one study, we controlled for socio-economic level, and in another we controlled for the "volunteer effect."[3] As Tables 1 and 2 show, student achievement data in both studies indicated improved learning by African Americans and white students taught by teachers who had participated in the SSI's sustained professional development. For example, the comparisons, shown in Table 1, between matched classes (e.g., seventh grade, general science) in the same school show that African American girls in classes of SSI teachers scored 9 percent higher on the science achievement test than did their peers in the classrooms of non-SSI teachers. This study controlled for socioeconomic level by using similar classes in the same school as its comparison groups.

Table 2, on the other hand, compares the predicted scores of students whose teachers had completed the SSI professional development to those whose teachers had applied to participate but had not yet done so. That is, all teachers were volunteers.

Table 1: Science Achievement Results for Students in Matched Classes Within the Same School

	Achievement results[a]		
	SSI Teachers	Non-SSI Teachers	Difference
African American			
Males	44	35	9
Females	40	31	9
White			
Males	60	50	10
Females	54	50	4

Note. Results are for tests given in 1995. *n* = 610. From "Effects of Inquiry Teaching on the Achievement Levels of Urban Middle School Science Students by Race and Sex," by J. B. Kahle and A. Damnjanovic, 1998, Submitted for publication. Adapted with permission.

[a]Achievement results are given as percent correct.

Table 2: Predicted Student Performance on the SSI Mathematics and Science Achievement Tests, Controlling for Urbanicity, Concentration of Poverty, and Grade Level, by Race and Gender (1995)

	SSI Teachers	SSI Applicant Teachers	Difference
Science achievement[a] (n=1,144)			
African American			
Females	47	44	3
Males	44	41	3
White			
Females	62	59	3
Males	60	56	4
Mathematics achievement[b] (n=1,230)			
African American			
Females			
Males	54	47	7
	54	52	2
White			
Females	66	59	7
Males	66	64	2

Note. All teachers had volunteered for the SSI professional development. SSI teachers had completed a six-week institute, while the SSI applicant teachers had not. From "Ohio's Project Discovery 1995 Discovery Test Student Results," by J. Supovitz, February 1996, Chapel Hill, North Carolina: Horizon Research, Inc. Adapted with permission.
[a,b]Science and Mathematics achievement results are given as percent correct.

The positive effect of the SSI's institutes is suggested by the higher scores on both the mathematics and science tests of students whose teachers had completed the sustained professional development.

As discussed earlier, paper-and-pencil inquiry tests were developed, using 1990 and 1992 NAEP public release items. Test items focused on process, not product, because the goals of Ohio's SSI were to increase conceptual understanding, as well as the skills needed to interpret and use scientific and mathematical information. Using disaggregated data, analyses indicated a decrease in the gender gap between boys and girls across and within racial groups. Further, the achievement gap between African American and white students (favoring whites) had narrowed, but it persisted. Most recently, therefore, achievement on performance items has been compared with achievement on comparable paper-and-pencil items (all were adapted from TIMSS). Neither test format favored girls or boys. However, in one urban school with over 80 percent African American students, achievement scores on identical test items were higher on the performance, compared with the paper-and-pencil, format. For example, 87 percent of the urban students were able to identify patterns in data on the performance assessment, but only 89 percent were able to identify identical patterns using the paper-and-pencil format. Similarly, 80 percent of the urban students were able to extrapolate information from a graph provided on a performance assessment. However, only 15 percent were able to extrapolate information from the graph provided on the paper-and-pencil assessment. In addition, the students demonstrated skills in data collection, presentation, and graphing while doing the performance assessment. Those skills could not be measured with the paper and pencil test format, because the data and graph were provided (Kelly & Kahle, 1999).

The nested research design used by Ohio's SSI produces fairly quick information at the survey (state) level to guide the reform and, at the district level, it provides ways (observation and interviews) to validate the survey data. Further, it promises to elucidate how systemic reform affects schools at different stages of readiness through its multiyear case studies in local schools. The nested design, extending across five years of Ohio's reform, provides one model for evaluating systemic reform of science and mathematics education. Another model is the *equity metric* (Kahle, 1998). It suggests a set of indicators to chart a system's (state, district, or school) progress toward equitable systemic reform, as well as critical times for assessing each indicator. Individually, each indicator assesses the progress of a reform component (increased enrollment in eighth grade algebra, for example), and collectively they track the progress of a system's reform. Both models address Corcoran's (1997) call for longitudinal, cross-jurisdictional studies to assess systemic reform. Although both need to be widely tested, initial results in Ohio indicate the efficacy of both models. From a researcher's perspective, the elucidation of one or more models for guiding research and evaluation has been an important step in the progress of systemic reform.

Conclusion

As discussed earlier, most of the systemic initiatives invested heavily in the professional development of teachers as their primary strategy for reforming mathematics and science education. Ohio's SSI selected professional development for middle school teachers as its wedge into the educational system. By carefully evaluating program outcomes, it was able to redesign its professional development programs in order to reach more teachers and to address local human and system capacity building. The SSI in Ohio relied heavily on research and evaluation to develop alternative strategies and to document changes in teaching practices and in student learning. As researchers involved in the evaluation, we attempted to lessen the problem of attribution by designing studies with different control groups and by adjusting the samples to reflect the progress of the reform. In addition, by widely disseminating research results in a very accessible way, Ohio's SSI was able to influence policies concerning teacher preparation and licensure and to garner support to continue its reform.

Further, the research indicates that the culture of teacher professional development was affected. During the SSI, Ohio experimented with two forms of professional development: the SSI's sustained model and a regional center model that of-

By widely disseminating research results in a very accessible way, Ohio's SSI was able to influence policies concerning teacher preparation and licensure and to garner support to continue its reform.

fered short (two- or three-day) workshops without follow-up activities. Using a random sample of over 100 schools, SSI and non-SSI teachers as well as principals, were asked to rank 10 strategies in order of importance to improve student learning in science and mathematics. Principals, whose teachers attended both models, and teachers, who experienced both, ranked professional development sustained over time significantly higher than professional development during the school day (Kahle & Boone, 1998).

Because it approached systemic reform from a researcher's perspective, all of Ohio's SSI activities were based on a design/research/redesign model. Both progress and outcomes were documented by NSF's evaluators, by Ohio's external evaluator (Horizon Research, Inc.), and by the SSI itself. *What have we learned*, therefore, refers not only to the information in the data collected but also to the value of research in guiding and defining systemic reform.

Notes

[1] The preparation of this paper was funded in part by grants from the National Science Foundation, Grant #REC 9602137 and Grant #OSR-92500 (J. B. Kahle, principal investigator). The opinions expressed are those of the author and do not necessarily reflect the position of NSF.

[2] Although the original TIMSS performance assessment involved 12 tasks (assigned randomly to samples of students), Ohio limited its test to four tasks. That decision was made in order to handle the amount of equipment needed and to accommodate the average length of science classes in Ohio. All tasks were taken from TIMSS' Population Two performance assessments (seventh and eighth graders). All Ohio personnel involved were trained by a TIMSS' trainer. Each student completed two of the four randomly assigned performance tasks. In addition, a small number of students were interviewed as they completed the tasks, while a few were videotaped.

[3] Evaluators of the systemic initiatives have cautioned that almost all of the professional development experiences are taken by teachers who volunteer to be involved. Systemic initiatives, including Ohio, have struggled to provide incentives to increase and diversify the pool of volunteer teachers. However, the concern remains that volunteer teachers are exceptionally good teachers or teachers who are ready for reform. The study of student achievement reported in Table 2, with all volunteer teachers, suggests that the sustained professional development enhanced the effectiveness of teachers in the volunteer pool.

References

Boone, W. J. 1998. Assumptions, cautions, and solutions in the use of omitted test data to evaluate the achievement of underrepresented groups in science—Implications for long-term evaluation. *Journal of Women and Minorities in Science and Engineering* 4:183–194.

Boone, W. J. 1998. *Test item measurement—Key steps to accurately calculating achievement measures*. Paper presented at the meeting of the National Association for Research in Science Teaching, April. San Diego, CA.

Cohen, D. K. 1995. What is the system in systemic reform? *Educational Researcher* 24(9):17–31.

Corcoran, T. B. 1997. The role of evaluation in systemic reform. In *Research on systemic reform: What have we learned? What do we need to know? Synthesis of the second annual NISE forum, Volume 1: Analysis* (Workshop Report No. 4), ed. W. H. Clune, S. B. Millar, S. A. Raizen, N. L. Webb, D. C. Bowcock, E. D. Britton, R. L. Gunter, & R. Mesquita, 64–68. Madison, WI: University of Wisconsin–Madison, National Institute for Science Education.

Corcoran, T. B., P. M. Shields, and A. A. Zucker. 1998. *The SSIs and professional development for teachers.* Menlo Park, CA: SRI International.

Harmon, M. 1991. Fairness in testing: Are science education assessments biased? In *Science assessment in the service of reform*, ed. G. Kulm & S. M. Malcom, 31–54. Washington, DC: American Association for the Advancement of Science.

Kahle, J. B. 1996. *Systemic reform: Lessons from the trenches.* Paper presented at the meeting of the National Research Council, Mathematical Sciences Education Board (MSEB), January. Irvine, CA.

———. 1997. Systemic reform: Challenges and changes. *Science Educator* 6(1):1–6.

———. 1998. Equitable systemic reform in science and mathematics: Assessing progress. *Journal of Women and Minorities in Science and Engineering* 4:91–112.

Kahle, J. B., and W. J. Boone. 1998. *Strategies to improve student science learning: Implications for science teacher education.* Manuscript submitted for publication.

Kahle, J. B., and A. Damnjanovic. 1998. *Effects of inquiry teaching on the achievement levels of urban middle school science students by race and sex.* Manuscript submitted for publication.

Kelly, M. K., and J. B. Kahle. 1999. A comparison of student achievement on performance and paper-and-pencil assessment tasks. Paper presented at the meeting of the National Association for Research in Science Teaching, March. Boston, MA.

National Science Foundation. 1996. *REC Indicator Series: The learning curve: What we are discovering about U.S. science and mathematics education* (NSF 96-53). Washington, DC: NSF.

———. (No date). *A brief primer on disaggregation of data.* Washington, DC: NSF.

Shields, P. M., T. B. Corcoran, and A. A. Zucker. 1994. *Evaluation of the National Science Foundation's Statewide Systemic Initiatives (SSI) program: First year report, Volume II: State summaries and indicator tables.* Arlington, VA: National Science Foundation.

Smith, M. S., and J. O'Day. 1993. Systemic reform and educational opportunity. In *Designing coherent policy*, ed. S. Fuhrman. San Francisco: Jossey-Bass.

Supovitz, J. 1996. *Ohio's Project Discovery 1995 student test results.* Chapel Hill, NC: Horizon Research, Inc.

———. 1996. *The impact over time of Project Discovery on teachers' attitudes, preparation, and teaching practice, Final report.* Chapel Hill, NC: Horizon Research, Inc.

Webb, N. L. 1998. Conditional equity metrics as tools for evaluating equity in schools and educational systems. *Journal of Women and Minorities in Science and Engineering* 4:141–160.

Witte, J. F. 1996. *Achievement testing in systemic educational reform: How to incorporate class, gender, race and disability differences.* Unpublished paper, University of Wisconsin–Madison, Robert M. La Follette Institute of Public Affairs.

The Colorado College Integrated Natural Sciences Program (CC-ISTEP): Putting into Practice Some Essential Principles of Teacher Development

Paul J. Kuerbis and Keith Kester

Paul J. Kuerbis is professor of education and director, Crown-Tapper Teaching and Learning Center at the Colorado College in Colorado Springs, Colorado.

Keith Kester is professor of chemistry at the Colorado College in Colorado Springs, Colorado.

The recently released Third International Mathematics and Science Study (TIMSS) reports (see, for example, Beatty, 1997) on how U.S. students achieve in mathematics and science internationally has created the catchy phrase that American K–12 science and mathematics education is "a mile wide and an inch deep." Could it be that American teacher development should also be described this way? If so, what might effective teacher development programs look like?

Everyone easily agrees that a prospective teacher's preparation has only started with the completion of a licensure program. As highlighted by the *National Science Education Standards* (NSES, National Research Council, 1996), becoming a teacher is "a continuous process that stretches across the life of a teacher, from his or her undergraduate years to the end of a professional career (p. 54)." Clearly, it is a process, not a single event: it calls for development that is thoughtful rather than superficial. The NSES go on to challenge all of us who work with teacher development, noting that "professional development must include experiences that engage prospective and practicing teachers in active learning that builds their knowledge, understanding, and ability."

How can liberal arts colleges better support teachers in becoming more effective teachers? In what ways can they collaborate with schools and school districts to create viable professional development programs that increase teachers' knowledge and understanding of both science and pedagogy? In this chapter, the authors describe a new program designed to provide answers to these questions and, in so doing, set forth some general principles that others can use as guides as they implement quality science teacher development in their communities.

Background

Three decades ago, Colorado College (CC) ended its offerings of masters degrees in subject areas and embarked upon a new degree aimed directly at teachers: the master of arts in teaching (MAT) degree. To those at CC, the advanced degrees in subject matter seemed the purview of major universities that could adequately support such content-specific programs. The CC faculty believed that a small liberal arts college could best support K–12 teachers by offering degrees aimed at improving their subject matter competence while simultaneously addressing concerns of improved pedagogy. This would be in keeping with CC's mission and the expertise of its faculty, who concentrated on teaching as a significant dimension of their scholarship. Only later would this broad definition of faculty scholarship, including the study and refinement of teaching, be espoused by such noted educators as Boyer (1989).

> *How can liberal arts colleges better support teachers in becoming more effective teachers?*

The first MAT degree established was the Arts and Humanities degree for elementary teachers, followed in the late 1970s by the Southwest Studies program for K–12 teachers. Until recently, however, no degree had been established in the natural sciences. With growing concern about the quality of science teaching in our public schools and with the willingness of a large number of natural science faculty to contribute and share the responsibilities of operating such a degree program, the master of arts in teaching integrated natural sciences (MAT-INS) degree was approved by the faculty in December 1993.

Faculty cannot simply create a program from the catalog of extant courses. Its goal was to simultaneously strengthen candidates' understanding of science concepts while asking them to reflect upon their teaching philosophies and approaches and embark on substantive changes in their classrooms. Recent literature on professional development, including NSES, created a plausible guiding framework for such a far-reaching program. Much conceptualizing and design work was necessary. In order to firmly establish the degree and ensure that it would become a lasting trademark of CC, the authors submitted a successful proposal to the National Science Foundation (NSF) for a four-year teacher enhancement program. This program, CC-ISTEP, with the MAT degree embedded in it, allowed the codirectors to explore ways to work with faculty to design and offer summer institutes. The institutes, which integrate pedagogy with science conceptual understanding, and which are complemented by supportive academic-year seminars, culminate in a master's research project and paper centered on the individual teacher-participant's development into a more effective classroom teacher of science.

In this chapter, the authors elaborate upon these successful efforts in a story we believe can be replicated anywhere a college or university and area schools want to work together to improve the teaching of K–16 science. Such efforts do not have to culminate in a master's degree; that is merely the vehicle chosen by Colorado College.

Many of the components of CC-ISTEP, along with its overarching philosophy, must be present to ensure lasting changes in how the clientele perceive their roles in helping K–12 students achieve the common national goals implied by the NSES: What do we want our students to *know, understand*, and be able to *do* in science?

Philosophical Basis of CC-ISTEP

CC-ISTEP has three goals: develop long-term collaboration among faculty and local educators in designing and implementing theme- or issue-based teacher institutes, improve the science backgrounds of teachers, and support teachers in implementing new strategies in their classrooms. In light of these goals and the emerging recommendations on professional development from groups like NSES, we decided that constructivist teacher education should provide the overall guide to how the program should be structured.

While multiple definitions, understandings, and misunderstandings of constructivist student learning abound, we believe and suggest that teachers engaged in constructivist learning involves their making sense of and putting into practice effective pedagogical approaches. This notion was first broached by one of the authors in the recommendations of the National Center for Improving Science Education and almost simultaneously in another article on technology education and professional development (Kuerbis & Loucks-Horsley, 1989). Those of us who are sometimes labeled "providers" have a role in creating experiences (e.g., lectures, labs, and classroom-based research tasks) that help teachers actively inquire into how to structure K–12 classrooms and engage in instruction that helps students come to both know and understand science. In the CC-ISTEP model, teachers become their own sources for growth, in this case carefully nurtured by the faculty that comprise the CC-ISTEP program. Moreover, the components described below provide a content structure within which the teachers are working at making sense of teaching. Over time, the teachers develop what Shulman (1988) calls Pedagogical Content Knowledge (PCK), an integration of science content understanding and strategies that might best help their students achieve this same knowledge and understanding of science. The approach that CC-ISTEP takes, where the teachers are active learners, models active learning in science and in pedagogy and encourages the teachers to inquire into practice by asking questions such as:

Those of us who are sometimes labeled "providers" have a role in creating experiences that help teachers actively inquire into how to structure K–12 classrooms and engage in instruction that helps students come to both know and understand science.

- ◆ Is this unit effectively sequenced to result in student understanding?
- ◆ Are all the students actively engaged in the learning activity that I've given them?

◆ Are there other ways to begin the lesson that allow me to assess students' prior knowledge?

This approach is a far cry from many teacher development approaches that focus only on teaching skills or that involve teachers only in copying modeled techniques, practicing them, and implementing them without ample reflection and examination of the larger picture of teaching and learning. We believe that all professional development should be guided by active learning principles that are more likely to result in skilled teachers of science that "have special understandings and abilities that integrate their knowledge of science content, curriculum, learning, teaching, and students" (National Research Council, 1996, p. 62). Several important components characterize the CC-ISTEP program.

The Components of CC-ISTEP

Given the philosophy of CC-ISTEP and the concerns of many about the need to structure teacher development in new ways that help teachers inquire into their practice, what features should characterize a thoughtful approach to professional development? Herein we describe the features of CC-ISTEP and note that many of these should characterize any viable plan by a district or university that wishes to help teachers of science improve their teaching and, consequently, the learning of their students.

Intensive summer institutes. These run for six weeks and operate for about five hours each day. They combine science content understanding through a theme or issue, with an equal emphasis on the participating teachers inquiring into pedagogical practice. The latter is largely achieved through modeling of active learning and teaching by the science and education faculty (comprising an institute's staff) and then asking the teachers to reflect with us on what we have been doing as teachers and learners and why. A crucial component of the intensive summer institutes is having the teachers experience being a science student at a level that is challenging to them as learners. In so doing, they become aware of their own misconceptions and struggle to reconstruct their understandings. They experience disequilibrium and learn how to ask questions and posit explanations to move past the disequilibrium, thus experiencing both the frustrations and joys of mastering scientific concepts.

The Summer 1997 Institute provides a good model of what all this means in practice. The institute, Plants in an Arid Landscape, was taught by a geologist, two field biologists, and the two authors who played both pedagogical and science roles. To set the stage for the study of plants and birds in a local park area west of the College, we spent four days "discovering" what we could about the geology of the area and ways that plant life was related to the geological features. Instead of lecturing on the geology of the Pikes Peak region—a truly remarkable area—Michael Hannigan, the institute's geologist, began by taking us to an overlook of the Garden of the Gods and Pikes Peak and asked us (repeatedly!), "What do you see?" We all shared our observations, and through our leader's gentle, persistent questioning, began to notice features of the landscape that we had not noticed before. This was the beginning of our individual attempts to make sense of the scenery and to construct a story of the Garden of the Gods. Anytime a teacher shared an observation or used a technical term, Michael (the geologist) would stop and ask the teacher to, "Tell us more." Or he would kid us that another "747" just flew by—telling us in a humorous way to avoid language that was conceptually over the heads of others. Frequently, however, we found that we were using terms without understanding the concept underlying the label—a probable reflection of how all of us had been taught. Indeed, we found we knew a lot, but understood very little! Michael continued to have us play with hypotheses and minitheories about the formation of the Garden of Gods and how to look for clues among the rock formations and vegetation patterns. The teachers felt comfortably challenged with the assessment of their work, telling in various ways a story of the creation of the Garden of the Gods, including text accounts supported with pictures, dioramas, time lines, and other "props" to demonstrate individual understanding and facility with a growing body of conceptual labels and terms.

All professional development should be guided by active learning principles that are more likely to result in skilled teachers of science that have special understandings and abilities that integrate their knowledge of science content, curriculum, learning, teaching, and students.

That geology work set the stage for how the field biology proceeded, and teachers eagerly scouted the 100-acre hilly site in their assigned teams. After selecting five different subareas of the main site, teams spent nearly a week under the guidance of the biologists learning the techniques of conducting a field study. They sampled the vegetation both on ridge tops and in riparian zones, for example, and identified species of birds, noted their feeding and nesting behaviors and took population counts. The study ended with a poster session presented by the five site-based teams of teachers—modeling what might transpire at a professional meeting. This also allowed the instructors to give feedback on the quality of the work and to share their own "rubrics" for grading the work of the teachers.

To cement the teachers' understanding of how to conduct a field study, we then took the institute to a remote campus that the college maintains in Colorado's San Luis Valley, near Crestone, Colorado. This high desert setting provided an opportunity for us to model for the teachers how once basic principles are learned, learners must have an opportunity to apply those ideas in new setting. This four-day experience also allowed us to model "embedded" and "authentic" assessments, and included time for a subgroup of the teachers to create and then use their own scoring rubric for another poster session.

The last two weeks of the institute allowed us to shift the focus from science content to more study of pedagogy, though still spending some time on other areas of science content. The teachers spent time reviewing and critiquing newer curriculum materials in light of NSES and the Benchmarks. We also looked, at their request, at some ways to use questions effectively in the classroom. The content study was individualized, with teachers having choices of some additional content-related areas: chemistry of photosynthesis or human uses of plants (dyes, health, etc.). This was also a time in which the teachers worked alone or in small teams on a module of study that they could implement in their classrooms the following academic year. This requirement (of all institutes) helps teachers develop further understanding of the institute's science content while examining instructional approaches for helping their students construct new understandings. This also helps them in the development of PCK.

Follow-up seminars. During the academic year, the program hosts a series of six all-day Saturday seminars, typically three in the fall and three in the spring. These are occasions for the teachers to share their teaching experiences, think more about pedagogical issues and continue the inquiry into practice that started in the summer. Several areas provide the content focus for these meetings: classroom-based research, further examination of constructivist models of teaching, curriculum adaptation, authentic assessment and leadership development.

We have found that *classroom-based research* is a highly effective strategy for helping the teachers develop as confident inquirers into pedagogy. Teachers typically pose one or more researchable questions around the modules they have designed and they then implement. Many have difficulty with this because they think that they are to research something we want researched or they fail to believe that they are capable of conducting informal studies that might better help them make instructional decisions. But once underway, teachers gain much information about their teaching and develop data gathering techniques that allow possible answers to their questions. They begin to teach from the perspective of, "I wonder if this approach or technique will impact my students and how?" They begin to think of themselves as professionals who are eager to share with their colleagues the results of their classroom research. We do this at a poster session during the summer institute following the school year in which they conducted their classroom-based research.

The educational literature contains several examples of *"constructivist teaching models"* (National Center for Improving Science Education, 1991). We introduce these to our students early on and continually reexamine them—sometimes in how a given institute exemplified one or more teaching models and, at other times, in how newer curriculum materials might use a model explicitly or reflect in the sequence of activities the use of a model (or not) by the developers. The CC-ISTEP teachers now have a common language and comfortably talk about the 5E, NCISE, Insights, or Kuerbis IDEA2 models. The power of the models is that they represent the very ways in which science knowledge is created—the beginning hunch, the tinkering that follows, the proposed explanation a scientist presents to colleagues, and finally the application of ideas that are research-based and appear sound. This 1997 Summer Institute was particularly effective at "modeling the models" and, therefore, provided a convenient way to introduce the models by analyzing teaching from time-to-time in what became known as "reflective debriefings." We encourage the reader to revisit the institute description and see if you can see how the institute began with elements of "Engage and Invite" with opportunities for Michael to assess for prior knowledge, then moved to time for "Explorations," followed by interspersed times for Michael and the teachers to provide "Proposed Explanations" and finally time for the teachers to "Take Action" and elaborate upon their de-veloping understandings by telling a story about the Garden of the Gods. The model, repeated again in the field studies and the entire institute, ended with teachers proposing ex-planations through the design of a module and then taking action in the subsequent implementation (and classroom-based research!) of their modules. It is important for teach-ers to *experience* the models, *reflect* on them, and then *use* them as guides to their module development—so they see how they can be used in a "macro" sense over longer peri-ods of time and also can be used in a "micro" sense for indi-vidual lesson design.

Teachers who have embarked on a constructivist way of instruction in their classrooms must also examine how they will assess their students in ways that are "constructivist compatible" yet meet more traditional district assessments.

Another important component of the seminar series is *curriculum adaptation*. So much has been made about cur-riculum adoptions and the five-to-seven year adoption cycle that districts typically experience—funds that may need to be spent on science, for example, in any given year. Yet in CC-ISTEP, we recognize that once an adoption has taken place, the real work lies in *adapting the adopted curriculum* for the local setting. The modules that our teachers create are just that—adaptations of extant materials that they have access to in their dis-tricts. Thus the adaptation process begins in each summer institute and continues during the year as teachers implement those modules, seek answers to their research questions, and discuss their findings in the seminars. Curriculum adaptation is a significant thread throughout the entire CC-ISTEP program.

We have already demonstrated how authentic assessment was an important part of the 1997 Institute. But our examination of *alternative assessments*—embedded, authentic, portfolios—continues during the seminars. Teachers who have embarked on a constructivist way of instruction in their classrooms must also examine how they will assess their students in ways that are "constructivist compatible" yet meet more traditional district assessments. Thus, we spend a considerable portion of the seminars exploring alternative assessments, revisiting (for many) the differences between norm- and criterion-referenced evaluation systems, and helping the teach-ers understand what nationally normed tests tell us and what locally developed as-sessments (including tests) tell us about the success of their teaching. As testing becomes an important part of science teaching, this area will no doubt continue to receive attention.

Because we cannot reach all teachers, we have designed CC-ISTEP to include a long-term commitment on the part of the participants that includes *leadership development* to prepare them to serve as teacher-leaders in their local settings. We are finding that the components naturally help teachers serve in multiple leadership roles. They function as examples of teachers who are successfully implementing active learning strategies with their students. They have frequent conversations with colleagues about teaching, about their modules, and about the findings of their research. They serve on countless district and building committees, helping analyze potential curriculum materials for adoption, designing assessments of student achievement, and creating supplemental programs for a variety of special needs students. They are confident in their teaching, in their ability to reflect on it and improve it, and in their ability to contribute beyond the confines of their own classrooms.

Preliminary evidence from the CC-ISTEP external evaluation, as well as the authors' informal observations of teacher-participants, lead us to suggest that districts and universities can make their own teacher development efforts more effective if they attend to most of these features. Teacher development is, indeed, complex and a lifelong undertaking. Just as the American science and mathematics curriculum has been described as a "mile wide and an inch deep," with a focus more on procedural knowledge (skills) than on understanding, so too can we describe most of current science teacher development. We believe, however, that those of us in teacher development can make that process more successful if we give ample attention to some underlying principles of teacher development and help our teachers look at content understanding and introduce them to pedagogical inquiry.

References

Beatty, A. 1997. *Learning from TIMSS: Results of the Third International Mathematics and Science Study*. Summary of a symposium. Washington, DC: National Academy Press.

Boyer, E. 1989. *Scholarship rediscovered*. New York: Carnegie Foundation.

Kuerbis, P. J., and S. Loucks-Horsley. The promise of staff development for technology education. In *The 1989 AETS Yearbook: Information technology and science education*, ed. J. D. Ellis. Columbus, Ohio: ERIC Clearinghouse for Science, Mathematics, and Environmental Education.

National Research Council. 1996. *National science education standards*. Washington, DC: National Academy Press.

National Center for Improving Science Education. 1991. *The High Stakes of High School Science*. Washington, DC: National Center for Improving Science Education.

Shulman, L. S. 1988. Knowledge and teaching: Foundations of the new reform. *Harvard Educational Review* 57:1–22.

It's All About Choices: Science Assessment in Support of Reform

Margaret A. Jorgensen

Margaret A. Jorgensen is the vice president for education product development at Harcourt Educational Measurement, a Harcourt Assessment Company. She received her Ph.D. in 1976 from The University of Chicago. Since then, she has written two assessment books and numerous articles and chapters. She has developed professional development programs in areas of test score interpretation and performance assessment and rubric development. For the past 25 years, Dr. Jorgensen has developed tests, conducted research, and pioneered innovative item types and assessment formats—all initiatives focused on more meaningful ways to systematically capture evidence about what students know and can do.

Science assessment can improve science teaching and learning. Both in classrooms and in high-stakes standardized environments, the structure and format of assessments imply choices about the meaning and use of the information derived. When teachers understand the range of possible choices and their consequences, they become better teachers. Thus, teacher involvement in the design, development, selection and interpretation of assessments can be a powerful lever for change, influencing how teachers teach and how they decide what to teach and when to teach it.

Although tests have often been acknowledged as driving instruction, test development has seldom been used to improve teaching. However, recent research supports such a use (Jorgensen, McDevitt, Wolfe, and Hensley, in press). This research does not indicate that teachers should develop traditional instructional or learning objectives and then write multiple-choice test questions that measure those objectives. Rather, it suggests an approach to professional development described in this chapter that requires a fundamental shift both in the way professional development is structured and in the way teachers think about tests, an approach that models the discipline of science by actively engaging teachers in inquiry.

For many of the more than 2.6 million teachers working in U.S. schools today (U.S. Department of Education, 1998a), education reform is likely to be empty rhetoric having no impact on the day-to-day operation of their classrooms. Even in states engaged in curricular restructuring through cooperative projects (e.g., The Council of Chief State School Officers State Collaborative on Assessment and Student Standards Projects), the impact of reform ideas at the classroom level on a daily basis is questionable. And for good reason—change is difficult.

But the need is clear. No number of reform documents will make a difference in what students know and can do if teachers do not change.

At a September 24, 1998, House Science Committee hearing on science and math education, the panel of witnesses—all educators— repeatedly emphasized the importance of the professional development of teachers to any attempts at science education reform. At this same session, Bruce Alberts, president of the National Academy of Sciences, declared that "standards-based reforms will take hold only when the nation's teachers of mathematics and science…are effectively enacting the ideas provided by standards in each of their individual classrooms (*Testimony of Bruce Alberts, 1997*)."

> *No number of reform documents will make a difference in what students know and can do if teachers do not change.*

The National Commission on Teaching and America's Future (1996) highlighted the important need for capable teachers by pointing to teacher quality as the most important determinant of student performance. As reforms based on standards sweep the country and educators grapple with ways to help an increasingly diverse student population realize its academic and social potential, the need for knowledgeable and highly skilled teachers grows.

This need was emphasized by a U.S. Department of Education Study (1998b) that science learning is not increasing in dramatic ways, even though millions of dollars have been spent on reform projects since 1970. Although there was a statistically significant "positive quadratic trend" for 9-, 13-, and 17-year-olds since 1970, viewing these results in terms of the dollars invested casts doubt on the effectiveness of the efforts to improve science teaching.

Teacher-trainers are faced with a fundamental question: If professional development is the critical factor in promoting systemic change for practicing teachers, supervisors, administrators, and ultimately the students, as suggested by the *National Science Education Standards* (NRC, 1996), what model or models for professional development will likely produce the greatest improvement?

Research and experience have demonstrated the limitations of the short-term "training" model—the one-shot workshop or "expert" lecture that transmits information or skills to passive recipients. Increasingly, that model has yielded to a more long-range, capacity-building approach that offers meaningful intellectual, social, and emotional engagement with ideas, with materials, and with colleagues both in and outside of teaching.

To ensure that all students have richer learning experiences and are enabled to reach more challenging goals, school systems must invest in developing the capacity of teachers to teach in ways that are effective for a range of different learners. "Without such support for teachers, standards and standards-based assessments could ultimately prove to have unintended harmful effects, particularly for those struggling students who are already least well-served by the education system" (Falk & Ort, 1998, p. 59).

Many science educators across the country (e.g., Duschl & Gitomer, 1991; Shymansky, Henriques, Chidsey, Dunkase, Jorgensen, & Yore, 1997; Pizzini, 1998) have explored the available choices. Considerable investments have been made in resources and creativity to design and implement teacher professional development that would result in sustained change. The Regional Improvement of the Standards in Education (RISE) and Parents, Activities, and Literature in Science (PALS) projects have pushed train-the-trainer models to their limits and have achieved some success in introducing change and in guiding teachers in implementing change. These projects have yet to demonstrate ongoing influence. Duschl and Gitomer (1991) persuasively argued that shift in the school culture is a necessary component for sustaining enhanced teaching and learning.

Shifting to which professional development model(s) for teachers would work best? This question challenged me to experiment with using assessment design to bring about change in teachers training that, in turn, would result in students achieving at higher levels. Gerald Wheeler, director of the National Science Teachers Association (NSTA), said: "Teachers are the key to any changes in education." He then identified three barriers to reform: lack of time for teachers to plan effective use of the standards, isolation from the plans and ideas of other teachers, and lack of resources and professional development opportunities that would help them implement the standards (*Testimony of Gerald Wheeler,* 1997). Professional development that focused on assessment, it occurred to me, could get over these barriers. It could convince teachers of the value of change, support them in their implementation of change, and engage them in ongoing critical refinement of change as knowledge about student needs and about teaching and learning evolves.

School systems must invest in developing the capacity of teachers to teach in ways that are effective for a range of different learners.

Through projects such as the Georgia Initiative in Mathematics and Science (GIMS), one of many statewide systemic projects funded by the National Science Foundation (NSF) in the 1990s, I participated in professional development initiatives designed to be train-the-trainer types of programs. Likewise, through the Rural Technical Assistant Center program funded by the U.S. Department of Education, I designed and conducted many train-the-trainer professional development programs. Ironically, in all of these programs the first-tier participants—those teachers usually designated as excellent teachers themselves and clearly nominated for their potential as trainers of their peers—often relied on teacher-centered delivery for peers rather than the student-centered constructivist model they advocated for student learning. In other words, they tended to be constructivists with students but autocratic with other teachers.

Voices spoke loudly and aggressively that "teachers don't have time to construct their own understanding," "teachers need a manual," "teachers need a step-by-step guide for implementation," and so on. Indeed, because of scheduling pressures, assessment training was often designed and delivered in short sessions (one to two days) with occasional follow-ups. Not surprisingly, little commitment to change resulted. One heard the phrases "authentic assessment" and "portfolio assessment" from time to time, but real changes in how teachers used or understood assessment were not visible in many classrooms.

At the same time that these systemic projects were under way, I had the opportunity to create a professional development model based largely on constructivist learning theories and focused on the design, implementation, and use of new forms of assessment in support of science education reform. This project—funded by NSF—spanned 30 months from 1992 to 1994. Twenty-four teachers participated (teams of four from six different school systems representing a wide range of resources, student populations, teacher expertise, administrative support, and district commitment to change vis-à-vis the National Science Standards movement). This project and the three-year project funded by the Rural Technical Assistance Center (Region IV) that followed it provided convincing evidence of the power of assessment design as a lever for sustained change in classrooms.

Theoretical Perspective

Lampert & Ball (1990) defined effective professional development as a "reciprocal process that enables participants in an educational community to construct meanings that lean toward a common purpose about schooling." What exactly is that reciprocal process? Jorgensen (1994) and Jorgensen, McDevitt, Wolfe, and Hensley (in press) defined it as the interchange of ideas between individuals in a challenging environment. The responsibility for gaining a full understanding of the issues at hand rests with each individual in the conversation. There are no assumptions made about "truth" or "acceptability." The product of the discourse and of the construction of meaning may be unpredictable, or it may be status quo, but participants make no assumptions about the nature or shape of the product (or solution) at any time during the process.

When this process happens within an educational environment, there are guiding principles, however. These include:

1. All students can learn at high levels.
2. Student-based learning supports student achievement.
3. Teachers' roles are to facilitate student learning.
4. A safe environment is essential for all participants in the teaching-learning process.
5. Administrative support is essential.

If the professional development effort is based on constructivist thinking, it is inappropriate at best and misleading at worst to presume a specific schedule, a specific outcome, or a specific process. What can and should be expected is a mutuality of purpose, shared values, and communities of memory that connect teachers and administrators who work in the same school/district and are in common efforts (Bellah 1985).

Because this approach to professional development requires flexibility in scheduling and in outcomes, it calls for a basic shift in the way administrators think about professional development. It also requires that those educators who participate change their expectations for the experience. Participants in a constructivist-based professional development program will work harder, experience more frustration, and likely gain far greater personal rewards than they will from other models of professional development.

Before exploring the details of a constructivist model for professional development focusing on assessment design and implementation, it is important to define that term. Like much of the language of education reform, constructivism has many definitions. Henriques (1997) presented a useful comparative framework for four different interpretations of constructivism. She called these information processing, interactive constructivism, social constructivism, and radical constructivism and defined them as shown in Table 1.

The constructivist theory that forms the professional development model described here is the Social Constructivist model, following the work of Henriques (1997). From my perspective there are two keys to this concept. One is that there are no right ways to teach for all learners, and likewise there are no right ways to learn for all learners. The other is that when teachers and learners become tolerant of individual differences in ways of constructing knowledge, exciting growth and learning results. As Pizzini (1998, p. 2) stated: "When actually engaged in reflective dialogue, adults become more complex in their thinking, more tolerant of diverse perspectives, and more flexible and open toward new experiences thus leading to professional growth and development."

Why Focus on Assessment?

Despite decades of research on the teaching and learning process, many teachers teach the same materials and in the same way as a century ago. Stepans and Miller (1992) suggested three major reasons for this inertia:

1. Many teachers are held accountable to follow a prescribed curriculum and/or textbook without having much input on the appropriateness of the materials or the sequence in which concepts are taught.
2. Many classroom teachers view most of the educational research reports by professional researchers as impractical, superficial, and difficult to interpret and apply.
3. The educational researchers have not allowed the participantion of the classroom teacher in the act of research.

Assessment can be the driving force that shifts perceptions, attitudes, and practices within the context of high quality pro-

The challenge in the current reform environment is to use new findings about student learning, information from and about standardized assessment, and available technologies to develop optimal new forms of assessment.

Table 1: Faces of Constructivism	
Constructivist Category	Characteristics
Information Processing	Utilizes a computer metaphor to illustrate learning in which a series of microprocesses generate ideas and analyze errors leading to closer and closer approximations of the correct answer. Learning is a process of identifying causal relationships between antecedents and outcome, establishing critical (essential, necessary, and sufficient) attributes of a concept, and acquiring accurate understanding of fixed entitles and relationships that exist independent of human activity.
Social Constructivism	Utilizes a context metaphor to illustrate learning in which group dynamics lead to multiple interactions that are resolved by social negotiations resulting in consensus and common understanding at the group level. Knowledge is perceived as a social artifact, not a representation of reality.
Radical Constructivism	Utilizes an organism metaphor to illustrate learning in which interpersonal deliberations and inner speech lead to equally valid unique interpretations that are internally assessed for personal consistency. Knowledge is perceived as an individualistic snapshot of a multiple reality.
Interactive Constructivism	Utilizes an ecology metaphor to illustrate learning in which dynamic interactions of prior knowledge, concurrent sensory experiences, belief systems, and other people in a social-cultural context lead to multiple interpretations that are verified against evidence and privately integrated (assimilated or accommodated) into the person's knowledge network. Knowledge is perceived as individualistic conceptions that have been verified by the epistemic traditions of a community of learners.

fessional development. One of the most exciting opportunities that has come to the measurement communities in the past 30 years is the call "authentic assessment." Those of us in the measurement field rail at the phrase because it impugns the value of traditional measures as inauthentic. Good measurement of all types captures important evidence about learners' knowledge and skills. The challenge in the current reform environment is to use new findings about student learning, information from and about standardized assessment, and available technologies to develop optimal new forms of assessment. Jorgensen (1994) advocated that the goal of new forms of assessment should be to "cause a student to demonstrate the best that they know and can do before they even realize they are being tested." Studies of new assessment initiatives indicate that carefully evaluating authentic student work can help teachers better understand what students know and can do by clarifying goals and expectations for teaching and learning, deepening teacher knowledge of the disciplines, and increasing teachers' understanding of students and their work (Falk & Ort, 1998).

Using new forms of assessment as a focus for constructivist professional development has two distinct advantages: all ill-defined product and a process unfamiliar to most classroom teachers. The value of novelty and uncertainty is that none of the participants knows exactly what should happen when. The burdens of this approach are that the facilitator must be comfortable with stress and the teacher participants must struggle to construct their own understanding of what is important student learning and how best to document that learning. Precedents for such adult student-centered learning models include training of medical doctors, medical training that blends case writing with discussions of educational goals, modes of teaching, curriculum structure, and classroom organization (Waterman, 1997).

Critical Choices for Assessment in a Reform Environment
The professional development model proposed here focuses on the development and use of assessment tools to capture evidence about what students know and can do that is not already being documented in systematic ways. This focus prompts dialogue about what is being taught, what is being learned, and how teachers, students, parents, and administrators can know this with certainty.

The model's specific goals are to:

1. Create reliable and valid assessments that closely mirror sound instructional strategies.
2. Investigate the effect of assessment formats on student learning.
3. Engage teachers in the work of developing assessments so they can serve as resident mentors for others who might wish to do similar work in science or other disciplines or content areas.
4. Incorporate ongoing assessment development and refinement into the teaching/learning process on a routine and regular schedule.

More generally, this type of professional development aims to engage teachers in gaining a common understanding of what is important for students to know and be able to do and to empower teachers to craft or modify assessment tools to best reflect what is important to document about the teaching and learning process. There are no right decisions or right answers or specific development rules within this constructivist approach. Each participant brings to the discussion a unique perspective and a particular bias. Likewise, groups from the same schools bring a unique and biased common perspective on what students should know and be able to do and which assessment types are meaningful, credible, and informative for a variety of audiences. The yardstick of success must also be constructed from the work of the group, their assumptions, and their values.

For teachers accustomed to short professional development activities, the arduous journey of the constructivist approach can be daunting and frustrating. Thus, it is critical to have a commitment from participants to persevere. I recommend working with school teams that have agreed to participate in the project for at least one year. Likewise, it is critical that responsible administrators actively and regularly join in the experience. To be successful in providing academic preparation for students, a program must work through the school system, with the full support and endorsement of the superintendent and the school principal.

Participants in a professional development program that focuses on assessment must begin by candidly discussing the myths about tests. Many unfounded myths are widely held among teachers. Among the most detrimental to reform is that "tests are meaningless tasks that take time away from real learing." Until this myth is challenged, little progress can be made in changing the way teachers think about learning and about what students should be engaged in while studying science. It is important to use whatever techniques or resources are available to cause the participants to question that myth. One technique is to share with the participants tests different from those typically used in their own school environment. For example, if the teachers tend to think of standardized commercial multiple-choice tests, examples of constructed response tests should be presented. If the teachers tend to think of subject-specific objective-referenced tests, then they should see examples of integrated assessments. If the teachers tend to think of tests as things that happen at the end of the year or at the end of a unit, they should have an opportunity to see examples of embedded assessments that are virtually invisible to the students as assessment tools.

For teachers accustomed to short professional development activities, the arduous journey of the constructivist approach can be daunting and frustrating.

This exposure to alternative tests should extend to examples of the different kinds of information they yield. If teachers tend to think about score reports generated from commercial tests that provide statistical information not directly connected to teaching and learning, it would be useful to share with them examples of score reports based on proficiency descriptions or rubric categories. The goal of this exposure is to cause teachers to begin to challenge their own understanding about what tests can do for them as managers of effective instruction.

Another approach to disrupt teachers' conventional understanding of tests is to get them to think about what assessments should look like and to how they should perform in the classroom to the benefit of both teachers and students. Often this can be accomplished by asking the participants how they would define a test. Typically, the responses are affective (e.g., anxiety producing, stressful) and format-related (e.g., multiple choice, unrelated to the way teachers teach and students learn). Seldom will teachers define tests in a functional manner. A reminder of a well-accepted definition of a test may help refocus this conversation: "A test is a systematic procedure for observing behavior and describing it with a numerical or categorical score" (Cronbach, 1970, p. 26). This definition allows for an open interpretation and discussion of what tests can be. It challenges the participants to think about how tests can be designed to model ideal instruction, elicit credible and meaningful evidence of learning consistent with the habits of the discipline of science, and yield sound information about individual learners.

Begin by sharing with teachers and administrators a brief overview of new forms of assessment. The examples shared should be chosen to broaden the teachers' perspectives of what a test *could* look like. This is a deliberate attempt to encourage the teachers to use instructional strategies as a base for assessment design. This initial information sharing gives the participants an opportunity to build a common understanding about the purpose, structure, limitations, and advantages of various forms of constructed-response (as opposed to only-choice) formats.

As the conversation continues and as teachers begin to stretch their understanding of what a test can be, challenge them to think about assessment design and format that maximizes the value of the information derived while at the same time maintaining the credibility of the tool by adhering to

If teachers tend to think of tests as things that happen at the end of the year or at the end of a unit, they should have an opportunity to see examples of embedded assessments that are virtually invisible to the students as assessment tools.

the essential elements of good measurement: objectivity, reliability, and validity. Bringing into balance high quality assessment that models ideal instruction and provides meaningful information to teachers, students, parents, and administrators, while being true to fundamental measurement characteristics, is a challenge. But it is only when all these qualities are present together that there is value in this approach to professional development.

Deciding When and How to Capture Evidence

After dealing with testing myths and discussing alternative tests, the participants should address two key questions:

- What is quality work in science at the grade levels of interest?
- How can evidence of science learning that is consistent with our understanding of quality work in science be captured?

Out of the intellectual struggles with these questions come solutions consistent with good practice in both teaching and assessment.

What is Quality Work in Science?

Task development begins with a critical conversation focused on the key question: What is quality work in science at the grade levels of interest? Teachers should identify the behaviors that an independent, competent student in x grade in science or in x-specific science course should be able to demonstrate upon completion. This task has proven to be exceedingly difficult if taken beyond specific curriculum objectives and set in a broader context of the *National Science Education Standards* (NRC, 1996). Providing a temporal anchor (such as end of year) helps focus the conversation.

Jorgensen, McDevitt, Wolfe, & Hensley (in press) found that typical responses to this question—regardless of content area focus—were superficial. Teachers respond with "student conducts an experiment approximately," "student knows how to set up an experiment," or "student understands basic properties." These types of responses are signals to the facilitator of the professional development program that the participants are not engaged in meaningful learning. It is only when teachers begin to challenge what students should know and be able to do in the broader context of the *National Science Education Standards* that they will change what happens in classrooms. If they are challenged to break away from the "canned programs" and think about learning outcomes in the discipline, this task will be a difficult one for most teachers.

Initially, participating teachers' focus tends to be on discrete instructional objectives or on science-process skills. Teachers should be challenged to make explicit what students must know and be able to be literate in science, as well as to be active agents in the classroom—making decisions on what to teach, when to teach, and how to teach, which many of the science curricula do not require. Many programs are virtually lockstepped for teachers. For all the value of the kit-based programs in terms of bringing hands-on science to the classroom, the fact that teachers do not have to think about how the tasks and activities and readings fit together can actually inhibit a reform environment. Likewise, using the published objectives as benchmarks without thinking critically about what is really important for students to know and be able to do inhibits reform.

Hard content means not just the facts and skills of academic work, but understanding concepts and the interrelationships that give meaning and utility to the facts and skills....The emphasis is on students learning to produce knowledge, rather than simply reproduce knowledge (Porter, Archbald, & Tyree, 1991, p. 11).

In order to expand their perspective, the participants might be challenged to make explicit the critical content, critical processes, and critical approaches to work that are essential to science. The insights teachers gain from this task can influence the format of the assessment tasks the teachers design and the standards of quality they develop for judging student achievement.

Participants in professional development programs modeled as I am advocating are often anxious at first. A typical elementary teacher acknowledged,

I was a little apprehensive about the task at hand....I did feel that there may have been a little too much...thrown at us in a short period of time,...but I realize that it was not the time factor itself that caused the problem...I was not as prepared and knowledgeable as I would have liked to have been (Jorgensen, 1996).

For high school teachers, the anxiety typically took a different form, more focused on "but I have x content to cover." Some even went so far as to say, "The only test that matters is the AP test." All these comments indicated resistance to change.

It is for the professional development facilitator to move the group forward, to suggest the benefits of new forms of assessment for the participants' classrooms.

Task development continues by taking up the key question: How can evidence of science learning that is consistent with our understanding of quality work in science be captured? The participants must answer the following corollary questions:

- What are they trying to describe, and how?
- What needs to be documented, and how is it best to do that?
- What are they trying to model through the assessment?
- Whom are they trying to inform and how?

The first question draws on participants' understanding of what is critical that students know and can do. The second question asks what types of evidence are required and how the evidence should be organized. The third question harkens back to the reality that "tests drive instruction" and challenges teachers to use assessment to model high quality instruction. "You teach what you assess and you assess what you teach" (Resnick, 1987, p. 7). The team's charge must be to develop assessment tasks with appropriate and engaging forms that will maximize the likelihood that students will be able to demonstrate important science learning in a systematic and credible manner.

Deciding How to Summarize and Interpret Evidence
Just as complex a task as the designing of an assessment is the crafting of the mechanism to communicate what is assessed. The inherent appeal of experiments as performance tasks in science is that the work itself is valued within the discipline. They are student-centered and model what many scientists do every day. Participants are often inclined to make experiments and lab assignments the assessment of choice. However, if asked the fourth and last development question—Whom are you trying to inform and how?—teachers must admit the lab report often falls short. How does a lab on identifying minerals or on measuring and altering pH levels speak to the critical things that students should know and be able to do in science? How can students, teachers, parents, or administrators use lab reports to guide teaching and learning in the broader context of the science standards? What information can confirm whether students are learning what is important in science?

The inherent appeal of experiments as performance tasks in science is that the work itself is valued within the discipline.

Professional development based on this social constructivist model encourages debate about these issues without suggesting solutions. Its value is to challenge teachers by asking them what evidence about individuals they would find useful to have from that end-of-year assessment discussed above. Would the ability to complete lab reports be high on their list? Perhaps. But I hope they would also want evidence about unstructured inquiry, question development, and strategies designed to answer questions—and to provoke new questions.

The character of the information sought determines the information available, as well as its utility. What does a score on a lab report say about inquiry in a general sense? What does performance on an unstructured inquiry task say about inquiry in science?

Frequently, teachers tend to move away from merely quantitative information to proficiency descriptors or standards-based information because the latter speak directly to teaching and learning. An example of an holistic rubric developed to summarize evidence of inquiry skills from elementary students is provided in Table 2.

Table 2: Scoring Guide—Science Observation		
Score	Category	Description
5	Exceptional	The student's drawing includes multiple relevant features with attention to many specific details (shape, size, color, texture, proportions, parts, unique features). Drawing is a clear visual representation; there is accurate use of scale. The written response describes the object(s) observed, noting the multiple relevant features and specific details (exacting, clarifying, unique descriptors). The written description is objective and precise in the use of descriptors and includes those features drawn. Additionally, the description includes those elements observed through senses other than sight.
4	Very Good	The drawing includes multiple relevant features with attention to some specific details. Drawing is a clear visual representation; there is accurate use of scale. The written response describes the object(s) observed, noting the multiple relevant features and some specific details. Overall, the written description is objective and precise in the use of descriptors and includes those features drawn. Writing is more than a listing.
3	Satisfactory	The drawing includes multiple relevant features with some attention to detail; irrelevant features may be included. Drawing is a clear visual representation; there is evidence of an understanding of scale, although scale may be imprecise. The written response describes the object(s) observed, noting multiple relevant features and some specific details; irrelevant features may be included. Overall, the written description is objective and precise in the use of descriptors and includes those features drawn.
2	Limited	The drawing includes few relevant features with little attention to detail. Drawing is identifiable but may be simplistic. There is a distortion of scale that demonstrates confusion about proportional relationships. There is an attempt to describe the object(s) observed, but with few relevant features or details. Overall, the written description is vague and may include inconsistencies when compared to the drawing.
1	Minimal	The drawing includes few relevant features with little attention to detail. Object is difficult to identify. Scale is distorted. There is an attempt to describe the object(s) observed, but with few relevant features or details. The written description is vague and may include inconsistencies when compared to the drawing.
0	Off Task	No attempt was made or student did not follow directions for task; there is not enough information to score.

This rubric is holistic in that the judgment of the quality of work is made on the complete whole rather than on the elements that make up the whole. The nature of what the rubric developers considered indicators of quality is explicit in the description of a score of 5. Note that excellent work is defined as including multiple relevant features and specific details; the written description is objective and precise and includes elements observed through various senses.

Another approach to rubric development is to look specifically at those important elements separately. Table 3 is an example of such an analytic rubric. This was also designed for elementary students and was tailored for observing a NASA astronaut who played with a wind-up car during a space mission to demonstrate the principles of free fall or microgravity, friction, momentum, work, energy, the law of conservation of momentum, and so forth.

Using rubrics such as these or developing proficiency descriptions associated with specific levels of performance on an assessment task enhances the value of the test information. In good rubrics and proficiency descriptions, the wording parallels or connects directly to learning goals and instructional emphases. Test information becomes real from the perspective of the student, teacher, parent, or administrator because the link to teaching and learning is clear.

There are many examples of rubrics in the literature; however, note that most are task-specific. For example, the classic "Soda Task" (Baron, Forgione, Rindone, Kruglanski, & Davey, 1989) includes an analytic rubric just for the evaluation of that experiment. In contrast, the examples included in this article can be used across various appropriate stimulus activities. Thus, the science "stimulus" for "Science Observation" can range across a variety of units, lessons, concepts, and so forth. Likewise, even though "Toys in Space" was developed for the NASA video activities, the descriptions of excellence would be appropriate across many other science activities. In contrast, when numbers alone represent test performance and levels of quality, the numbers' meaning is often not clear. Some frame of reference for the number is often required—a comparison group, standard, or trend.

Making Assessment Meaningful and Useful

Measurement specialists work hard to make information derived from tests useful to their clients. Teachers will face similarly hard work as they design and implement new forms of assessment. They will have to balance available time for development, administration, and scoring against the value and utility of the information derived. They will have to make decisions about when they *really* need to capture evidence of student learning in a systematic and standard manner and when they can use less formal assessments. They will have to think carefully about how best to communicate the information from tests so that the message is heard.

There are no right or wrong ways to proceed here except within certain circumstances, and the participants best know those circumstances. The facilitator's job is to keep asking the question: How will this information be most meaningful to its audience(s)?

Table 3: Analytic Scoring Guide—Toys in Space

Score	Behaviorial Description
	Prediction (What do you think the car will do? Why?)
0	No attempt, or a prediction unrelated to the experiment
1	Prediction with no rationale
2	Prediction with a rationale
3	Accurate prediction with a rationale
4	Exemplary (includes accurate prediction and appropriate rationale for the variables involved)
	Drawing (Draw a picture of what the car did.)
0	No attempt
1	Attempt (includes car and track)
2	Appropriate (includes car and track, shows motion)
3	Accurate representation (includes car and track, shows motion, and demonstrates free flight of car away from the track)
	Narrative (What did you notice? Why do you think the car did what it did?)
0	No attempt
1	Attempt (mentions car and track)
2	Appropriate (includes car and track, mentions motion)
3	Accurate representation (includes car and track, mentions motion, and discusses free flight of car away from the track)
4	Exemplary (includes car and track; shows motion; discusses free flight of car away from the track; includes reference to term or concept of gravity, microgravity, etc.)
	Contrast of space with Earth (sixth-grade students only) (In your classroom...? Explain.)
0	No attempt
1	Attempt
2	Appropriate (but no evidence of extension of scientific concepts or principles)
3	Accurate attempt (some evidence of extension of scientific concepts or principles)
4	Exemplary (demonstrates evidence of extension of scientific concepts or principles, indicates logical "next step" in the investigation)
	Question (What question about the toy car would you like to ask the astronaut?)
0	No Attempt
1	Attempt (but not appropriate, given task)
2	Appropriate (but no evidence of extension of scientific concepts or principles)
3	Accurate attempt (some evidence of extension of scientific concepts or principles)
4	Exemplary (demonstrates evidence of extension of scientific concepts or principles, indicates logical "next step" in the investigation)

Continuous Improvement for Science Education Through Effective Assessment

The impact of training programs like those described above on teachers' thinking about learning in science and about how to better create engaging student-centered learning environments will be known only five or 10 years from now. But there is room for optimism. One administrator whose teachers participated in a professional development program modeled after this social constructivist approach provided support for this optimism, as well as an objective view on how hard the work is:

> *The journey was difficult. We were so uncertain of whether or not we were right! Just like the students—we wanted to know immediately if we had understood the assignment correctly. Had we followed directions? Had we produced quality work?*
>
> *By the end of the year, we had produced twelve innovative performance-based tasks! We had crafted meaningful scoring guides that reflected increasing sophistication in student understanding and we had tried out these tasks on students. Well, guess what? They worked, and the students liked them!*
>
> *For us, the "What's next?" question came quickly. We reflected on how much we had grown in terms of understanding. We recognized how valuable the products of our work had already been in making high quality work an expectation—a norm, not a distant goal in our school. Answering that critical question of "What is quality work?" and then moving to the creation of systematic ways to document and judge quality have made this learning journey the most powerful that I, as a former teacher, have ever been on. Never again will we look at assessment or instruction in some way. All students at our school will benefit from this work* (Wolfe, S., 1996)!

Such testimonials are encouraging for the future of this approach. However, it is essential that those who embark on this learning journey realize that the target for excellence in teaching and learning will be forever a moving one. Science standards evolve. We are all learners and experimenters who must keep open minds as we learn more about pedagogy and about cognition; as science grows and changes, what teachers expect from students will need to change. It is this reality that makes the social constructivist approach to professional development reasonable and exciting.

References

Baron, J. B., P. D. Forgione, D. A. Rindone, H. Kruglanski, and B. Davey. 1989. *Toward a new generation of student outcome measures: Connecticut's common core of learning assessment.* Paper presented at the annual meeting of the American Educational Research Association, April. San Francisco, CA.

Bellah, R. N. 1985. Creating a New Framework for New Realities. Social Science as a Public Philosophy. *Change* 17(2):35–39.

Cronbach, L. J. 1970. *Essentials of psychological testing.* New York: Harper & Row.

David, C., and B. Matthews. 1995. The teacher internship program for science (TIPS): A successful museum-school partnership. *Journal of Elementary Science Education* 7(1):16–28.

Duschl, R. A. 1985. Science education and philosophy of science education: Twenty-five years of mutually exclusive development. *School Science and Mathematics* 85:541–555.

Duschl, R. A., and D. H. Gitomer. 1991. Epistemological perspectives on conceptual change: Implications for educational practice. *Journal of Research in Science Teaching* 28:839–858.

Ellis, J. D., and D. E. Maxwell. 1995. *Intervening in the professional development of science teachers: The Colorado science teaching enhancement program. Interim report of the formative evaluation of CO-STEP.* Washington, DC: National Science Foundation.

Essig, S. R. 1995. *Long term effects study: Participants of the science in rural California teacher enhancement project.* ED 392–740.

Falk, B., and S. Ort. 1998. Sitting down to score teacher learning through assessment, *Phi Delta Kappan* 80(1):59–63.

Feldman, A. 1994. *Teachers learning from teachers: Knowledge and understanding ion collaborative action research.* Paper presented at the Annual Meeting of the American Educational Research Association, New Orleans, LA.

Finson, K. D. 1994. Science alternative assessment models in Illinois. *Journal of Science Teacher Education* 5(3):97–110.

Henriques, L. 1997. A study to define and verify a model of interactive-constructive elementary school science teaching. Unpublished Ph.D. dissertation, Iowa City, IA: University of Iowa.

Jorgensen, M. A. 1994. *Assessing habits of mind—performance assessment in mathematics and science.* Columbus, OH: Eisenhower Center for Science, Mathematics, and Environmental Education.

———. 1996. *Rethinking portfolio assessment in mathematics and science.* Columbus, OH: Eisenhower Center for Science, Mathematics, and Environmental Education.

Jorgensen, M. A., M. A. McDevitt, S. Wolfe, and T. Hensley. (in press). Capturing the gist—performance assessment in reading. *Florida Journal of Educational Research.*

Lampert, M. 1984. Teaching about thinking and thinking about teaching. *Journal of Curriculum Studies* 16:1–8.

Lampert, M., and D. Ball. 1990. *Using hypermedia technology to support a new pedagogy of teacher education* (Issue paper 90-5). East Lansing, MI: National Center for Research on Teacher Education.

Lieberman, A. 1995. Practices that support teacher development: Transforming conceptions of professional learning. *Phi Delta Kappan* (April):591–96.

National Commission on Teaching and America's Future. 1996. *What matters most: Teaching for America's future.* New York: National Commission on Teaching and America's Future.

National Research Council. 1996. *National science education standards,* Reston, VA: National Academy Press.

Office of Policy and Planning (OPP). 1993. *Improving the teaching of science: staff development approaches.* Washington, DC: OPP.

Pizzini, E. L. 1998. Teacher leaders, professional staff development and the implementation of the reform initiatives in science and mathematics education in Iowa. [pub?]

Porter, A. C., D. A. Archbald, and A. K. Tyree. 1991. Reforming the curriculum: Will empowerment policies replace control? In *The politics of curriculum and testing*, ed. S. H. Furhman & B. Malen, 63–80. London: Falmer Press.

Resnick, L. B. 1987. *Education and learning to think*. Washington, DC: National Academy Press.

Resnick, L. B., and D. P. Resnick. 1989. Tests as standards of achievement in schools. *Proceedings of the ETS Invitational Conference*, 63–80. Princeton, NJ: Educational Testing Service.

Sheingold, K., J. I. Heller, and S. T. Paulukonis. 1995. *Actively seeking evidence: Teacher change through assessment development*. Princeton, NJ: Educational Testing Service.

Shepardson, D. F. 1995. *Twenty-four out of thirty = change*. Paper presented at the Annual Meeting of the Educational Research Association.

Shymansky, J. A., S. Enger, J. L.Chidsey, L. D. York, M. A. Jorgensen, L. Henriques, and E. W. Wolfe. 1997. Performance assessment in science as a tool to enhance the picture of student learning. *School Science and Mathematics,* 97(4):172–183.

Shymansky, J. A., L. Henriques, J. L. Chidsey, J. Dunkase, M. A. Jorgensen, and L. D. Yore. 1997. A professional development system as a catalyst for changing science teachers. *Journal of Science Teacher Education* 8(1):29–42.

Shymansky, J. A., C. A. Marberry, and M. A. Jorgensen. 1997. Science and mathematics are spoken and written here: Promoting science and mathematics in the classroom. [CD-ROM]. *Reform in Math and Science Education: Issues in the Classroom.* Columbus, OH: Eisenhower National Clearinghouse.

Stepans, J. I., and K. W. Miller. 1992. *Teacher, administrator, and science educator form a TRIAD.* Paper presented at the Area Conference of the National Science Teachers Association, December. Charlotte, NC.

Testimony of Bruce Alberts, President, National Academy of Sciences, before the Committee on Science, U.S. House of Representatives. 1997. Available: http://www.house.gov/science/alberts_9-24.html [1999, February 16].

Testimony of Dr. Gerald F. Wheeler, Executive Director, National Science Teachers Association, Arlington, VA. for the U.S. House of Representatives Committee on Science Hearing on Science, Mathematics, Engineering, and Technology Education in America. 1997. Available: http://www.house.gov/science/wheeler_9-24.html [1999, March 10].

U.S. Department of Education, Office of Educational Research and Improvement. 1998a. *Digest of Education Statistics 1997*. Washington, DC: USDE, Office of Education Research and Improvement.

U.S. Department of Education, Office of Educational Research and Improvement 1998b. *NAEP Facts* 3(3). Washington, DC: USDE, Office of Education Research and Improvement.

Waterman, M. A. 1997. *Curriculum and teacher development in biology via case writing* (ED407409). Paper presented at the Annual Meeting of the American Educational Research Association, March. Chicago, IL.

Defining Teacher Quality Through Content: Professional Development Implications from TIMSS

William H. Schmidt
Michigan State University

William H. Schmidt is a professor of education at the Michigan State University, College of Education and serves as the national research coordinator for the Third International Mathematics and Science Study.

The major evidence around which the theme of this paper is built comes from data gathered as part of the Third International Mathematics and Science Study (TIMSS). TIMSS was the most extensive and far-reaching cross-national comparative study of mathematics and science education ever attempted (see Schmidt and McKnight, 1995; Beaton, Martin, Mullis, Gonzalez, Smith, & Kelly, 1996). It included comparing the official curricula, textbooks, teacher practices, and student achievements of many countries (20 to 50 countries, depending on the particular comparison). Thousands of official documents and textbooks were analyzed. Thousands of teachers, principals, and other experts responded to survey questionnaires. More than half a million children in over 40 countries were tested in mathematics and science. These tests were conducted for 9-year-olds (grades 3 and 4 in the United States), 13-year-olds (grades 7 and 8 in the United States), and for students in the last year of secondary school (12th grade in the United States).

The focus of this chapter is on the science portion of the TIMSS study. Achievement testing results are reviewed and discussed in the context of the curriculum and instruction provided in those countries. A special focus in the chapter is on the policy implications of TIMSS for professional development, especially in the sciences.

Achievement Results

Fourth-Grade Achievement

The brightest spot for the United States in the TIMSS achievement results was fourth grade science (Figure 1). The United States tied for second among TIMSS countries on the overall science score (NCES, 1997). U.S. students were outperformed only by those from Korea and performed significantly better than most others (19 countries out of 26, including England, Canada, Hong Kong, and Singapore). The same cannot be said about fourth-grade mathematics achievement results, where, overall, the United States placed somewhat above the international average.

Figure 1: U.S. Average Science Performance: Population 1

Nations with Average Scores Significantly Higher than the U.S.		Nations with Average Scores Significantly Lower than the U.S.	
Nation	*Average*	*Nation*	*Average*
Korea	597	England	551
		Canada	549
Nations with Average Scores Not Significantly Different from the U.S.		Singapore	547
		Slovenia	546
		Ireland	539
Japan	574	Scotland	536
United States	**565**	Hong Kong	533
Austria	565	Hungary	532
Australia	562	New Zealand	531
Netherlands	557	Norway	530
Czech Republic	557	Latvia	512
		Israel	505
		Iceland	505
		Greece	497
		Portugal	480
		Cyprus	475
		Thailand	473
		Iran	416
		Kuwait	401

Eighth-Grade Achievement

The TIMSS eighth-grade science results, presented in Figure 2, revealed the United States as slightly above the international average (NCES, 1996). Students in several countries performed significantly better than those in the United States (including Singapore, Japan, Korea, Hungary, and the Netherlands, among others). Many countries (such as England, Russia, Switzerland, and Germany) had scores that did not differ significantly from those of the U.S., and several had scores significantly lower.

The TIMSS eighth-grade mathematics results were not as strong as the science results. Essentially, the United States scored below the international mean in almost every area. U.S. students were better than only seven countries—Colombia, Kuwait, South Africa, Iran, Portugal, Cyprus, and Lithuania. There was a large number of countries that scored significantly better than the United States, including most of Europe and Asia.

The comparison of fourth to eighth grade for both science and mathematics showed that students consistently performed better at fourth grade than at eighth, especially in science. U.S. students did not start behind, they fell behind.

Figure 2: U.S. Average Science Performance: Population 2

Nations with Average Scores Significantly Higher than the U.S.

Nation	Average
Singapore	607
Czech Republic	574
Japan	571
Korea	565
Bulgaria	565
Netherlands	560
Slovenia	560
Austria	558
Hungary	554

Nations with Average Scores Significantly Lower than the U.S.

Nation	Average
Spain	517
France	498
Greece	497
Iceland	494
Romania	486
Latvia	485
Portugal	480
Denmark	478
Lithuania	476
Belgium (Fr)	471
Iran, Islamic Republic	470
Cyprus	463
Kuwait	430
Colombia	411
South Africa	326

Nations with Average Scores Not Significantly Different than the U.S.

Nation	Average
England	552
Belgium (Fl)	550
Australia	545
Slovak Republic	544
Russian Federation	538
Ireland	538
Sweden	535
United States	**534**
Germany	531
Canada	531
Norway	527
New Zealand	525
Thailand	525
Israel	524
Hong Kong	522
Switzerland	522
Scotland	517

Twelfth-Grade Achievement

The downward trend in terms of the U.S. ranking internationally, which was evidenced in TIMSS from fourth to eighth grade, was further continued when the 12th grade results were examined (NCES, 1998). In science, two different tests were given to two different groups of students. The first type was given to a general cross-section of students completing secondary school and surveyed students' general knowledge of both science and mathematics. From an international perspective, the content of this general knowledge test was drawn from curricular topics addressed in grades seven to nine. U.S. performance in science general knowledge is shown in Figure 3. Statistically, in both the mathematics and science general knowledge areas, there were only two countries that U.S. students outperformed: Cyprus and South Africa. Thus, the decline in relative international standing continued its downward trend to the bottom of the international distribution. It must be noted that the Asian countries, such as Hong Kong, Singapore, Korea, and Japan, which were among the highest performing nations at both of the two younger student populations, opted not to participate in the end of secondary school testing.

> *Statistically, in both the mathematics and science general knowledge areas, there were only two countries that U.S. students outperformed: Cyprus and South Africa.*

The second type of test given was a specialist examination—one in advanced

---

Figure 3: U.S. Average Science Performance: Population 3

Nations with Average Scores Significantly Higher than the U.S.		Nations with Average Scores Not Significantly Different than the U.S.	
Nation	*Average*	*Nation*	*Average*
Sweden	559	Germany	497
Netherlands	558	France	487
Iceland	549	Czech Republic	487
Norway	544	Russian Federation	481
Canada	532	**United States**	**480**
New Zealand	529	Italy	475
Australia	527	Hungary	471
Switzerland	523	Lithuania	471
Austria	520		
Slovenia	517	**Nations with Average Scores Significantly Lower than the U.S.**	
Denmark	509	*Nation*	*Average*
		Cyprus	448
		South Africa	349

mathematics and another in advanced physics. Each nation was to define those students taking the most advanced course of study in each of these two areas. For much of Europe, this population was well-defined as specific tracks or courses of study with clearly defined students. Such tracks have about 15 percent to 20 percent of the end of secondary students in them. For the United States, the advanced students in physics were defined as those taking a college-level preparatory course in physics or advanced placement (AP) physics.

Even students taking the most advanced course work in physics do not compare well with their counterparts in the other TIMSS countries.

The results of the advanced physics test are presented in Figure 4. This startling result placed U.S. students literally at the bottom of the international distribution. All the participating countries, except Austria, outperformed the United States. These results call into question a seriously held belief that the problems of American education reside mostly with those students with average or poor ability levels but certainly not with the most able of students. Even students taking the most advanced course work in physics do not compare well with their counterparts in the other TIMSS countries.

Figure 4: U.S. Average Science Performance: Population 3 Physics Students

Nations with Average Scores Significantly Higher than the U.S.		Nations with Average Scores Not Significantly Different than the U.S.	
Nation	*Average*	*Nation*	*Average*
Norway	581	Austria	435
Sweden	573	**United States**	**423**
Russian Federation	545		
Denmark	534	**Nations with Average Scores Significantly Lower than the U.S.**	
Slovenia	523		
Germany	522	*Nation*	*Average*
Australia	518	(None)	--
Cyprus	494		
Latvia	488		
Switzerland	488		
Greece	486		
Canada	485		
France	466		
Czech Republic	451		

Summary

The TIMSS achievement results painted a disappointing picture. It is a picture of decline in relative standing internationally from fourth through eighth to 12th grade. The pattern holds both in science and mathematics. While acknowledging the difficulties of making comparisons among countries at the end of secondary school, the overall pattern is unmistakably clear. The middle grades (5–8) are central in understanding that decline. The next section examines U.S. achievement in science more closely.

A Closer Look at Science Achievement in Grades 4 and 8

A characteristic feature of much American thinking on achievement testing is that once a test is labeled as "science," if it is properly developed (which usually means meeting various psychometric criteria), it essentially yields the same information as that from another psychometrically well-developed "science" test. Put more simply, it is the belief in educational circles that a test is a test is a test.

TIMSS data suggests that a science test is not a science test; that the use of different curriculum-specific measures when comparing countries can lead to very different conclusions.

Using TIMSS data as reported elsewhere (Schmidt, Jakwerth, & McKnight, 1998), a set of analyses suggests that a science test is not a science test; that the use of different curriculum-specific measures when comparing countries can lead to very different conclusions. In this section, curriculum-specific measures in science are used to portray U.S. performance relative to other countries, providing a much more precise characterization of student achievement results.

Fourth-Grade Achievement

Data for 15 areas of science for the upper of the two grades containing most 9-year-olds (fourth grade in the United States: see Schmidt, McKnight, Cogan, Jakwerth, & Houang, 1999, for a similar analysis of a subset of the 41 countries presented here) showed that no countries outperformed U.S. students in the areas: "organs and tissues," "interactions of living things," "human biology and health," and "scientific processes." U.S. students performed the best, relatively speaking, in "interactions of living things," where only the Netherlands outperformed the United States by about one percentage point. The weakest area was "forces and motion." Students' average scores were higher than the international means in all but four areas: "earth in the universe," "life cycles and genetics," "matter," and "forces and motion."

Eighth-Grade Achievement

Figure 5 (pp. 148–156) presents science data for the upper of the two grades with the most 13-year-olds (eighth grade in the United States; again, see Schmidt, McKnight, Cogan, Jakwerth, & Houang, 1999). This is similar to the fourth-grade science data referred to in the previous section. Data are presented for 17 content areas. Because overall science score's standing was high at fourth grade and around average at eighth, one might expect a set of mostly lower rankings. However, there was substantial variation in the U.S. ranking across the 17 content areas.

In "life cycles and genetics," the United States was not significantly outperformed by any country at the eighth-grade level. In fact, in "life cycles and genetics" the United States was only one-half percentage point from sharing the number one ranking with the Czech Republic. In "scientific processes," "earth in the universe," and "chemical changes," the United States was significantly outperformed by only one or two countries. The relatively worst areas for the United States were "physical changes," "properties and classification of matter," and "forces and motion," being outperformed by 15 to 18 countries. However, the United States did not perform significantly below the international average in any of the 17 science topic areas.

Generally, the United States did best at both fourth and eighth grade in earth science, in particular "earth processes." U.S. students also did well in life science at both levels, although the specific content areas differed—"organs and tissues" and the "interactions of living things" at fourth grade, but "life cycles and genetics" at eighth grade. This reflected the general tendency among elementary and middle-school teachers to focus most of their instruction on biology and earth science.

The worst area at both levels was in physical science—"forces and motion," "physical and chemical changes," and "matter" at fourth grade, and "physical changes," "properties and classification of matter," and "forces and motion" at eighth grade.

Eighth-grade science achievement is somewhat difficult to interpret, given the lack of agreement as to what constitutes the eighth-grade curriculum.

Eighth-grade science achievement is somewhat difficult to interpret, given the lack of agreement as to what constitutes the eighth-grade curriculum. By eighth grade, the typical science curriculum pattern in U.S. educational systems is to have students take a course oriented to a specific broad area of science (earth science, life science, and physical science) or, less frequently, a mixed course in "general science." As a result, not all students were taking or had recently studied all areas of science. At both seventh and eighth grade, around 30 percent of U.S. students take a general science course. For the specific disciplines, the differences between seventh and eighth grade are rather pronounced. At seventh grade, almost 60 percent took life science, whereas 10 percent were in an earth science course and less than 5 percent took physical science. By contrast, at eighth grade about 30 percent each had a physical or an earth science course and only 10 percent took life sciences.

Figure 5: Country science scores for specific content areas for upper-grade 13-year-olds in selected countries compared to the U.S. mean (national % correct in each area)

Earth Features		Earth Processes		Earth in the Universe	
Slovenia	69.5	Ireland	66.9	Sweden	70.7
Czech Republic	67.1	England	66.7	Norway	70.1
Hungary	67.1	Singapore	66.7	Netherlands	67.5
Korea	65.3	Belgium (Fl)	65.4	Czech Republic	66.9
Singapore	64.6	Netherlands	62.5	**Japan**	**66.7**
Bulgaria	63.1	Norway	62.3	Thailand	66.0
Ireland	62.9	Austria	61.0	Bulgaria	66.0
Austria	61.8	**United States**	**60.9**	Singapore	64.9
Belgium (Fl)	61.1	Russian Federation	60.8	**Switzerland**	**64.8**
Slovak Republic	61.0	Canada	60.6	Slovenia	64.7
Sweden	60.5	Sweden	60.0	Korea	64.4
Thailand	59.7	Slovenia	59.6	Slovak Republic	63.8
Russian Federation	59.2	Korea	59.0	Austria	63.6
Norway	59.2	**Japan**	**58.5**	**United States**	**63.3**
Japan	**59.0**	Slovak Republic	58.1	Germany	62.8
England	58.7	New Zealand	57.3	Spain	62.8
Switzerland	**58.2**	Czech Republic	57.2	Australia	62.7
Netherlands	58.0	Australia	56.7	Belgium (Fl)	61.8
Australia	57.5	Thailand	56.0	New Zealand	61.7
Germany	75.2	**Switzerland**	**56.0**	Greece	61.5
United States	**57.1**	Scotland	55.8	Canada	61.2
Canada	56.6	Spain	55.5	England	59.0
Israel	56.1	France	55.0	Ireland	58.5
Spain	55.9	Israel	54.7	Hungary	58.5
New Zealand	55.9	Germany	53.9	Iceland	58.2
International	55.4	International	53.5	Hong Kong	58.0
France	55.1	Bulgaria	52.9	Israel	56.2
Romania	54.8	Hong Kong	52.3	International	58.2
Hong Kong	54.1	Hungary	51.3	Russian Federation	56.9
Lithuania	52.9	Portugal	51.1	Denmark	55.9
Latvia	52.5	Iceland	50.1	Portugal	55.0

Figure 5: continued

Greece	52.3	Belgium (Fr)	48.5	France	53.2
Scotland	51.9	Denmark	48.5	Scotland	52.7
Belgium (Fr)	50.8	Cyprus	46.3	Kuwait	52.5
Iceland	50.1	Greece	45.3	Latvia	52.4
Iran	49.3	Romania	44.5	Cyprus	51.7
Portugal	47.9	Latvia	43.1	Belgium (Fr)	49.3
Cyprus	47.2	Iran	41.8	Philippines	48.3
Denmark	45.8	Lithuania	40.5	Lithuania	48.0
Kuwait	42.1	Philippines	40.0	Iran	47.5
Philippines	40.6	Colombia	38.9	Romania	45.5
Colombia	39.7	Kuwait	38.8	Colombia	38.5
South Africa	27.2	South Africa	27.6	South Africa	28.8

Diversity & Structure of Living Things		Life Processes & Functions		Life Cycles & Genetics	
Japan	**75.9**	Singapore	72.3	Czech Republic	81.8
Singapore	74.2	**Japan**	**70.4**	**United States**	**81.2**
Hong Kong	73.4	Korea	68.2	England	80.4
Korea	72.5	Slovenia	65.2	Ireland	79.6
Czech Republic	72.3	Czech Republic	63.7	Netherlands	79.3
Netherlands	71.6	Thailand	63.0	Israel	79.0
Bulgaria	70.4	Belgium (Fl)	62.9	Belgium (Fl)	78.9
Thailand	68.8	Bulgaria	62.6	Canada	78.4
Sweden	67.7	Netherlands	60.7	Austria	78.3
Hungary	67.1	Austria	60.1	Sweden	78.2
Austria	66.7	Hungary	59.9	Norway	78.1
Australia	66.7	Russian Federation	59.4	Scotland	76.5
Germany	65.7	England	59.3	Korea	75.9
Russian Federation	65.7	Germany	58.1	France	75.7
Slovak Republic	65.3	**United States**	**58.0**	Denmark	75.6
Slovenia	65.1	Australia	57.4	Russian Federation	75.5
England	64.5	Canada	57.2	Germany	75.5
United States	**63.9**	Israel	57.1	**Switzerland**	**75.1**

Figure 5: continued

Canada	63.3	Hong Kong	56.3	**Japan**	**74.8**
Belgium (Fl)	62.9	New Zealand	56.1	Bulgaria	74.2
New Zealand	62.3	Ireland	56.1	Iceland	74.0
Iceland	61.9	Spain	55.9	New Zealand	73.9
Spain	61.3	Sweden	54.9	Hungary	73.7
International	61.3	Slovak Republic	54.8	Australia	73.0
Switzerland	**61.0**	International	54.5	Spain	71.1
Israel	60.4	**Switzerland**	**54.2**	Slovak Republic	71.0
Belgium (Fr)	59.6	Norway	54.2	Slovenia	70.8
Ireland	59.4	France	53.8	International	70.2
Norway	59.2	Romania	52.3	Lithuania	69.6
France	58.4	Belgium (Fr)	52.0	Portugal	69.2
Scotland	57.6	Greece	51.5	─Singapore	68.6
Cyprus	57.5	Scotland	51.4	Belgium (Fr)	67.4
Romania	56.0	Iceland	50.8	Thailand	67.3
Lithuania	55.7	Portugal	50.5	Romania	66.5
Denmark	55.5	Denmark	48.4	Hong Kong	65.3
Greece	55.3	Latvia	47.7	Greece	61.9
Latvia	55.2	Lithuania	46.0	Latvia	61.7
Portugal	54.2	Iran	45.4	Cyprus	59.0
Iran	50.9	Cyprus	44.5	Kuwait	52.4
Kuwait	49.1	Colombia	39.5	Philippines	51.6
Colombia	48.4	Kuwait	39.2	Iran	48.9
Philippines	41.0	Philippines	36.4	Colombia	45.3
South Africa	32.0	South Africa	22.4	South Africa	33.7

Interactions of LivingThings

Korea	68.8
⇐Singapore	65.6
Japan	**65.0**
Thailand	64.1
Hungary	63.1

Human Biology & Health

─Singapore	74.0
Czech Republic	71.6
Austria	71.1
Netherlands	71.2
Bulgaria	71.2

Properties & Classification of Matter

Japan	**66.6**
─ Singapore	66.6
Korea	65.4
Slovak Republic	62.4
Bulgaria	61.6

Figure 5: continued

Australia	62.0	**Japan**	**69.4**	Czech Republic	60.4
England	61.5	Belgium (Fl)	69.3	Slovenia	58.4
Norway	59.9	Hungary	68.7	Netherlands	58.3
Canada	58.2	England	68.3	Belgium (Fl)	57.9
Czech Republic	57.6	Israel	67.6	Hungary	57.3
Slovenia	57.2	Germany	67.6	Sweden	57.2
Ireland	56.0	**United States**	**66.8**	Austria	56.5
New Zealand	55.9	Thailand	66.5	Hong Kong	56.4
Netherlands	55.8	Australia	66.5	Canada	55.7
Slovak Republic	54.8	Korea	65.5	Norway	54.8
United States	**54.3**	Ireland	65.4	Australia	54.7
Germany	52.9	Slovenia	65.3	England	54.7
Belgium (Fl)	52.9	Canada	65.3	Germany	54.9
Spain	52.9	Sweden	63.9	Russian Federation	54.3
Russian Federation	52.3	New Zealand	63.7	New Zealand	53.5
Austria	52.2	Spain	63.2	Israel	53.5
Sweden	52.1	Russian Federation	63.1	France	52.3
Romania	51.5	Scotland	62.6	International	51.6
Scotland	51.1	Norway	62.6	Ireland	51.5
International	51.0	Slovak Republic	62.0	**Switzerland**	**51.1**
Israel	50.2	Iceland	61.5	Scotland	51.0
Iceland	50.2	**Switzerland**	**61.4**	Denmark	50.7
Switzerland	**49.8**	International	61.2	**United States**	**49.9**
Greece	48.8	Hong Kong	59.9	Spain	49.6
Denmark	48.0	Belgium (Fr)	57.4	Greece	47.9
Latvia	47.4	Portugal	57.0	Latvia	47.9
Portugal	47.3	Greece	56.9	Iceland	47.4
Hong Kong	46.6	Denmark	56.9	Cyprus	47.3
Iran	45.5	Romania	56.2	Portugal	47.2
France	44.8	France	55.7	Lithuania	47.0
Bulgaria	43.0	Latvia	53.9	Thailand	46.7
Kuwait	40.3	Lithuania	52.9	Belgium (Fr)	45.4
Belgium (Fr)	40.0	Iran	51.8	Romania	45.0
Colombia	37.4	Cyprus	50.9	Iran	39.1

Figure 5: continued

Lithuania	37.2	Colombia	50.2	Kuwait	36.6
Cyprus	37.1	Kuwait	47.9	Colombia	36.1
Philippines	30.0	Philippines	41.1	Philippines	29.6
South Africa	20.9	South Africa	28.1	South Africa	28.2

Structure of Matter		Energy & Physical Processes		Physical Changes	
Bulgaria	63.0	Singapore	71.2	**Japan**	**66.7**
Russian Federation	56.4	**Japan**	**68.8**	Singapore	63.1
Slovak Republic	54.9	Korea	67.2	Czech Republic	62.9
Hungary	53.9	Bulgaria	64.7	France	61.9
Czech Republic	54.2	England	64.1	Slovenia	61.8
Singapore	53.2	Netherlands	63.8	Israel	61.4
Greece	51.8	Austria	63.1	Sweden	61.3
Romania	51.0	Czech Republic	62.3	Slovak Republic	61.2
Spain	51.0	Belgium (Fl)	62.2	Netherlands	61.1
Slovenia	50.0	Slovenia	61.2	Hungary	61.0
Lithuania	49.3	Australia	61.1	Norway	60.0
Austria	48.7	Slovak Republic	60.9	Austria	59.4
United States	**48.2**	Scotland	60.4	England	58.9
Israel	44.7	Hungary	60.2	Belgium (Fl)	58.7
Sweden	42.7	New Zealand	59.9	Canada	58.5
Korea	42.1	Canada	59.9	Denmark	57.5
Japan	**41.1**	Hong Kong	59.5	Korea	57.3
Portugal	40.8	Israel	59.5	Australia	57.1
Ireland	40.1	Germany	59.3	Russian Federation	57.0
Hong Kong	40.0	**Switzerland**	**58.7**	Iceland	56.4
International	39.6	Russian Federation	58.4	**Switzerland**	**54.0**
Australia	38.7	Ireland	58.0	Germany	53.6
England	38.1	**United States**	**57.1**	Thailand	53.2
Latvia	37.8	Norway	56.6	Spain	53.1
Canada	37.1	Sweden	56.6	Latvia	53.0
Colombia	36.1	International	56.4	International	52.8
Germany	35.2	Thailand	55.3	Lithuania	52.8

Figure 5: continued

New Zealand	34.5	Spain	55.2	New Zealand	52.8
Iran	34.0	France	54.6	Ireland	51.5
Scotland	31.9	Iceland	54.4	Cyprus	50.9
Norway	31.9	Greece	54.2	Iran	50.9
Thailand	30.6	Denmark	52.2	Belgium (Fr)	50.1
Cyprus	30.4	Latvia	52.1	Scotland	50.0
Netherlands	30.0	Belgium (Fr)	51.9	**United States**	**49.1**
France	29.4	Iran	50.6	Hong Kong	48.8
Philippines	28.9	Lithuania	50.2	Greece	46.1
Switzerland	**28.6**	Portugal	49.4	Romania	45.3
Kuwait	28.0	Romania	49.0	Portugal	44.2
Belgium (Fl)	27.4	Kuwait	47.6	Bulgaria	37.2
Denmark	26.1	Cyprus	47.2	Kuwait	32.4
Iceland	25.0	Philippines	41.3	Philippines	31.6
Belgium (Fr)	24.6	Colombia	38.6	Colombia	31.0
South Africa	22.2	South Africa	28.6	South Africa	22.1

Chemical Changes		**Forces & Motion**		**Science, Technology & Society**	
Singapore	73.5	Czech Republic	78.1	Korea	74.3
Iran	67.2	**Japan**	**73.6**	Hungary	73.3
Bulgaria	66.6	Singapore	73.4	Netherlands	67.4
Korea	65.9	Netherlands	71.2	Sweden	66.9
Hungary	65.4	Korea	69.6	Singapore	66.4
Austria	65.1	Hong Kong	69.4	Belgium (Fl)	65.2
Czech Republic	64.2	**Switzerland**	**68.8**	New Zealand	60.4
England	63.7	Hungary	68.7	**Japan**	**60.1**
Japan	**63.5**	Slovak Republic	68.4	Thailand	59.2
Australia	61.9	Slovenia	68.4	Ireland	58.2
Russian Federation	61.8	England	67.6	England	57.2
United States	**61.4**	Sweden	67.5	Hong Kong	54.8
Slovak Republic	60.9	Australia	67.2	Scotland	54.6
Ireland	60.8	Norway	67.1	Austria	53.0
Germany	60.7	Canada	66.3	Canada	52.5

Figure 5: continued

Israel	60.6	Germany	66.9	**Switzerland**	**52.5**
Slovenia	60.1	Austria	66.8	Norway	52.1
Canada	59.6	New Zealand	65.6	Czech Republic	51.9
New Zealand	59.4	Belgium (Fl)	65.2	Australia	51.5
Cyprus	59.3	France	63.8	Israel	51.3
Scotland	58.9	Denmark	63.5	Slovenia	50.3
Hong Kong	58.2	Belgium (Fr)	63.3	Iceland	50.1
Spain	58.1	Bulgaria	62.6	Denmark	49.6
Netherlands	57.6	Spain	62.6	International	47.9
Greece	57.2	Lithuania	62.5	**United States**	**47.5**
Sweden	57.1	Ireland	62.2	Germany	47.3
Portugal	56.3	Russian Federation	62.1	Slovak Republic	46.0
International	56.5	**United States**	**61.3**	Bulgaria	44.9
Belgium (Fl)	55.6	International	61.2	Spain	44.1
Switzerland	55.4	Scotland	61.1	Belgium (Fr)	43.6
Norway	53.4	Latvia	59.1	France	42.9
France	52.5	Iceland	57.7	Greece	42.4
Latvia	52.0	Portugal	56.2	Russian Federation	40.4
Thailand	50.9	Israel	54.9	Portugal	33.4
Kuwait	50.4	Thailand	56.4	Kuwait	32.2
Romania	50.3	Romania	53.7	Iran	31.6
Lithuania	50.1	Greece	53.6	Latvia	31.2
Iceland	49.4	Cyprus	46.1	Romania	29.7
Belgium (Fr)	46.8	Iran	45.3	Lithuania	29.6
Denmark	42.5	Colombia	41.7	Cyprus	29.4
Philippines	36.1	Philippines	40.3	Colombia	28.6
Colombia	32.9	Kuwait	39.5	Philippines	22.9
South Africa	29.2	South Africa	30.8	South Africa	12.4

Environmental & Resource Issues		**Scientific Process**	
Singapore	73.1	Singapore	74.6
Thailand	70.1	Korea	64.2
Ireland	67.7	Netherlands	65.2

Figure 5: continued

England	67.2	Slovenia	62.9
Australia	64.7	France	62.2
Netherlands	65.1	Bulgaria	62.1
Korea	62.7	Czech Republic	60.7
Bulgaria	62.1	Australia	60.6
Japan	**61.7**	**Japan**	**60.1**
Canada	61.5	England	60.0
New Zealand	61.4	Canada	59.2
Scotland	60.2	**United States**	**58.9**
United States	**59.9**	Hungary	57.3
Belgium (Fl)	59.7	Hong Kong	57.2
Czech Republic	59.1	Belgium (Fl)	56.9
Spain	58.6	New Zealand	56.7
Norway	58.2	Belgium (Fr)	56.6
Austria	56.6	Slovak Republic	56.3
Slovenia	53.7	Austria	55.4
Hong Kong	53.3	Thailand	55.3
International	53.0	Scotland	54.9
Sweden	51.8	Germany	53.4
Israel	51.6	Latvia	53.2
Greece	51.6	Israel	51.8
Slovak Republic	50.8	**Switzerland**	**53.3**
Switzerland	**50.3**	International	53.1
Germany	50.1	Sweden	52.4
Hungary	49.4	Ireland	52.1
France	48.5	Norway	52.1
Iceland	47.8	Greece	51.8
Colombia	47.4	Russian Federation	51.2
Cyprus	47.3	Spain	49.6
Russian Federation	46.8	Iceland	49.4
Portugal	45.9	Denmark	49.2
Denmark	44.9	Cyprus	48.4
Kuwait	43.1	Portugal	47.6
Romania	41.9	Lithuania	44.3

Figure 5: continued

Latvia	41.9	Romania	42.4
Iran	39.5	Philippines	37.3
Belgium (Fr)	39.2	Kuwait	37.0
Philippines	37.8	Iran	36.2
Lithuania	36.0	Colombia	34.7
South Africa	27.3	South Africa	23.7

Mathematics Topic Areas Related to Science

A similar discussion of achievement in the specific topic areas of mathematics can be found elsewhere (Schmidt, McKnight, Cogan, Jakwerth, & Houang, 1999). We focus here on that part of the mathematics achievement results especially germane to science achievement. Because much of science depends on the appropriate measurement of physical phenomena, the knowledge eighth-grade students possess of measurement topics would be critical for science learning, especially as laboratory experiences become more a part of the curriculum. The worst areas of performance in mathematics for U.S. eighth-grade students relative to the rest of the TIMSS countries were measurement and geometry. The relatively poor performance in measurement included topics other than just measurement units and, therefore, suggested a general weakness in measurement-related knowledge that could have a profound impact on science learning.

The worst areas of performance in mathematics for U.S. eighth-grade students relative to the rest of the TIMSS countries were measurement and geometry.

Curriculum Makes a Difference

A major conclusion to draw from the data presented above is that the fourth- and eighth-grade performances varied depending on the specific content area. U.S. performance was far from monolithic, as was also the case for virtually all other countries. U.S. students performed much better in some areas of science than in others. In fact, in some areas, such as "earth processes" and "earth in the universe," U.S. students were among the top tier of performing countries. In one area at eighth grade, U.S. students were virtually at the top, statistically outperformed by no other country—an area of biology focusing on life cycles and genetics.

The story is simple: U.S. science performance had both strengths and weaknesses. An understanding of the U.S. performance in science demands a more careful examination of these data. This leads to a more sophisticated understanding of the strengths and weaknesses of U.S. curricula and instructional practices. One conclusion is clear from a discussion of these results: curriculum does matter (Schmidt, McKnight, Cogan, Jakwerth, & Houang, 1999). It is difficult to imagine that curriculum does not matter when confronted with data in which no one country dominates performance in all areas of the curriculum and in which a country's performance in one area of the curriculum can be so radically different from its performance in another area. (Bulgaria having the number one ranking in the "structure of matter" but being 36th in the rankings in "physical properties of matter" is a good example.)

The U.S. Science Curriculum

There is no single intellectually coherent vision that dominates U.S. practice in science. We as a nation do not have a coherent view of what we want children to know in science. Why is this remarkable? Because most other nations of the world have such a vision. That vision is reflected in their national standards and curricula. Why is that important? If the vision at the core of the system is coherent, then it can be argued that the system itself has a chance of being coherent. If, on the other hand, the vision is fragmented or splintered, then the system is not likely to be coherent (Schmidt, McKnight, & Raizen, 1997).

A Lack of Focus

The U.S. curriculum lacks serious focus. It tries to cover many more topics each year, compared to the rest of the TIMSS countries. This is not a new idea, as science reformers have long talked about how a pared focus—a "less is more" approach—is needed. What is new is the empirical evidence that actually shows that among the TIMSS nations, the United States stands out in terms of how many topics we expect children to learn in each grade (Schmidt, McKnight, & Raizen, 1997). That is true for the state frameworks that define the official intentions of what children should learn. It is also true for textbooks, and it is true in terms of what is actually taught by teachers in the classroom. U.S. teachers teach more topics than is the case in most of the other TIMSS nations (Schmidt, McKnight, Cogan, Jakwerth, & Houang, 1999).

> *The U.S. curriculum lacks serious focus. It tries to cover many more topics each year, compared to the rest of the TIMSS countries.*

This lack of focus can be illustrated throughr textbooks. Science textbooks from approximately 50 countries were content analyzed line by line (Schmidt, Raizen, Britton, Bianchi, & Wolfe, 1997). Figure 6 (Schmidt, McKnight, & Raizen, 1997) shows the distribution of the number of topics in science textbooks over the sampled countries. There are three grade levels represented. They are the ones that correspond to the TIMSS-tested grades: population one, which is fourth grade in the United States; population two, which is eighth grade; and population three, which in the United States are the 12th-grade students taking advanced physics.

The rectangle in Figure 6 represents the distribution. The 25th percentile and the 75th percentile are the two ends of the rectangle, and the black line in the middle is the 50th percentile. U.S. textbooks have more topics in them than do any other TIMSS

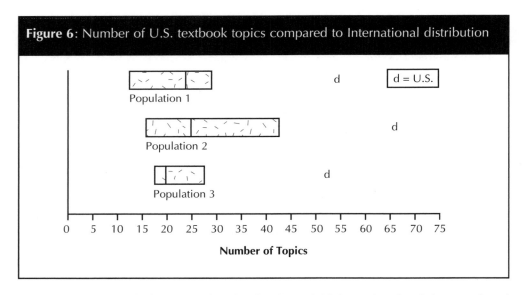

Figure 6: Number of U.S. textbook topics compared to International distribution

country's books. This is true at fourth, eighth, and 12th grade—implying a cultural phenomenon that is not idiosyncratic to a particular grade level or to a particular subject matter (see Schmidt, McKnight, & Raizen, 1997, for an analysis of the mathematics textbooks). To illustrate the magnitude of the difference, at eighth grade approximately 65 topics on average are found in U.S. science books, compared to around the 25 typical of other TIMSS countries.

The U.S. science textbooks analyzed were discipline-specific textbooks. There were earth science books, life science books, and physical science books. A remarkable finding from the content analyses of these books was that the content profile of each book was not restricted to topics defining the discipline used as the title of the book. In fact, these books covered topics from all four of the disciplines (earth science, biology, chemistry, and physics) in spite of the title of the book. U.S. science textbooks resembled general science books, in spite of their titles. They play a major role in the splintering or fragmenting that occurs in U.S. science education. U.S. eighth-grade science textbooks were 700 pages long, hardbound, and resembled encyclopedia volumes. By contrast, most other countries' textbooks were paperbacks with around 200 pages (Valverde, Bianchi, Schmidt, Wolfe, & Wiley, in press).

A Lack of Coherence

The U.S. curriculum is not very coherent. Science is about big ideas—theories that connect facts and integrate ideas even across disciplines. Yet, when one looks at U.S. state frameworks and textbooks, they are like long laundry lists of topics to be covered. Rarely in our analysis of these materials did we find the topics explicitly connected into larger and more coherent wholes. The lack of explicit connections among the major ideas likely impacts how students think about science, but just as importantly, it likely impacts how teachers think about science as a discipline. Teachers in elementary or middle school who do not have strong science backgrounds will view science through those documents. If they are presented with a laundry list, then that is what science is likely to be for them and how they are likely to teach it. They will focus on a collection of topics, teaching them one at a time in an unconnected way. Relatedly, the TIMSS video data revealed that this type of pattern characterized U.S. instruction in eighth-grade mathematics (Stigler, n.d.).

A Lack of Rigor

The last characteristic of the U.S. curriculum has to do with the lack of intellectual rigor, at least as defined internationally. Perhaps here one may find a strong hypothesis as to why the United States' relative performance in science declined from fourth to eighth grade. Causality is very difficult to establish, especially from survey data, but when one looks at the middle school curriculum, a very powerful potential explanation for this drop in U.S. academic performance emerges.

The following empirical definition was used in TIMSS to define an international standard of rigor: If 70 percent of the countries had a particular topic in their curriculum, and it was in their curriculum for all students, then at least internationally the topic was considered basic and fundamental (Schmidt, Raizen, Britton, Bianchi, & Wolfe, 1997).

At fourth grade, what U.S. teachers teach is consistent with the TIMSS notion of basic. The TIMSS international standard was a curriculum focusing on classification—the classification of earth's features, the solar system, animals, plants, and the organs of the body. It also focused on weather. Perhaps this consistency of U.S. instruction to the world standard is related to the strong U.S. performance at fourth grade.

The U.S. curriculum lacked a serious intellectual rigor at eighth grade, as defined by what other countries intended for coverage at their equivalent of U.S. eighth grade.

The middle school curriculum, from an international point of view, shifted to a stronger focus on the physical sciences—chemistry and physics. Biology was also present in many countries, but the topic shift was away from identifying organisms and organs to the biological, physical, and chemical processes underlying the metabolic and other functions of living organisms. U.S. teachers, however, reported teaching many of the same topics that were done in earlier grades, including ecology, environmental science, and the classification of organs, animals, rocks, bodies of water, etc. (Schmidt, McKnight, Cogan, Jakwerth, & Houang, 1999). This may, in part, have reflected those topics with which they were most comfortable. The U.S. curriculum lacked a serious intellectual rigor at eighth grade, as defined by what other countries intended for coverage at their equivalent of U.S. eighth grade.

Teachers and Teaching

In the past, when confronted with the relatively low international rankings of the United States, the nation has often decided that the fault lay with teachers. Yet what the TIMSS results suggested is that teachers are simply doing what they have been asked to do—trying to teach all officially intended topics while being supported by materials that are a "mile wide and an inch deep" (Schmidt, McKnight, & Raizen, 1997, p. 62). The traditional response in the past has been that the way to make U.S. public schools better is to improve the quality of teaching.

What does it mean to improve the quality of teachers or teaching? This political or reform cry has little meaning and has had little success, we have argued, because teachers don't teach, they teach something, and public policy aimed at reform often ignores the "something" by setting policy about the quality of teaching in the abstract and without explicit reference to the content of the curriculum (Schmidt, McKnight, Cogan, Jakwerth, & Houang, 1999). Attempts are made to improve teaching without first addressing the issue of the vision from which instruction derives. One of the implications of TIMSS was that in addressing the issue of teacher quality, it is often approached in a backward fashion, trying to improve teaching without first addressing the "what" of teaching—the subject matter.

The necessary but not sufficient condition for improving science instruction, we argue, is to decide upon a focused, coherent, challenging, and rigorous vision or set of standards. Those standards must clearly articulate what all students at each grade level need to know and to understand conceptually. Additionally, those concerned with education reform must help teachers understand the content undergirding the standards, as well as the ways in which the subject matter can be meaningfully communicated to students so that they can conceptually understand it, solve problems with it, and be able to use theories, principles, and facts derived from it. The latter must, however, proceed from the former.

Teacher Beliefs About Subject Matter
What and how teachers teach are affected by their conceptions of the subject matter disciplines defining science. A typology of teacher beliefs (Schmidt, McKnight, Cogan, Jakwerth, & Houang, 1999) was constructed based on beliefs about the discipline itself and about the discipline as represented in school. What follows are the definitions of these typologies as presented by Schmidt, McKnight, Cogan, Jakwerth, & Houang (1999).

> …[F]our categories were constructed empirically into which teachers could be classified. The first group of teachers might be characterized as discipline-oriented teachers, understanding "discipline" in the sense of subject matter. Teachers in this group took a more formal, as opposed to a real-world, view of their disciplines…. [These teachers] more often indicated that science was essentially abstract, and that the "real world use" of [science] was less important… [T]eachers in this group… more often indicated that creativity was not particularly important in learning science.
>
> The second group might be considered process-oriented teachers. In general, they did not take a formal, abstract view of their discipline, but indicated

that the real-world use of their discipline was important. They also tended to emphasize creativity and to think about [science] more conceptually.

The third group shared most things in common with the first group, but were more concerned with emphasizing the real-world use of [science]. This group is perhaps best characterized as procedure-oriented teachers, concerned with [science] as a discipline, but one that employs useful representations of the real world. These teachers did not hold as consistently a formal view of their discipline as was the case for discipline-oriented teachers.

The fourth group is quite different. They tended to indicate a high level of importance for most things.... They preferred a more formal view of their discipline.... Science teachers in this group did not view creativity as important. Perhaps the most appropriate label for this group is eclectic teachers.... We use "eclectic" in this sense of blending, without distinction, elements of all approaches. They were both somewhat discipline-oriented and somewhat real-world-oriented, but also seemed to favor more conceptual process-oriented approaches in some cases (pp. 82–83).

U.S. science teachers for seventh- and eighth-grade students were distributed among the four categories. Nearly half fell into the category of eclectic teachers. They viewed science formally, but also emphasized the importance of real-world applications and creativity. About half or more of the teachers from Australia, Spain, Singapore, Canada, and Thailand fell into this category.

Less than 10 percent of U.S. 13-year-olds' science teachers (8 percent) fell into the discipline-oriented category. In contrast, about one-third of Japanese, Korean, Dutch, German, Czech, and Belgian (Flemish) 13-year-olds' science teachers fell into this category, as well as around one-fourth to one-third of the teachers in most other TIMSS countries. Only Canada, Spain, and Thailand had less than 10 percent fall into this category like the United States.

Another 20 percent of U.S. science teachers at this level fell into the process-oriented teacher category. In contrast, nearly twice as many (around 40 percent or more) of the French, Swedish, Swiss, and Norwegian science teachers fell into this category, but only around 10 percent of those from Singapore, Hong Kong, and Germany did so.

About 50 percent of U.S. science teachers held a fundamentally formal approach to science as it was to be presented in school (defined as the discipline-oriented and eclectic teachers combined). The United States was not alone in its teachers' orientation to formal discipline, as Japan was very similar (58 percent). Others, such as Singapore, Hong Kong, Australia, Israel, Germany, and Thailand, had 60 percent or more of their counterparts who shared similar views. The similarity between the U.S. and Japanese teachers ended, however, at this global level. The largest proportion of both Japanese mathematics and science teachers fell into the discipline-oriented category. Nearly one-half of U.S. seventh- and eighth-grade mathematics and science teachers were in the category of eclectic teachers. Fewer than 25 percent of either science or mathematics teachers in Japan were in the eclectic category that also emphasized a formal view of the discipline.

We propose that a teacher's understanding and conception of subject matter is one of the major aspects that defines teacher quality. A country can have a rigorous and challenging curriculum, supported by materials providing good pedagogy, but if the teacher does not understand the science content, it is very difficult for the instruction to be good instruction. On the other hand, we argue that teachers with a strong subject matter background will find it similarly difficult to provide good instruction in a country that lacks a well-defined, rigorous, and challenging curriculum.

The science reform movements articulated by the American Association for the Advancement of Science and the National Academy of Sciences encourage the development of conceptual understanding and involvement in empirical data collection, including the design of such studies and the associated analyses. What happens when such an approach is given to teachers whose background in science content is weak, we hypothesize, is a separation of content and pedagogy (or the associated processes). Such teachers do not understand the science content, but they believe they understand the processes or the pedagogy. The false dichotomization (false, because this is not the design or intention of the reform) and the suppression of the science content creates a set of instructional activities that has children engaged in "neutered" processes, e.g. doing such things as cooperative learning or manipulating physical objects void of real science content. When such processes are separated from the science content, the activities appear to be inane to parents, and their frustration with schools mounts because their children are not learning science. This then creates the functional equivalent of "fuzzy mathematics." The biggest challenge for science reform efforts is to develop a process by which teachers may develop the subject matter knowledge needed to support the standards so they can implement both aspects of current science reform—that is, meaningful science content presented in challenging ways that engage students not only in the factual aspects of science but also at the more meaningful conceptual and problem-solving level. The key is that the conceptual problem-solving aspect, together with the attendant pedagogical approaches, must be imbedded in real science content.

> *A country can have a rigorous and challenging curriculum, supported by materials providing good pedagogy, but if the teacher does not understand the science content, it is very difficult for the instruction to be good instruction.*

Professional Development

We have argued that content knowledge is a critical component in the definition of teacher quality. We further argued that content is critical to defining quality instruction. First, the vision that guides the educational system should provide a focused, coherent, and intellectually rigorous set of standards (including both content and

performance expectations). Such standards are the necessary condition that provides a context that supports quality
instruction. Without such a focused and coherent definition,
U.S. teachers continue to cope with a system guided by a
splintered vision and supported by "mile-wide-inch-deep"
textbooks, themselves the product of an incoherent system.
This argues that effective teaching must be viewed and ad-
dressed in a systemic context. The call for a national consensus as a means of articu-
lating a coherent vision then should be viewed as addressing quality teaching as
well.

Content knowledge is a critical component in the definition of teacher quality.

The second way in which content is critical is as a component of teacher quality and
relates to the content knowledge possessed by the teacher. A clearly articulated and
challenging set of standards can only set the expectations and provide a coherent context. The delivery of the instruction is accomplished through the teachers' knowledge
and understanding of the subject matter. Thus, both aspects of content are critical to the
definition of instructional quality—one defining the context in which it is delivered
and the other influencing the delivery itself.

Implied by TIMSS and supported elsewhere is the reality that many teachers,
especially in the elementary and middle grades, do not have strong science backgrounds. Given the argument made in the previous paragraphs, the development of a
coherent set of standards is not enough. Something must be done to ensure a stronger
subject matter knowledge on the part of teachers. The long-term solution may be
certification requirements that are more stringent in terms of subject matter preparation and the corresponding requirements at the university level in terms of teacher
preparation.

Even under such ideal conditions, and especially in the current context, this will
not be adequate to address the content aspect of instructional delivery. It is here that
professional development becomes critically important. But given the expanded definition above of teacher quality, which includes not only pedagogical skills but also
content knowledge, this implies the need for an expanded conception of professional
development, one that focuses more attention on helping teachers acquire the subject
matter knowledge associated with the curriculum standards applicable to the grade
in which each teacher is teaching. Coupled with that preparation is the topic-specific
pedagogy that enables teachers to bring the content to the students in a meaningful
and engaging way that fosters both a deep and rich conceptual understanding that
engenders scientific reasoning, theorizing, and problem solving, as well as factual
and algorithmic knowledge.

Generic pedagogy (i.e., instructional practices not imbedded in science content),
such as the use of manipulatives or cooperative learning, often the topic of current
professional development in the United States, is not what is needed. If content is an
important part of quality instruction and if teachers often lack such content specific
knowledge, then professional development should be geared to facilitate such an ac-

quisition and bridge the gap. Here again the systemic nature of professional development is clear. Such professional development is really possible only if the content goals or standards are common to the teachers for whom the professional development is intended, for example, all sixth grade teachers in a district, state, region, or nation. This, of course, is realistic only in the presence of clearly articulated standards.

So the systemic nature of teacher quality and the means of enhancing it—professional development—are dependent on a coherent vision, or set of standards and the corresponding curricular materials and assessments that are aligned with it. It may or may not take a village to raise a child, but it clearly takes a village to enhance quality teaching and, through this, to educate a child.

References

Beaton, A. E., M. O. Martin, I. Mullis, E. J. Gonzalez, T. A. Smith, and D. L. Kelly. 1996. *Mathematics Achievement in the Middle School Years: IEA's Third International Mathematics and Science Study.* Chestnut Hill, MA: Center for the Study of Testing, Evaluation, and Educational Policy, Boston College.

Beaton, A. E., M. O. Martin, I. Mullis, E. J. Gonzalez, T. A. Smith, and D. L. Kelly. 1996. *Science Achievement in the Middle School Years: IEA's Third International Mathematics and Science Study.* Chestnut Hill, MA: Center for the Study of Testing, Evaluation, and Educational Policy, Boston College.

National Center for Education Statistics (NCES). 1996. *Pursuing Excellence: A Study of U.S. Eighth-Grade Mathematics and Science Teaching, Learning, Curriculum, and Achievement in International Context* (NCES 97-198). Washington D.C.: U.S. Department of Education. National Center for Education Statistics.

———. 1997. *Pursuing Excellence: A Study of U.S. Fourth-Grade Mathematics and Science Achievement in International Context* (NCES 97-255). Washington D.C.: U.S. Department of Education. National Center for Education Statistics.

———. 1998. *Pursuing Excellence: A Study of U.S. Twelfth-Grade Mathematics and Science Achievement in International Context* (NCES 98-049). Washington D.C.: U.S. Department of Education. National Center for Education Statistics.

Schmidt, W. H., P. M. Jakwerth, and C. C. McKnight. 1998. Curriculum-sensitive assessment: Content *does* make a difference. *International Journal of Educational Research* 29:503–527.

Schmidt, W. H., C. McKnight, L. S. Cogan, P. M. Jakwerth, and R. T. Houang. 1999. *Facing the Consequences: Using TIMSS for a Closer Look at US Mathematics and Science Education.* Dordrecht/Boston/London: Kluwer.

Schmidt, W. H., C. McKnight, and S. Raizen. 1997. *A Splintered Vision: An Investigation of U.S. Science and Mathematics Education.* Dordrecht/Boston/London: Kluwer.

Schmidt, W. H., and C. C. McKnight. 1995. Surveying educational opportunity in mathematics and science: An international perspective. *Educational Evaluation and Policy Analysis,* 17(4):337–353.

Schmidt, W. H., S. A. Raizen, E. D. Britton, L. J. Bianchi, and R. G. Wolfe. 1997. *Many Visions, Many Aims, Volume II: A Cross-National Investigation of Curricular Intentions in School Science.* Dordrecht/Boston/London: Kluwer.

Stigler, J., et al. (in preparation). *The TIMSS Classroom Videotape Study.* Washington, DC: U.S. Department of Education. National Center for Education Statistics.

Valverde, G. A., L. J. Bianchi, W. H. Schmidt, R. G. Wolfe, and D. E. Wiley. (in press). *Structure and pedagogy of textbooks.* Dordrecht/Boston/London: Kluwer.

The Teacher Speaks: Using Achievement Data to Modify Teaching Practice

Judy K. Sink

Judy K. Sink is an elementary teacher at Hardin Park School in Boone, North Carolina. She also teaches a science lab for pre-service teachers at Appalachian State University. Judy is a National Board Certified Teacher in the Early Child Generalist area. She is a Presidential Award Winner for Elementary Science Teaching and an Albert Einstein Outstanding Educator. She was a member of the Committee to Develop the National Science Education Standards.

Such has been written during the last decade about the need for change in the teaching and learning of science. The role of the teacher has become one of facilitating instruction through careful preparation of a learning environment that encourages real inquiry and offers quality opportunities for students to engage in meaningful science learning. The emphasis has changed to students gaining an understanding of scientific concepts and being able to apply their knowledge and understanding in new situations and in the real world.

This paradigm shift in our thinking regarding the teaching and learning of science has brought the need for new and better methods of assessment that can truly show us what students know and can do in science. We have *National Science Education Standards* to guide us as we begin to evaluate our existing science programs. The *Standards* provide a road map that can assist us as we move toward the vision of what a good science program can and should be for students. So what does this mean for the classroom teacher? How does one come to understand this new role in teaching as presented in the *Standards*? What is the role of assessment and how can we determine what students know and can do in science? How can student achievement data assist the teacher in modifying teaching practice? What is the role of professional development in this process? These are a few of the questions that I hope to discuss in this writing.

First, I wish to describe my own professional growth as an elementary teacher, and how my own practice changed because of what I came to believe about the teaching and learning of science. Perhaps my experiences will assist others who teach children, as well as those who teach teachers. I tell the interns and student teachers with whom I work that a degree in education is merely preparation to enter the teaching profession. I am explicit in telling them that good teachers evolve over a lifetime and that their journey in this process is one that never really ends until they cease to be a teacher.

It took me many years, a multitude of people (including my students), and many diverse experiences to get to where I am now. I still have a long way to go, but my excitement for teaching grows every year with each new group of students assigned to my care. Additionally, I find that the more I learn along the way, the better prepared I become in meeting the challenges of the classroom today.

For me, the greatest change in my teaching has been in the area of science. Perhaps it is because this is where I had the greatest need for change. I used to be one of those teachers who read the chapter, discussed its content with students, and assigned the questions at the end of the chapter. Occasionally we did an experiment, step by step, as directed by the textbook. I ended the chapter by giving a test to find out what my students had been able to retain—not what they understood or could do. I cannot assume all the responsibility for this ineffective teaching or the lack of meaningful learning on the part of my students. This approach is what had been modeled for me as a student in elementary, junior high, and senior high school, and even in my instructional methods classes in college. We tend to teach how we were taught, and that is what I did.

For me, the greatest change in my teaching has been in the area of science. Perhaps it is because this is where I had the greatest need for change.

It was later in my teaching career—and due, in part, to effective professional development that modeled hands-on experiential teaching—that I risked taking my first steps toward constructivist science teaching. The first step was being willing to take the risk, because I believed that my students could learn best by doing science. I began to discover the power of providing quality opportunities for children to engage in scientific inquiry. It became clear to me that children want and need to understand how their world works. I learned that experiential science is the hook that grabs their attention and nurtures the natural curiosity that they so enthusiastically bring with them to school every day. I then began to seek ways to teach more effectively and more efficiently by using science as the content through which I could integrate the basic skills of reading, writing, and mathematics. It is the science content that excites children and motivates them to write about their experiences. Their innate curiosity motivates them to read books to find out more about an idea or a concept they are exploring. I have seen young children spend endless hours searching through books and periodicals, determined to find out more about a concept experienced first-hand through scientific investigation. I know of many times when young children could scarcely wait to write about what happened during a science experiment, to draw a sequence of pictures to communicate observations, and then to share them with other students.

Two Challenges

My first challenge for those who conduct professional development, then, is to turn teachers onto science—to excite them to value science learning by engaging them in quality opportunities that model experiential teaching and constructivist learning. One cannot simply tell teachers about the importance of science learning or that science is best learned through a constructivist approach: They must experience for themselves the excitement and wonder of learning new things. By becoming the learner and constructing their own understanding of scientific phenomena, teachers can begin to value such learning for children and can begin to understand this new role of teachers as facilitators of instruction. Professional development must begin where teachers are. They must first experience and embrace this new way of teaching and learning science before they are open to changing their practice.

I participated in a very effective two-week professional development institute for teachers in environmental education. The staff consisted of university professors who assisted with the content knowledge and teacher consultants who worked with participants, shared their expertise, and served as group leaders during peer teaching sessions. We spent part of the two weeks in classroom discussion, but many days were packed with field experiences with teachers actually doing science. For example, teachers spent one day participating in a field and stream experience with participants making observations, collecting data, and doing the kinds of investigations they could later do with students in their classes. Teachers worked in pairs, collecting and describing water samples; measuring the temperature of the stream water; measuring the width and depth of the stream in various locations; and observing, describing, and comparing the organisms found in the stream. During the afternoon, teachers explored a heavily wooded site looking for and comparing organisms within habitats, making rubbings of a variety of textured materials, measuring and comparing shadows at various times of the day, and graphing the kinds of ferns found in the area. The following day, participants returned to the classroom and used the data collected on Venn diagrams to write a comparison of two organisms found in the field or stream. Questions during the sharing of their writings led to additional small group work to find answers. These teachers were engaged in inquiry and meaningful science learning. Their enthusiasm, comments, and evaluations made it clear that they would offer similar opportunities to their students.

Professional development must begin where teachers are. They must first experience and embrace this new way of teaching and learning science before they are open to changing their practice.

Such professional development takes time and cannot be achieved in a few short sessions. Additionally, teachers must feel supported as they risk changing their practice. They must be encouraged to "hang in there," especially when they become discouraged and frustrated. They need immediate support and feedback, whether it comes from another teacher or an administrator. They need to feel that they are not alone in this process of teaching and implementing change.

This brings me to my second challenge for professional development—inclusion of administrators. Administrators must know and understand how science teaching is changing and be able to recognize and value scientific inquiry when they see it. They, too, must be partners in the teaching and learning process by helping to locate necessary resources and providing teachers with the planning time needed for quality science instruction.

Administrators must know and understand how science teaching is changing and be able to recognize and value scientific inquiry when they see it.

Several years ago, I was involved in planning staff development for middle school teachers to learn how to use LEGO Dacta to teach problem solving and critical thinking. Because of the cost of such a program to a school and the need for teacher support, each participating school was required to send a team consisting of a teacher, a student, a parent, and an administrator. Each team worked together to build their "machine" and then programmed their computer to operate it. The dynamics were amazing as the team members worked together to determine why their machine would not operate according to their plan. Through a process of sharing ideas, they revised their plan and tested it. It was obvious that the teams were eager to implement the new program in their schools. Teams were then asked to meet to develop an implementation plan. After six weeks, a follow-up session brought them back to share the results. Parents had not only used their new skills to volunteer their assistance in the classroom with this new program, but they had been successful in seeking additional funding from PTA and civic groups to purchase more materials. Likewise, administrators volunteered their time with students and, whenever possible, had arranged for changes in scheduling for teachers who needed additional planning and computer time for program implementation. Students attending the training had served as peer teachers, thus freeing the teacher to work with groups needing special assistance. Additionally, parents experienced the importance of critical thinking and problem solving in science learning.

The Role of Assessment

Let us assume that all teachers value experiential science and are willing to take initial steps toward constructivist teaching. They have a strong, developmentally appropriate curriculum with a clear, constructivist philosophy. Let us also assume that because they have the support of administrators and parents, they have the time for planning and the necessary resources they need to embark on this exciting journey in science teaching. Where and how do they begin? How will they know what their students learn and can do as a result of their school science program? Where and how does assessment fit into an inquiry-based science program?

As my own skills grew in constructivist teaching, I became increasingly aware of the need for change in how I assess student learning in science. I began to see the need to begin instruction with assessment in order to gain a clearer understanding of what my students know and understand (or don't understand) before I begin to plan for their learning. For example, my students spend the better part of a semester learning about life cycles. We begin this in-depth study by investigating plants and seeds and later move on to different kinds of organisms. Before I begin to plan for their instruction, we gather as a class and I ask them to tell me what they know about seeds. They enthusiastically volunteer answers to my question. Usually, they tell me that seeds have different shapes, sizes, and textures and that seeds grow and need certain things, such as water, soil, and sun. Together we make a chart listing everything they know about seeds, including any misconceptions that they might have. I make no value judgments; I simply add their statements to our chart. I know that we will revisit this chart often as we learn about seeds, always checking to see if what we found out supports what we thought we knew. As we discuss, sometimes one student will challenge the thinking of a peer; sometimes, a child will express disbelief in what another child says. I encourage challenge and skepticism because from such interaction, I can determine which of my second-graders are developing scientific attitudes and dispositions. I can also assess what my children know before I start to plan specifically for their instruction, as well as any misconceptions that must be addressed. This information is invaluable as a tool in planning for science learning.

As my own skills grew in constructivist teaching, I became increasingly aware of the need for change in how I assess student learning in science.

My next step is to ask students what they want to find out about seeds. Here, the sky is the limit. They usually want to know if seeds can grow without water or soil. Sometimes they want to know the biggest seed and the smallest. They may want to know if all seeds will grow or how they will change. Such questions shape my teaching by providing me with questions students want to have answered—insights into their interests. These questions may later provide inquiries for small-group planning of investigations to find answers. I also can make decisions about how I might group children for small-group work.

When to Assess

Assessment prior to instruction is essential. Not only does it help me to plan for instructional needs, but it saves valuable time. I do not need to teach those things that students already know and understand. I like doing this as a whole-group activity, because I can observe group dynamics and social interactions. Also, one child's thinking might stimulate and challenge that of another child. Sometimes a shyer student will be stimulated to contribute. In my classroom, we applaud risk taking. I work hard to establish a climate that says it is okay to answer without fear of saying the wrong thing.

I have learned that assessment must also occur on a daily basis if I am truly to plan for children's learning and to build on prior understanding. This does not mean that I formally assess children's learning every day. Rather, I use a variety of methods to gain insights into what they know and can do at that particular time before I plan how and in what direction I must proceed. Teacher observations, student journal entries, scientific data collections (such as charts, graphs and diagrams), small-group discussions, student-designed models, reports, and student drawings are all ways to check into student understanding and provide valuable insights in planning for future learning.

It is student achievement data that guides me in making decisions about when my students are ready to move on to a new concept.

For example, after my class investigated plant parts to find seeds, students planted the seeds, tracked their growth, and observed the germination and development of roots, stems, leaves, and tendrils. Students then experimented to find answers to their inquiries. Later, we applied what we had learned by planting a raised garden bed just outside our classroom. The children planned what seeds they would plant and brought in a variety of seed packets from home. After we examined the seed packets, noting the kinds of information we could learn about planting the seeds, I planned an art integration project by having students create their own seed packets. I provided them materials, and they eagerly drew plants on their seed packets depicting the kind of seed inside and writing directions for planting the seeds. It was my plan to display these on a bulletin board outside our classroom. When the children finished, I mounted the packets on construction paper. I read their directions as a quick check on writing progress and to assess their knowledge of planting seeds. The colorful drawings on the packets indicated that several of the children had chosen beets, carrots, and radishes growing in a garden similar to the one we had planted. However, the carrots, beets, and radishes were growing on top of the soil, rather than under the ground. Then I realized many of the children did not understand how these plants grow. They did not understand that a carrot, for example, is a root that we eat. I modified my plans for the next day to provide time for students to plant carrots, radishes, and beets in our garden. Once these seeds germinated, my students would track their growth and begin to replace their misconceptions with more accurate scientific information. Sometimes achievement data comes in a variety of packages and takes us by surprise. We simply have to be open to recognize it when we least expect to see it.

I want to emphasize the importance of ongoing assessment. It is student achievement data that guides me in making decisions about when my students are ready to move on to a new concept. That does not mean that learning is concluded, for there will be many times throughout the remainder of the year when as a class we will revisit prior learning—applying, integrating, and making connections to new concepts.

What to Assess

Much of what I have read about assessment discusses the need to assess that which we value. I value the following things, but not necessarily in the order I am listing them.

First, I value content knowledge and understanding. Content is important. After all, we cannot ask children to process nothing. Content is probably the easiest to assess. If I ask a short-answer question, I usually ask children to explain their answer, or to tell me how they know what they know. This way I can assess not only children's ability to think and reason, but also their ability to communicate their thinking. Additionally, I can gauge whether or not a child is learning to rely on data to verify scientific explanations. For young children who have not yet developed good writing skills, I often do interviews, asking questions and seeking explanations to gain insights into a child's thinking and understanding.

For example, once I asked students to use a Venn diagram to record objects that sink or float. In their trials, they learned that some objects do both depending on how they place them in the water. They recorded these objects in the intersecting lines of the circles. Kenny, a special needs child with writing skills far below grade level, could not accomplish this task. In his persistence to record his findings, he drew a picture of each object, being careful to draw them in the correct location on the Venn diagram. He clearly understood the concept, and I observed his strong determination to find a way to communicate his findings.

The second area that I value in assessment is process. Process is very important to me because this informs my instruction as I learn what a child can actually do. For example, I spend a great deal of time planning for instruction in measurement at the beginning of the year. I maintain a measurement center throughout the year with changing tasks for students to do during center time. Measurement tools are always available in this center for students to use on their own. Not only do students learn how to measure length, weight, volume, and temperature, but also they learn which tools to use and how to use them appropriately. Exact measurements are of less importance than correct process.

Teacher observations and notes in student portfolios concerning progress in measurement are ongoing throughout the year. Such data helps me to plan for those students who need particular help in one or more areas. Once students have had sufficient experience in measuring, I administer a performance assessment to find out what each child knows and can do. One task is to measure the temperature of a liquid in a cup. As the student performs the task, I observe carefully and gather data according to the clearly defined rubrics that I have developed for this task. As I develop the rubrics, I must first determine what it is that I want the child to know and be able to do. Then I divide the task into the various steps through which the student must progress to demonstrate competence. For example, the student scores a one for selecting the thermometer for measuring temperature. The student scores a two for placing it in the liquid correctly and allowing sufficient time for the alcohol to stop moving in the thermometer. If the child continues to hold the thermometer in the liquid while reading the temperature, then a score of three is given. Finally, if the child reads the temperature correctly, allowing a range of plus or minus two degrees as a correct answer, a score of four is given. So a child can actually miss the reading on the thermometer by three or

Although formal assessments provide valuable information about student learning, informal observations of my students often provide even greater insight into student understanding of the concept.

more degrees and still get a score of three out of four for the correct choice of a tool and the correct process. If I find that a significant number of my students are having difficulty with a particular portion of the task, then perhaps I did not thoroughly or effectively teach the skill or concept. I then revise my plans and take a modified approach to teaching the skill or concept in a different way. If I find just a few students with the same difficulty in completing a task, then I plan for the small group to have additional experience to acquire the skill or to understand the concept.

I use the same process assessment for measuring weight, volume, and length with different rubrics used for each task. When I have finished, I have a clear picture of what each student can do and how I must proceed in planning for specific needs.

A third area that I value in assessing science learning is that of the child's ability to apply his or her understanding of a concept learned. In my classroom, I sometimes do this by a formal assessment and sometimes by a more informal teacher observation. In the concept and process of measuring weight, a formal assessment might take the form of the previously mentioned task of finding weight. Although formal assessments provide valuable information about student learning, informal observations of my students often provide even greater insight into student understanding of the concept. The following example will explain why I believe this to be true.

One day Katie brought her hamster to school to show during our morning sharing time. It also happened that I had a furry teddy bear hamster named Edison in our classroom animal center, cared for by the children on a daily basis. Katie eloquently detailed how she had acquired her new hamster, how she had decided on a name for it, and the kind of care the hamster required. Later that same day, some of the children were crowded around Katie and her hamster during center time. One of the children asked which hamster would have more weight—the one belonging to Katie, or Edison, the classroom pet. After a brief argument, one of the children suggested that Edison weighed more because he looked bigger than Katie's hamster. Another child argued that Katie's hamster would have more weight, because Edison was a different kind of hamster with longer, fuzzier hair that only made him appear to weigh more. After a few minutes of heated discussion, Katie marched over to the measurement center, located the scales, and placed her hamster in one of the balance pans. Kevin, who was holding Edison, quickly placed him in the other pan. The children watched as the pan with Katie's hamster lowered. "There," several of them shouted. "We were right! Katie's hamster weighs more." "How much more?" asked another child. Katie picked up a paper clip and began to add one at a time to Edison's pan until both pans balanced. Then she carefully removed the last paper clip she had added, checking to see if the pans were more balanced with or without the final paper clip. She made her decision and placed it back in the pan. "About eight paper clips," she announced. "That's about eight grams."

I watched in amazement from my desk, scribbling a few notes in Katie's portfolio. I clearly could see that she understood how to weigh objects and when it was appropriate to do so. I could see that she understood how to use the balance scales to compare the weight of one thing with another. Katie also remembered that we had begun measuring weight by using nonstandard, uniform weights and that a paper clip weighed about one gram. When asked how much more her hamster weighed than Edison weighed, she knew how to add weights to the lighter pan until both pans were balanced. A teacher must always be open to opportunities to assess student learning. I used what I learned about Katie's understanding of measuring weight to place her in a small group as a peer helper to other students having difficulty with this concept.

Sometimes my assessment of student application of knowledge is more formal and planned. For example, the first half of the year my students study interaction and systems. One of the concepts they investigate is electrical interaction. In groups of two, they construct electric circuits and identify the evidence of interaction within the circuit. They build on this understanding as they investigate open and closed circuits and identify various objects that can close the circuit. To assess their understanding I ask each child individually to choose what they need from the materials provided and to construct a closed circuit. Once they have successfully constructed their circuit, I ask them how they know the circuit is closed. They generally identify the movement and hum of the motor, or the lighted bulb, depending on which objects they chose from those provided. I use the same procedure to see if they can demonstrate an open circuit. I then give them a bag containing a variety of objects and ask them to test the objects and place them in two piles—objects that can close the circuit and those that cannot. One of the objects for testing is a clothespin made of both wood and metal. Some children test the clothespin by touching the wood or the metal and then placing it in one of the two groups. Other children will test it both ways, first using the metal and then the wood. They announce to me that it can close the circuit depending on how you test it, because it is made of two different materials— wood and metal. I can clearly see that these children show persistence in their investigations and the ability to think and reason based upon evidence.

This brings me to the fourth area that I value and attempt to assess in children's science learning—attitudes toward science and the development of scientific attitudes and dispositions. Through careful observations, I can gather data to help me determine if a child shows interest in voluntarily undertaking science activities beyond his or her day at school. Every morning we begin the day with an opportunity for sharing something new or noteworthy. Often items brought in for sharing include a rock collected from a special (or not-so-special) place, a feather found outside while playing, or an insect in some form of its life cycle. Occasionally, children bring or tell about a salamander, a frog or toad, a science picture from a recently read book, a science program watched on television, or an article from the newspaper. Then I know that they are keen observers and that their interest extends beyond the classroom. I celebrate their skepticism when I do a discrepant event and then challenge them to ask yes-or-no questions of me until they can figure out what happened. As they do so, I can clearly see those who persist in asking questions until they arrive at a reasonable explanation. I can also observe creative thinking and students' abilities to make scientific inferences. It matters to me when students collect data and I see them explain their findings based on observations and the data they have gathered. By using a simple checklist, I can quickly note when a child has exhibited one or more of these attitudes. I can track students who have poor social skills and continually have difficulty working with a partner or with a small group. I then modify instruction by offering more opportunities for those children to work in small groups, to share materials, and to collaborate in their investigations. I may even arrange for a student to work alone or with just one other child until social skills have improved.

Assessment Embedded in Teaching

How then can professional development help teachers to learn how to use student achievement data to modify teaching practices? Let's assume once again that teachers value providing the kind of opportunities for science learning outlined in the *National Science Education Standards* and that they have taken the initial steps toward the kind of science teaching called for in the *Standards*. We are now ready to move forward in helping them to understand that assessment and teaching are so closely tied together that they are inseparable. We must begin with where teachers are: What do they know and believe about the teaching and learning of science? Are they ready to take beginning steps toward this new way of teaching science? If so, then we must begin to look at assessment practices as a critical part of teaching.

Many elementary teachers are generalists, and because they teach all subjects, their knowledge base is more general rather than specific. They are often afraid to teach science for fear of not knowing enough content. Often they come into the classroom without the preparation and self-confidence they need to teach science. Perhaps their student teaching experience did not offer many opportunities to observe or to model effective strategies in teaching science. A strength that many elementary teachers bring to the classroom is that of knowing their students and understanding their students' development. For me, the beauty of elementary teaching lies in being able to plan for the child's total educational needs. I can nurture a child's strengths while helping him or her to overcome weaknesses. A classroom is a community of learners. The learner and teacher share the responsibility for learning. I can integrate learning and help children use new skills and make connections between content areas, and relate their knowledge and understanding to the real world. For example, when my students eagerly harvest lettuce, radishes, and onions from the garden they have planted to make a tossed salad, they understand the value of learning about plant life cycles and how it is useful to them in real life.

My own professional growth has come from a variety of sources. The most meaningful growth has not come through the kind of workshops that teachers like most to attend—workshops filled with a variety of activities to do on Monday morning. We will never realize the *Standards* with fun activities that simply fill the day. Meaningful science learning comes through carefully planned, developmentally appropriate instruction that provides for in-depth learning of fewer concepts. Such learning should be coupled with appropriate assessment that measures what we value most—a child's understanding of content, a child's ability to do science, and a child's understanding of how to make a new application of a concept on his or her own. Teachers must learn that assessment is a critical part of the teaching process; it is ongoing and extremely important to one's ability to plan effectively for each day's science learning.

Meaningful science learning comes through carefully planned, developmentally appropriate instruction that provides for in-depth learning of fewer concepts.

Final Challenge

The greatest challenge, in my opinion, for those doing professional development of teachers is to engage teachers in the same inquiry-based, experiential learning process as that of our students—to get them hooked on science. Only then will they take that first step toward constructivist teaching. The second step will lead them to consider the effectiveness and efficiency of integrating the skills of reading, writing, and mathematics into the teaching of science concepts. In some states, this will be more difficult than in others. Some states have identified science as basic to children's education and expect teachers to teach science on a regular basis to all students. Other states have placed educational priorities on reading, writing, and mathematics and (perhaps, unknowingly) have allowed science and social studies to suffer. Science end-of-course testing has been eliminated in some schools, and teachers are not held accountable for science learning in the same way they are held accountable for other curriculum areas. I was pleased to discover that the National Board for Professional Teaching Standards has placed a high priority on science teaching and learning by making it a part of certification as an Early Childhood Generalist and Middle Childhood Generalist.

In summary, all teachers must come to value science and experience the power of inquiry in motivating children to learn. Teachers can learn to integrate the skills of reading, writing, and mathematics with science content and process for efficient teaching that truly maximizes students' learning. Teaching and assessment are inseparable. We should use appropriate assessment to measure what we value in science—content, process, application, and scientific attitudes and dispositions. Assessment strengthens teaching when used as a tool for planning for science learning. Teachers need ongoing professional development that allows them to build on their content knowledge. Additionally, professional development must model for teachers how to teach and assess science. There must be continual follow-up, along with administrative and community support. Teachers must have the time to collaborate with each other as they begin to change their practice. Only then will our nation's classrooms reflect the vision of the *National Science Education Standards*.

Guided Index

Issues in Science Education: Professional Development Planning & Design													
		Issue Matrix (see numbered descriptions below)											
Chapter	First Author	1	2	3	4	5	6	7	8	9	10	11
1	Bybee, R.		x	x				x		x	x	x
2	Loucks-Horsley, S.		x	x						x		
3	Lederman, N.		x	x						x		
4	Gilbert, S.		x		x			x		x		
5	Collins, A.							x		x		
6	Gadsden, T.	x								x		
7	Texley, J.		x		x			x		x		
8	Gess-Newsome, J.		x	x				x		x		
9	Kahle, J.		x	x			x	x	x	x		
10	Keurbis, P.		x	x		x		x	x		x	x
11	Jorgensen, M.		x					x	x			
12	Schmidt, W.								x		x	
13	Sink, J.			x	x	x		x				

1. **Online learning**

    A variety of new online delivery methods are available for professional development. They allow presentation to diverse audiences, provide resources beyond the range of any program planner, and are easily accessible. As in all delivery methods, there are good and bad ways to use online instruction. For discussion of the variety and use of online learning methods, see:

    Gadsden, T. & Roempler, K.S., pp. 69–80.

2. **Teaching techniques in professional development**

As in teaching students, working with educators can benefit from proven techniques in accomplishing learning goals. Engaging teachers in inquiry and building instruction around assessment are a few methods described in this book. As you plan a professional development program, refer to the following chapters:

Bybee, R. W. & S. Loucks-Horsley, pp. 1–12.
Gess-Newsome, J., pp. 91–100.
Gilbert, S., pp. 43–58.
Jorgensen, M., pp. 123–140.
Kahle, J. B. & Kelly, M. K., pp. 101–114.
Keurbis, P., & Kester, K., pp. 115–122.
Lederman, N., Abd-El, Khalick, F., & Bell, R. L., pp. 25–42.
Loucks-Horsley, S., & Stiles, K. E., pp. 13–24.
Texley, J., pp. 81–90.

3. **Building a professional development program**

There may be a range of goals and outcomes you are planning in any level of professional development program. The following chapters offer insight into program design:

Bybee, R. W. & S. Loucks-Horsley, pp. 1–12.
Gess-Newsome, J., pp. 91–100.
Kahle, J. B. & Kelly, M. K., pp. 101–114.
Keurbis, P., & Kester, K., pp. 115–122.
Lederman, N., Abd-El, Khalick, F., & Bell, R. L., pp. 25–42.
Loucks-Horsley, S., & Stiles, K. E., pp. 13–24.
Sink, J., pp. 167–178.

4. **Motivation**

Students at every age learn better when they are in charge of their own learning. Motivational methods for professional development include such topics as constructivist processes and leadership development. See:

Gilbert, S., pp. 43–58.
Sink, J., pp. 167–178.
Texley, J., pp 81–90.

5. **Community Collaboration**

Successful school programs often benefit from community resources beyond the school, and professional development programs are no exception. Applying for grants, using informal science learning centers, tapping local cultural resources, and adopting systemic initiative strategies are a few methods described here. See chapters:

Kuerbis, P., & Kester, K., pp. 115–122.
Sink, J., pp. 167–178.

6. **Equity/Diversity Issues**

It is critical that we provide quality science education for all students in order to ensure a viable workforce and to meet the demands of society in the future. To do so, those who are currently underrepresented in those fields—women and minorities—must participate in greater numbers. For various ways professional development can help meet these needs, see chapters:

Kahle, J. B. & Kelly, M. K., pp. 101–114.

7. **Promoting Change**

Change is very difficult for most people, but it is essential if we are to have hope of meeting the recommendations found in reform documents. The change process can be facilitated in a number of ways through professional development. See the following chapters:

Bybee, R. W. & S. Loucks-Horsley, pp. 1–12.
Collins, A., pp. 59–68.
Gess-Newsome, J., pp. 91–100.
Gilbert, S., pp. 43–58.
Jorgensen, M., pp. 123–140.
Kahle, J. B. & Kelly, M. K., pp. 101–114.
Keurbis, P., & Kester, K., pp. 115–122.
Sink, J., pp. 167–178.
Texley, J., pp. 81–90.

8. **Assessment and Evaluation**

Since the United States Department of Education issued *A Nation at Risk* in 1983, numerous reform efforts have emerged to try to remedy the problems outlined in the report. The issue of whether these efforts have made a difference in student learning and teacher practice has been the topic of much of the recent research in science education. For a review of assessment and/or evaluation of professional development in the reform era, see:

Jorgensen, M., pp. 123–140.
Kahle, J. B. & Kelly, M. K., pp. 101–114.
Keurbis, P., & Kester, K., pp. 115–122.
Schmidt, W. H., pp. 141–166.

9. **Reform**

An in-depth understanding of the current reform efforts is essential if programs and curricula are to be aligned with them. Reform documents outline such topics as what students should know and understand at various grade levels, teaching, content, assessment, and professional development. See the following chapters for information on the nature of science and these documents in general:

Bybee, R. W. & S. Loucks-Horsley, pp. 1–12.
Collins, A., pp. 59–68.
Gadsden, T. & Roempler, K.S., pp. 69–80.
Gess-Newsome, J., pp. 91–100.
Gilbert, S., pp. 43–58.
Kahle, J. B. & Kelly, M. K., pp. 101–114.
Lederman, N., Abd-El, Khalick, F., & Bell, R. L., pp. 25–42.
Loucks-Horsley, S., & Stiles, K. E., pp. 13–24.
Texley, J., pp. 81–90.

10. **Curriculum Development**

    Numerous curricula and curricular changes have been developed to reflect recommendations from reform documents. Discussion of the successes and challenges of implementing these changes are found in chapters:

    Bybee, R. W. & S. Loucks-Horsley, pp. 1–12.
    Kuerbis, P., & Kester, K., pp. 115–122.
    Schmidt, W. H., pp. 141–166.

11. **Leadership Development**

    Leadership development is critical to widespread implementation of reform efforts. For details of successful elements of leadership development, see:

    Bybee, R. W. & S. Loucks-Horsley, pp. 1–12.
    Keurbis, P., pp. 115–122.